Time and Space
in Haggai-Zechariah 1–8

Studies in Biblical Literature

Hemchand Gossai
General Editor

Vol. 24

PETER LANG
New York • Washington, D.C./Baltimore • Bern
Frankfurt am Main • Berlin • Brussels • Vienna • Oxford

Seth Sykes

Time and Space in Haggai-Zechariah 1–8

A Bakhtinian Analysis of a Prophetic Chronicle

PETER LANG
New York • Washington, D.C./Baltimore • Bern
Frankfurt am Main • Berlin • Brussels • Vienna • Oxford

BS
1655.2
.S95
2002

Library of Congress Cataloging-in-Publication Data

Sykes, Seth.
Time and space in Haggai-Zechariah 1-8:
a Bakhtinian analysis of a prophetic chronicle / Seth Sykes.
p. cm. — (Studies in biblical literature; vol. 24)
Includes bibliographical references and index.
1. Bible. O.T. Haggai—Criticism, interpretation, etc. 2. Bible.
O.T. Zechariah I–VIII—Criticism, interpretation, etc. 3. Bible. O.T.
Haggai—Comparative studies. 4. Bible. O.T. Zechariah I–VIII—Comparative
studies. 5. Babylonia—Historiography. 6. Bakhtin, M. M. (Mikhail
Mikhaælovich), 1895–1975. I. Title. II. Series.
BS1655.2 .S95   224'.9706—dc21   99-053037
ISBN 0-8204-4596-7
ISSN 1089-0645

Die Deutsche Bibliothek-CIP-Einheitsaufnahme

Sykes, Seth:
Time and space in Haggai-Zechariah 1-8: a bakhtinian analysis
of a prophetic chronicle / Seth Sykes.
–New York; Washington, D.C./Baltimore; Bern;
Frankfurt am Main; Berlin; Brussels; Vienna; Oxford: Lang.
(Studies in biblical literature; Vol. 24)
ISBN 0-8204-4596-7

The paper in this book meets the guidelines for permanence and durability
of the Committee on Production Guidelines for Book Longevity
of the Council of Library Resources.

Printed in the United States of America

I dedicate this book to Lisa, Adam and Wesley

TABLE OF CONTENTS

Contents

EDITOR'S PREFACE

More than ever the horizons in biblical literature are being expanded beyond that which is immediately imagined; important new methodological, theological, and hermeneutical directions are being explored, often resulting in significant contributions to the world of biblical scholarship. It is an exciting time for the academy as engagement in biblical studies continues to be heightened.

This series seeks to make available to scholars and institutions, scholarship of a high order, and which will make a significant contribution to the ongoing biblical discourse. This series includes established and innovative directions, covering general and particular areas in biblical study. For every volume considered for this series, we explore the question as to whether the study will push the horizon of biblical scholarship. The answer must be *yes* for inclusion.

In this volume Seth Sykes applies Bakhtinian literary theory to an analysis of Haggai and Zechariah 1–8. To this end Sykes explores the relationship between Haggai and Zechariah 1–8, and the chronotope of the Babylonian chronicles to determine both the socio-historical context and the socio-political function of the chronistic genre. Using the Bakhtinian analysis, Sykes demonstrates the radicality of the prophets' function in the original socio-historical context. This study is original and its arguments and proposals will have to be reckoned with in any future scholarly study of Haggai and Zechariah 1–8. The horizon has been expanded.

Hemchand Gossai, General Editor

ABBREVIATIONS

ABC A. Kirk Grayson (ed.), *Assyrian and Babylonian Chronicles*, Texts from Cuneiform Sources (Locust Valley, N.Y.: J. J. Augustin, 1975)

ANET J. B. Pritchard (ed.), *Ancient Near Eastern Texts relating to the Old Testament*, 2d ed. (Princeton: Princeton University Press, 1955)

ARAB D. D. Luckenbill (ed.), *Ancient Records of Assyria and Babylonia*, vol. 2 (Chicago: University of Chicago Press, 1927)

BDB F. Brown, S. R. Driver, and C. A. Briggs, *Hebrew and English Lexicon of the Old Testament*

BZAW Beihefte zur *ZAW*

CBQ *Catholic Biblical Quarterly*

ETL *Ephemerides theologicae lovanienses*

Ev.T *Evangelische Theologie*

GKC *Gesenius' Hebrew Grammar*, ed. E. Kautzsch, tr. A. E. Cowley

FOTL   The Forms of Old Testament Literature

IEJ   *Israel Exploration Journal*

JBL   *Journal of Biblical Literature*

JCS   *Journal of Cuneiform Studies*

JETS   *Journal of the Evangelical Theological Society*

JJS   *Journal of Jewish Studies*

JSOT   *Journal for the Study of the Old Testament*

KAT   E. Sellin (ed.), Kommentar zum A.T.

PEQ   *Palestine Exploration Quarterly*

VT   *Vetus Testamentum*

VTSup   *Vetus Testamentum* Supplements

ZA   *Zeitschrift für Assyriologie*

ZAW   *Zeitschrift für die alttestamentliche Wissenschaft*

INTRODUCTION

The literary location of Haggai and Zechariah 1–8 within the prophetic corpus of the Hebrew Bible compels readers of these books to classify them as prophecy. By classifying these books as prophecy, readers consequently read them with certain expectations. In other words, their preconceptions about the prophetic genre affect their interpretation of the individual texts of Haggai and Zechariah 1–8. For example, on the basis of this generic classification, readers expect to find, in Haggai and Zechariah 1–8, certain prophetic themes that are arranged in a certain literary sequence.

Some scholars, notably W. A. M. Beuken, suggest an alternative generic classification. Beuken classifies Haggai and Zechariah 1–8 as chronicles. The purpose of this present study is to re-read Haggai and Zechariah 1–8 as chronicles and to examine how this generic classification affects our interpretation of these texts. Specifically, this study analyzes the use of the chronistic genre in Haggai and Zechariah 1–8 by comparing these texts with other examples of the genre, notably, the Babylonian chronicles.

In terms of methodology, this study offers a Bakhtinian analysis of Haggai and Zechariah 1–8. The goal of a Bakhtinian literary analysis is to understand the text as a communication event by analyzing its particular use of a genre. The "Bakhtin circle" of Mikhail Bakhtin (1895–1975), Pavel Medvedev (1891–1938) and Valentin Voloshinov (1884/5–1936) proposed an illuminating way of differentiating genres. According to the "Bakhtin circle," each genre conveys a distinctive understanding of time, space and the human actor. Bakhtin labeled this literary conceptualization of time, space and the human actor "chronotope."

This study compares the chronotope of the Babylonian chronicles with the chronotope of Haggai and Zechariah 1–8. On the basis of this comparison, we will argue that the single, combined text of Haggai-Zechariah 1–8 is a prophetic transformation of the chronistic genre. According to the chronistic chronotope, the earthly king, by his cultic and military actions, protects and enriches the capital city. The composer of Haggai-Zechariah 1–8 transforms and subverts this chronistic chronotope by portraying Yahweh as the divine king who protects and enriches Jerusalem.

In the field of biblical studies, scholars have detected other examples of generic transformations. The best known example is George Mendenhall's argument that the covenant form, in the Hebrew Bible, is modeled on the ancient Near Eastern suzerainty treaty.[1] In the covenant, according to Mendenhall, the Israelite nation swears allegiance to Yahweh in the same way that subservient nations swear allegiance to a greater power, such as the Hittite or Assyrian empires. In the light of the parallels between the covenant form and the international or suzerainty treaty, Walter Reed suggests, in his Bakhtinian reading of the Hebrew Bible, that the whole Pentateuch could be understood as "a large-scale transformation of the international treaty."[2] Similarly, this study argues that Haggai-Zechariah 1–8 is a prophetic transformation of the chronistic genre.

According to the "Bakhtin circle," a chronotope is the literary expression of a particular socio-political discourse. Consequently, a Bakhtinian analysis seeks to relate the chronotope to a concrete communication event. Within a particular socio-historical context, a chronotope performs a certain socio-political function. Using the terminology of Paul Ricoeur, a chronotope performs either an ideological function or a utopian function.[3] This study argues that the chronotope of Haggai-Zechariah 1–8 offers a utopian vision of the future. As such, this prophetic vision is a theological critique of the ideological worldview of the chronistic genre.

According to Paul Ricoeur, theological discourse oscillates between the ideological pole of imagination and the utopian pole of imagination.[4] Many biblical scholars have observed a similar dialectic operating within the theology of the Hebrew Bible. For example, Moshe Weinfeld contrasts the royal ideology of the ancient Near East with the utopian visions of the biblical prophets.[5] Paul Hanson traces the development of biblical apocalyptic eschatology to a socio-political conflict within the post-exilic Judean community. On the one hand, a priestly party sought to defend the political status quo by means of ideological theological statements. On the other hand, a visionary party offered a utopian vision of the future.[6] More recently, Walter Brueggemann characterizes biblical theology as a dialectic between a "conserving, constructive tradition" and a "transformative, critical tradition."[7]

According to many scholars, the prophets Haggai and Zechariah, as well as the books that bear their name, provided ideological justification for the existing socio-political order. For example, according to Paul Hanson, Haggai and Zechariah "dedicated themselves to continuity, to preservation of the pre-exilic structures, to maintenance of the status quo."[8] In contrast, this study argues that Haggai-Zechariah 1–8 critiques Persian imperial ideology by offering a utopian vision of the future.

In the next six chapters of this study, I will apply Bakhtinian literary theory to an analysis of Haggai and Zechariah 1–8. In chapter one, I will summarize the history of research on three critical questions that arise when we analyze the chronistic form of Haggai and Zechariah 1–8. I will also introduce Bakhtinian literary theory. In chapter two, I will examine the relation between Haggai and Zechariah 1–8. On the basis of this examination, I will argue that Haggai-Zechariah 1–8 is a unified literary utterance. In chapter three, I will analyze the chronistic genre by examining the chronotope of the Babylonian chronicles. This chronotopic analysis will provide insights about the socio-historical context and the socio-political function of the genre. In chapter four, I will examine the biblical evidence to determine whether the chronistic genre also existed in ancient Israel. In chapter five, I will examine the distinctive use of the chronistic form in Haggai-Zechariah 1–8 by comparing its chronotope with the chronotope of the Babylonian chronicles. This comparison will enable us to understand Haggai-Zechariah 1–8 as a communication event. On the basis of this chronotopic analysis, I will reconstruct the socio-historical setting and the socio-political function of Haggai-Zechariah 1–8. Finally, I will conclude this study by summarizing the results of our Bakhtinian analysis and propose some avenues for future research.

NOTES

[1] George E. Mendenhall, *Law and Covenant in Israel and the Ancient Near East* (Pittsburgh: Biblical Colloquium, 1955).

[2] Walter L. Reed, *Dialogues of the Word* (New York: Oxford University Press, 1993), 51.

[3] Paul Ricoeur, *Lectures on Ideology and Utopia*, ed., George H. Taylor (New York: Columbia University Press, 1986).

[4] Paul Ricoeur, "Excursus: Ideology, Utopia, and Faith," in *Protocol of the Colloquy of the Center for Hermeneutical Studies in Hellenistic and Modern Culture* 17 (1976): 21–28.

[5] Moshe Weinfeld, "Zion and Jerusalem as Religious and Political Capital: Ideology and Utopia," in *The Poet and the Historian: Essays in Literary and Historical Biblical Criticism*, ed., Richard Elliot Friedman (Chico, California: Scholars Press, 1983), 75–115.

[6] Paul D. Hanson, *The Dawn of Apocalyptic: The Historical and Sociological Roots of Jewish Apocalyptic Eschatology* (Philadelphia: Fortress Press, 1979).

[7] Walter Brueggemann, *Old Testament Theology: Essays on Structure, Theme, and Text*, ed., Patrick D. Miller (Minneapolis: Fortress Press, 1992), 118. In his theology of the Old Testament, Brueggemann argues that biblical speech about God is either ideological or elusive; Israel's testimony about God is either authoritarian or ambiguous. See Walter Brueggemann, *Theology of the Old Testament: Testimony, Dispute, Advocacy* (Minneapolis: Fortress Press, 1997), 723.

[8] Hanson, *The Dawn of Apocalyptic*, 247. Similarly, according to Carol and Eric Meyers, the composite work of Haggai-Zechariah 1–8 stood as "the repository of words which expressed the ideological basis for the Second Commonwealth." See Carol L. and Eric M. Meyers, *Haggai, Zechariah 1–8* (New York: Doubleday and Company, 1976), xliii.

CHAPTER ONE
Preliminary Issues

The books of Haggai and Zechariah 1–8 have a distinctive literary structure that differentiates them from their canonical neighbors. Unlike the other books in the Minor Prophets, Haggai and Zechariah 1–8 have a chronological structure. This distinctiveness led W. A. M. Beuken, in 1967, to re-examine the chronistic form of Haggai and Zechariah 1–8 in order to reconstruct their tradition history.

W. A. M. Beuken, in his traditio-historical study of Haggai and Zechariah 1–8, argues that the same final redactor edited Haggai and Zechariah 1–8. This final redaction took place within a "Chronistic milieu."[1] By "Chronistic milieu," Beuken means a historical setting that was similar to, although not necessarily identical with, the setting of the Chronicler. As evidence, Beuken refers to the chronistic form of both books. In both Haggai and Zechariah 1–8, the final redactor transformed a prophetic collection into a chronicle. By composing and adding an editorial frame to the oracles and visions, the final redactor converted dated prophecies into chronistic reports.[2] To the dated prophecies, the final redactor added an introductory superscription that included a word event formula and often an address that did not correspond to the content of the oracles. In Hag. 1 and Zech. 1:1–6, the final redactor also added a concluding historical notice that described the audience's response to the prophetic word.[3] Since a chronicle is a series of chronistic reports in chronological order, Beuken argues that Haggai and Zechariah 1–8 are chronicles.[4]

As the title of his book suggests, Beuken is primarily interested in reconstructing the tradition history of Haggai and Zechariah 1–8. However, his argument concerning the genre of these two prophetic books raises three important questions that deserve further consideration. First, what is the literary relation between Haggai and Zechariah 1–8? Second, what is the relation between the chronistic form and the prophetic content? Finally, what is the relation between the form of the text(s) and the socio-historical context? This present study will propose solutions to these three questions. In this chapter, I will examine previous scholarly solutions to these questions.

I will address these questions by means of a Bakhtinian analysis of Haggai and Zechariah 1–8. A Bakhtinian analysis employs the literary theories of a group of Russian theorists known as the "Bakhtin circle." This circle consists of Mikhail Bakhtin, Pavel Medvedev and Valentin Voloshinov. The goal of a Bakhtinian literary analysis is to understand the text as a communication event by analyzing its particular use of a genre. This present study will interpret Haggai and Zechariah 1–8 by analyzing its particular use of the chronistic genre.

The Problem

The relation between Haggai and Zechariah 1–8

The first critical issue raised by Beuken's classification of Haggai and Zechariah 1–8 as chronicles concerns the literary relation between Haggai and Zechariah 1–8. According to Beuken, the use of a chronistic form in both Haggai and Zechariah 1–8 demonstrates that the same final redactor edited both books. This editor belonged to the same school of tradition as the composer of 1 and 2 Chronicles.[5] In his study, Beuken sought to identify the final redactor. Therefore, his primary goal was to discern the formal and thematic links between Haggai-Zechariah 1–8 and other texts from the same "milieu." Consequently, Beuken did not examine, in any detail, the formal and thematic connections between Haggai and Zechariah 1–8.

Prior to Beuken's study of Haggai and Zechariah 1–8, Peter Ackroyd had already argued that Haggai-Zechariah 1–8 was a single combined text, edited by the same final redactor. This final redactor combined the two originally separate prophetic collections into a single text. This same editor added Zechariah 8:9–23 as a concluding summary and exhortation. Like Beuken, Ackroyd argues that the editor of this combined text belonged to a "Chronistic milieu."[6]

More recently, Carol and Eric Meyers have argued that either Zechariah himself or a disciple of Zechariah composed Haggai and Zechariah 1–8 as a single, combined work.[7] They base their argument on similarities in form and content. First, a major theme in both Haggai and Zechariah 1–8 is the restoration and reorganization of the Judean community in the early years of the post-exilic period. For example, both texts emphasize the leadership roles of Joshua and Zerubbabel. Apart from this general thematic correspondence, we also find more specific thematic and stylistic correspondences between Haggai and Zechariah 7–8.[8] For example, in both Haggai 1–2 and Zechariah 7–8, we find not only an oracular question (Hag. 2:11ff and Zech. 7:3ff) but also the use of the phrase, "house of Yahweh Sebaoth" (Hag. 1:14 and Zech. 7:3; 8:9).

Second, Carol and Eric Meyers also draw attention to the use of dates. The use of a chronological framework in Haggai and Zechariah 1–8 creates a structural unity in the combined work. The structural arrangement of the dates into a 7+1 pattern draws the reader's attention to the refoundation ceremony on December 18, 520 BCE. This important cultic event is mentioned in Hag. 2:18 and Zech. 8:9.[9] The composer also uses a 7+1 structural pattern in the arrangement of Zechariah's visions (p. liv–lviii). The date in Zech. 1:1 reinforces the structural unity of Haggai-Zechariah 1–8 by dating the beginning of Zechariah's prophetic ministry in the month prior to December 18, 520 BCE. In other words, according to the chronological framework of the combined text, Zechariah was a prophetic contemporary of Haggai. Consequently, as Carol and Eric Meyers observe: "Their prophetic missions in time and in content are made interlocking and thus complementary" (p. 98).

According to the preceding scholars, the formal and thematic similarities between Haggai and Zechariah 1–8 demonstrate that the same editor composed both texts. Other scholars have emphasized the literary differences between Haggai and Zechariah 1–8. For example, according to David Petersen, the use of different prophetic genres suggests that Haggai and Zechariah 1–8 were edited at different times by different redactors. Haggai consists of oracles whereas Zechariah 1–8 consists of a combination of oracles and visions. Petersen suggests that Zechariah 1–8 was a literary "response" to the book of Haggai. In contrast to Haggai, whose book contains no visions, Zechariah 1–8 portrays Zechariah as a prophet "who used the full repertoire of oracle and vision to exercise his role."[10]

In a recent article, Peter Marinkovic contends that Haggai and Zechariah 1–8 also have different themes. He argues that Zechariah 1–8 has a different understanding of "the house" of Yahweh from that of Haggai.[11] Although both Haggai and Zechariah 1–8 refer to "the house" of Yahweh, Marinkovic argues that they each have a distinctive interpretation. Drawing upon the analogy of 2 Sam. 7, which distinguishes between the understanding of בַּיִת as the physical building of the temple and the understanding of בַּיִת as a royal dynasty, Marinkovic argues that a similar distinction exists in Haggai and Zechariah 1–8. Whereas Haggai emphasizes the rebuilding of the temple, Zechariah 1–8 emphasizes the restoration of Yahweh's community.[12]

In summary, Beuken's study raises the question of the literary relation between Haggai and Zechariah 1–8. Are Haggai and Zechariah 1–8 separate literary entities or a single combined chronicle? Scholars remain divided over this issue. Like Beuken, I will argue that Haggai-Zechariah 1–8 is a unified chronicle. I will defend this argument on the basis of a Bakhtinian analysis.

The relation between the chronistic form and the prophetic content

The second question that Beuken's study raises concerns the relation between the chronistic form and the prophetic content. Is the chronistic form merely "an artificial editorial technique" of providing a coherent structure to a prophetic collection, or does the combination of chronistic form and prophetic content exhibit an "overall unity of purpose"?[13] This question addresses the issue of the motivation behind the composer's use of a chronistic form to shape a collection of prophetic material.

According to Beuken, the use of a chronistic form displays a historiographic interest on the part of the final redactor. The redactor situates the prophetic word within the historical confines of a particular time and place.[14] This historiographic concern is also reflected in the contrast drawn between the obedience of the community in rebuilding the temple in the days of Haggai and Zechariah (Hag. 1:12–14; Zech. 1:6b) and Israel's rejection of the "former prophets" (Zech. 1:4; 7:9–12; p. 332). In spite of this obvious historiographic interest, Haggai-Zechariah 1–8 also contains symbolic visions (Zech. 1:7–6:8) and salvation oracles (Hag. 2:20–23; Zech. 8) and, therefore, remains a genuine prophecy with a message for the future (p. 332). Unfortunately, Beuken does not explain why an editor linked his historiographic interest in the past, as it is reflected in the chronistic form, with the predictions and optimistic message for the future, as it is contained in the prophetic words of Haggai and Zechariah.

H. W. Wolff also argues that the final redactor of Haggai was motivated by a historiographic concern. According to Wolff, the final redactor sought to write a chronicle about the temple rebuilding project.[15] However, the

Haggai-chronicler was also motivated by a political concern. The final redactor sought to emphasize Zerubbabel's role in this rebuilding project (p. 20). Zerubbabel was the appointed governor of the Judean province of Judah. The redactor's political concern to legitimate Zerubbabel's power is especially evident in the chronistic redaction of Hag. 1. According to Wolff, the purpose of the original scene-sketch, which consists of vv. 4–11, 12b–13, was to show how the people, as a whole, were brought to fear God (p. 54).[16] By adding vv. 1–3, 12a, 14, the Haggai-chronicler transforms this scene-sketch into a chronistic report about the beginnings of the temple's rebuilding. In these additions, the chronicler claims that Zerubbabel, in his official capacity as the governor of Judah, was primarily responsible for initiating the rebuilding project (p. 54–55).[17] According to Wolff, the content of Haggai's last recorded oracle (Hag. 2:21b–23) was the prophetic motivation behind the political concern of the final redactor (p. 19–20). In this prophecy, Haggai uses royal terminology to designate Zerubbabel as Yahweh's servant.

In his commentary on Haggai, David Petersen agrees that a historiographic concern was an important motivation for the composer of the book. This concern is demonstrated in the prose narrative discourse that introduces Haggai's words and in the chronological ordering of Haggai's activity.[18] However, Petersen argues that the prophetic content of the book suggests a more comprehensive purpose than just a memorialization of the temple rebuilding project (p. 33). On the basis of N. Lohfink's research on the genre of the *historische Kurzgeschichte*,[19] Petersen claims that Haggai is "a brief apologetic historical narrative" (p. 35). This short prophetic apologia serves at least four functions. First, it memorializes the rebuilding of the temple. Second, it highlights the role of Haggai. Third, it claims that obedience to Haggai's words will yield prosperity. Fourth, it encourages the people to support the temple compound and its cultus (p. 36).

Carol and Eric Meyers provide two other interpretations of the relation between the chronistic form and the prophetic content.[20] First, the use of the regnal years of a foreign ruler (Darius I) in the chronological framework of Haggai and Zechariah 1–8 reflects an acknowledgment of Persian domination in Judah.[21] This acceptance of Persian rule is based on the perception that Darius, in allowing the Jerusalem temple to be rebuilt and in granting semiautonomy to Judah, was fulfilling the will of Yahweh (p. 37–38).[22] The references to Zerubbabel and Joshua, in both the editorial frame of Haggai and the symbolic visions of Zechariah 1–8, also demonstrate an acceptance of Persian rule. For example, the editorial frame of Haggai refers to Zerubbabel as the governor of Judah, i.e., a Persian appointee (p. 39). In addition, the visions of Zechariah, in general, and Zech. 4, in particular, reflect an acceptance of the Persian establishment of a diarchic rule of high priest and governor in Judah (p. xl–xli, 220–221).

Second, Carol and Eric Meyers also connect the chronological framework of Haggai and Zechariah 1–8 with prophetic expectation. The prophet Jeremiah had predicted seventy years of God's wrath (Jer. 25:11–12; 29:10). According to Carol and Eric Meyers, the specificity of the chronological headings demonstrates a belief that the period of judgment was about to end (p. 6). Thus, in Zech. 1:7–17 and Zech. 7–8, the prophet declares an end to the seventy-year period of judgment (see especially, Zech. 1:12 and 7:5) and a beginning of a period of blessing when Yahweh will dwell among the people in the rebuilt temple of Jerusalem (see especially, Zech. 1:13–17 and 8:1–8).

In summary, scholars have proposed different interpretations of the relation between the chronistic form and the prophetic content of Haggai and Zechariah 1–8. All the preceding scholars agree that the use of the chronistic form indicates a historiographic interest. However, disagreements arise when these same scholars discuss the "overall unity of purpose." In this study, on the basis of a Bakhtinian analysis, I will propose a new interpretation of this overall purpose of Haggai-Zechariah 1–8.

The relation between the chronistic form and the socio-historical context

The third question that Beuken's study raises is the question of the relation between the chronistic form and the socio-historical context. What does the chronistic form tell us about the authorship and the historical setting of Haggai and Zechariah 1–8? As we will discover, scholars disagree about both the social identity of the composer(s) and the date of composition.

According to Beuken, the final redactor composed Haggai-Zechariah 1–8 within a "Chronistic milieu." In other words, the final redactor was influenced by, and may have belonged to, the school of tradition that also composed 1 and 2 Chronicles, Ezra and Nehemiah. Thus, Beuken dates the final redaction to the late fifth century or early fourth century BCE. Beuken provides three types of evidence to support his argument: formal, thematic, and stylistic.

The most obvious formal correspondence between Haggai-Zechariah 1–8 and the literature of the Chronistic School is the use of a chronological framework. Other formal correspondences include the following examples. First, the final form of Hag. 1 presents a particular theological sequence of human actions. The people break the covenant. The people repent of their sins. The people renew the covenant. This sequence is also present in other chronistic texts (see Ezra 9–10; Neh. 9–10; 2 Chr. 29:5–11; 14:8–15:8).[23] Second, according to the chronistic frame of Hag. 1, Haggai now addresses the prophetic word to the two leaders of Judah, Zerubbabel and Joshua. Originally, Haggai addressed the oracle to the whole community. Similarly, in 1 and 2 Chronicles, the prophetic word is always addressed to the king (p. 32). Third, Hag. 2:4–5, which Beuken considers to be an addition of the final redactor, is in the form of an "installation to office" genre. According to Beuken, the only other examples of this genre are found in Chronistic texts (1 Chr. 22:11–16; 28:10; 28:20; 2 Chr. 19:11; 25:7f; Ezra 10:4; p. 53–54). Finally, Beuken argues that Zech. 1:3–6a is a "levitical sermon." The closest literary parallel, in form and content, is 2 Chr. 30:6–9 (p. 88–91).

Beuken detects three types of thematic correspondences between the final form of Haggai-Zechariah 1–8 and other texts from the Chronistic tradition (p. 331). The first thematic correspondence is a concern to maintain a historical record of the rebuilding of the temple. This historiographic concern is present in both Haggai and Ezra 1–6. Haggai-Zechariah 1–8 and the Chronistic tradition also share a common interest in the figure of Joshua, the high priest. According to Beuken, the chronistic redactor of Zechariah 1–8 added Zech. 3:6f, 4:11–14, and 6:13 to the original vision cycle. In all these additions, the redactor emphasizes the importance of Joshua, the high priest. Similarly, in Ezra, Joshua is given a prominent role alongside Zerubbabel (p. 133). Finally, both Haggai-Zechariah 1–8 and the Chronistic tradition share a general historiographic concern to retell the story of Israel's past history. This latter interest is most obvious in Zech. 1:1–6 and 7:7–14.

Beuken also detects stylistic correspondences between Haggai-Zechariah 1–8 and the Chronistic tradition. Let me cite three examples. First, both the final redactor of Haggai (Hag. 1:13) and the Chronicler (2 Chr. 36:15–16) refer to the prophets as Yahweh's "messengers" (p. 38). Second, the phrase "Yahweh stirred up the spirit" (רוח את יהוה ויער), in Hag. 1:14, is a "chronistic expression" (see 1 Chr. 5:26; 2 Chr. 21:16; 36:22; Ezra 1:1, 5; p. 31). Third, in Zech. 1:3, the composer of the "levitical sermon" uses a stylistic pattern in which the same verb is used for both a human action and a reciprocal divine action. Thus, Yahweh will "return" if the people will "return." This pattern is a prominent stylistic feature of Chronistic texts (p. 94).[24]

As we have seen, Ackroyd also argues for a Chronistic setting. Ackroyd suggests that the final redactor of Haggai-Zechariah 1–8 may have shared the same apologetic aims as the composer of 1 and 2 Chronicles. Namely, both composers sought to defend the legitimacy of the Jerusalem temple against the rival claims of the Samaritan temple.[25]

In his article on the editorial framework of Haggai, Rex Mason criticizes Beuken's insistence on a late date for the final redaction.[26] On the basis of the retention of the Zerubbabel prophecy (Hag. 2:21–23) within the final form of the text, Mason argues for an early redaction rather than late (p. 417). According to Mason, the editorial framework of Haggai is the first attempt to relate Haggai's predictions to the historical situation that emerged shortly after the prophet actually made those predictions. Rather than being part of the same "milieu" as the Chronicler, the final redactor of Haggai probably belonged to a group "farther upstream, but in the same waters which nourished the Chronicler" (p. 420).

In his later book, *Preaching the Tradition*, Mason re-examines the editorial framework of Haggai.[27] Mason acknowledges many stylistic and thematic correspondences between the editorial framework of Haggai and the so-called "addresses" in 1 and 2 Chronicles. Rather than talk about a common setting within a "Chronistic milieu," however, Mason suggests that the editor of Haggai functioned within a "temple milieu" (p. 195). The correspondences reflect the style, themes and interests of temple "preachers" who preserved, developed and taught the "received tradition."[28]

David Petersen uses the final form of Haggai to argue for a Deuteronomistic redaction. As we have already seen, Petersen argues that Haggai is in the form of an "apologetic historical narrative." This genre was developed in the sixth century BCE. Other examples of this genre are found in texts composed by Deuteronomistic tradents (Jer. 26 and 36; Jer. 37–41; 2 Kings 22–23).[29]

In his Ph.D dissertation, Michael Prokurat argues that "the school of Zechariah" supplied a Deuteronomic/Deuteronomistic edition of Haggai-Zechariah 1–8 within approximately one generation of the completion of the temple. The two distinctive features of the editorial emendations of this school were: "they desired to show the prophecies of Haggai and Zechariah to be true prophecy" and "they furthered the Deuteronomic/Deuteronomistic theology."[30]

Carol and Eric Meyers also assign an early date to the final edition of Haggai-Zechariah 1–8. According to Carol and Eric Meyers, the absence of any reference to the rededication ceremony for the Jerusalem temple in 515

BCE suggests that the final redactor composed Haggai-Zechariah 1–8 before the rededication took place. They also suggest that the anticipation of the rededication ceremony motivated the use of the chronological framework to create the combined text of Haggai-Zechariah 1–8.[31] This early date for the composition of Haggai-Zechariah 1–8 raises the distinct possibility that Zechariah himself, or a close disciple, was the composer (p. xlvii).

In summary, scholars have proposed different explanations of the relation between the chronistic form and the socio-historical context of Haggai and Zechariah 1–8. To some scholars, the chronistic form suggests a setting within a "Chronistic milieu" and a late date of composition. Other scholars subscribe to an early Deuteronomistic editing theory. In this study, on the basis of a Bakhtinian analysis of Haggai-Zechariah 1–8, I will propose my own interpretation of the socio-historical setting of the text.

A Bakhtinian Methodology

Since I will be re-examining the chronistic form of Haggai and Zechariah 1–8, this study is a form critical enterprise. Rather than use traditional form critical methods, however, I will apply the literary theories of a group of Russian theorists known as the "Bakhtin circle." The "Bakhtin circle" consists of Mikhail Bakhtin (1895–1975), Pavel Medvedev (1891–1938) and Valentin Voloshinov (1884/5–1936).[32]

A Bakhtinian analysis begins with the premise that a literary text is a "dialogic utterance;" it is an act of speech communication. As such, the author of the text communicates a particular point of view to a specific audience in a concrete socio-historical situation.[33] Moreover, each utterance not only responds to previous utterances ("already-spoken") but also anticipates the audience's response ("not-yet-spoken"). The text contributes to a never-ending, eternal dialogue.[34]

As a "dialogic utterance," a literary text must have clear-cut boundaries in order that the audience might know when it is appropriate for them to respond. Those boundaries are determined by "a *change of speaking subjects*, that is, a change of speakers" (p. 71). This change of speakers is most obvious in conversational dialogue. However, Bakhtin insists that any utterance, from a simple conversation to a complex multi-volume text, has "an absolute beginning and an absolute end" (p. 71). In an oral communication, we detect a change of speaker by a change in accent and tone. In a written communication, we detect a change of speaker by a change in the linguistic style, thematic content, and structural composition of the text.

Every complete text or "whole utterance" is in the form of a particular genre. Genres are the typical forms of whole utterances (p. 78). As such, genres allow us to communicate with each other. Thus, Bakhtin claims:

> Speech genres organize our speech in almost the same way as grammatical (syntactical) forms do. We learn to cast our speech in generic forms and, when hearing others' speech, we guess its genre from the very first words.... If speech genres did not exist and we had not mastered them, if we had to originate them during the speech process and construct each utterance at will for the first time, speech communication would be almost impossible (p. 78–79).

Genres guide not only the writer as she composes an utterance but also the reader as he attempts to understand the utterance. According to this perspective, a genre is not a fixed entity that exists in a pure state but rather "an open or virtual class which describes a possibility."[35] Genres become real only in the speech-act of the utterance. Genres provide the "potential" or the "given;" utterances provide the "actual" or the "created."[36]

The "Bakhtin circle" proposed a distinctive way of analyzing a genre. According to Bakhtin and his colleagues, every genre has a "two-fold orientation in reality."[37] On the one hand, each genre has a particular way of perceiving reality (the "intrinsic orientation" or the "worldview" of a genre). On the other hand, a genre also has a socio-historical setting in life (the "extrinsic orientation" or the *Sitz im Leben* of a genre).

In the first place, a genre "is oriented in life, from within, one might say by its thematic content" (p. 131). The form and content of a genre convey a particular worldview. Just as seeing and representation merge in the act of painting, so form and content interrelate to create a generic worldview.[38] By reading an actual example of a genre, one begins to see the world through the "lens" of the genre. Like eyeglasses with a particular prescription, each genre prescribes a particular worldview.[39]

In his essay, "Forms of Time and of the Chronotope in the Novel," Bakhtin distinguishes various novelistic genres according to how each genre conveys its view of time (*chronos*) and of space (*topos*).[40] The chronotope is Bakhtin's term for the literary conceptualization of time, space, and the human actor. Each genre prescribes a particular temporal and spatial context for the occurrence of human actions and events.[41]

From a literary representation of the world (time, space and the human actor), a Bakhtinian analysis of a genre must progress to the actual socio-historical context that generated this particular chronotope. A chronotope is organically related to the time and the place in which it was created. For example, Bakhtin associates the literary chronotope of the "rhetorical biography" of ancient Greece with the "real-life" situation of the agora where civic leaders were praised and memorialized (p. 131). Similarly, Bakhtin relates the chronotopic significance of "parlors and salons" in the novels by Stendhal and Balzac to the social and political life of nineteenth century Paris (p. 246–247). In other words, the chronotope of a genre provides insights about the *Sitz im Leben* of a genre. Therefore, an analysis of the chronotope can be the means by which we can relate a literary text to its socio-historical context.[42]

The "Bakhtin circle" also proposed a particular understanding of the *Sitz im Leben* of a genre. According to Medvedev, "(t)he conceptualization of reality develops and generates in the process of ideological social discourse."[43] As members of a social group interact, they create genres to communicate with each other and with other social groups. Consequently, these genres reflect the worldview of a particular social group at a particular point in history. A Bakhtinian analysis of a genre seeks to reconnect the worldview preserved in the chronotope to the discourse of a particular social group, at a particular point in time, under the conditions of a particular social situation.

A Bakhtinian analysis of a genre concludes with an examination of the socio-political function of the chronotope. As the worldview of a particular social group in a particular historical setting, a chronotope either preserves the socio-political order (ideological function) or subverts it (utopian function). Thus, a Bakhtinian analysis includes ideological criticism as part of its analysis.

Like other ideological critics, members of the "Bakhtin circle" consider literary texts to be "socially symbolic acts" or "ideological acts."[44] The Bakhtinian approach to genre is determined by a desire to critique the ideology of certain texts and genres by contrasting them with other texts and genres that offer a utopian view of the individual and of society. As Michael Gardiner observes, Bakhtin's ideological critique from a "utopian" perspective is very similar to Paul Ricoeur's dialectic of ideology and utopia.[45] By examining Ricoeur's dialectic, therefore, we can better understand Bakhtin's theory of ideology.[46]

Ricoeur places ideology and utopia within the "single conceptual framework" of "social and cultural imagination."[47] According to Ricoeur, ideology and utopia represent the two poles of cultural imagination and, as such, they operate at the same three levels of socio-political discourse. In addition, ideology and utopia can operate in both constructive and destructive ways. Ricoeur begins by analyzing the pole of ideology.

On the first level, ideological discourse provides a symbolic model for social praxis and social identity. The various ideological discourses are "symbolic systems constitutive of action itself" (p 317). Therefore, ideology performs the constructive function of providing a symbolic template or blueprint through which we shape our experience of the social world.[48] On the second level, whenever the problem of authority and power arises, ideological discourse legitimates the authority of a particular social group. Ideological discourse is an attempt to "fill up the credibility gap" between the claim to legitimacy, raised by the rulers, and the belief in that legitimacy, conceded by the ruled.[49] On the third level, ideological discourse usually legitimates the authority of the rulers by distorting reality. The particular interests of the ruling social group are distorted and, subsequently, presented as the general interests of society as a whole (p. 313).[50] At this point, ideological discourse has the potential of becoming destructive in its socio-political intent.

Although utopia is usually understood to be a literary genre, Ricoeur analyzes the socio-political function of the utopian "spirit."[51] In other words, just as Bakhtin reconstructs the worldview of novelistic genres, so Ricoeur reconstructs the worldview of the utopian genre. Like ideological discourse, utopian discourse operates at the same three levels of socio-political discourse. First, in contrast to ideological discourse which provides a symbolic template of existing reality, utopian discourse "defamiliarizes" the existing social world by opening "a field for alternative ways of living" (p. 320). Second, in contrast to ideological discourse which seeks to "legitimate" the political authority of a particular social group, utopian utterances "always imply alternative ways of using power" and thereby "call established systems of power into question" (p. 321). Third, the danger of utopian discourse is that it can result in a form of "escapism" if it is not connected with a concrete course of action (p. 322).[52]

Viewed from Ricoeur's perspective, a generic chronotope is a "symbolic medium" through which a social group either preserves its social identity (ideology) or offers an alternate way of living (utopia).[53] As such, a chronotope can either legitimate (ideology) or subvert (utopia) the political authority of a social group. Moreover, a chronotope can either distort reality (ideology) or flee from reality (utopia). Therefore, a Bakhtinian analysis of a genre concludes by determining whether a chronotope functions as an ideology or as a utopia.

In his writings, Bakhtin contrasts "strictly straightforward" genres, which "preserve" the social order and "legitimate" the authority of powerful social groups, with "parodying" genres, which "challenge" the social order and "subvert" the political order.[54] For example, in his essay "Epic and Novel," Bakhtin contrasts and critiques the generic worldview of the epic, which emphasizes the "absolute past" and "tradition," with the generic worldview of the novel, which emphasizes the "openness" of the present.[55] In his "Chronotope" essay, Bakhtin contrasts and critiques the "transcendent and hierarchical worldview" of medieval texts with the "harmonious" worldview of the Rabelaisian chronotope.[56] In each contrasting pair, the latter "parodying" genres disclose a "utopian" worldview from which Bakhtin can critique the ideology of the former "serious" genres.

In summary, the unifying concern of Bakhtinian literary theory is to discern "the nature of discourse."[57] A literary text is an utterance, a communication event. The goal of a Bakhtinian analysis is to understand the nature of this communication event.[58] Just as genres allow us to communicate with each other, so genres enable understanding. By analyzing the genre of a text, we can begin to understand the nature of the discourse underlying the literary text. The chronotope of the genre is the means by which we can reconstruct the socio-historical context and the socio-political function of the genre. On the basis of this reconstruction, we can then analyze the specific use of the generic chronotope in the literary text.

A Bakhtinian analysis seeks to understand a concrete utterance by examining its use of a generic form. Consequently, it is ideally suited for this particular examination of Haggai and Zechariah 1–8. Specifically, a Bakhtinian analysis will help us to resolve the three critical issues that were summarized in the previous section.

The first critical issue is the relation between Haggai and Zechariah 1–8. This issue concerns the literary "boundaries" of the utterance. Are Haggai and Zechariah 1–8 a single utterance or two separate utterances? As we have seen, a Bakhtinian analysis of a literary text is concerned with determining the limits of the "whole utterance." The Bakhtinian understanding of chronotope is particularly relevant in this examination of Haggai and Zechariah 1–8. First, in their use of a chronistic form, Haggai and Zechariah 1–8 display a particular interest in time. This concern for chronology suggests that Haggai and Zechariah 1–8 have a particular perspective on time that is related to their use of the chronistic genre. Second, a genre conveys a chronotopic perspective by means of the form-content totality. Form and content interrelate to produce a generic representation of reality. Thus, a Bakhtinian analysis of the chronotope seeks to discern the relation between the form and content of a text. Third, a chronotope is organically related to the time and place in which it was created. In other words, an analysis of the chronotope is the means by which we can relate the literary text to its socio-historical context.

In the next four chapters of this study, I will apply Bakhtinian literary theory to an analysis of Haggai and Zechariah 1–8. Specifically, I will undertake the following tasks. First, I will examine the relation between Haggai and Zechariah 1–8 in order to determine the structural limits of the utterance. Second, I will analyze the chronotope of the Babylonian chronicles in order to determine the socio-historical context and the socio-political function of the chronistic genre. Third, I will examine the biblical evidence to determine whether the chronistic genre existed in ancient Israel. Finally, I will compare the chronotope of Haggai-Zechariah 1–8 with the chronistic chronotope in order to determine the socio-historical context and socio-political function of Haggai-Zechariah 1–8.

NOTES

[1] W. A. M. Beuken, *Haggai-Sacharja 1–8: Studien zur Überlieferungsgeschichte der Frühnachexilischen Prophetie* (Assen: Van Gorcum, 1967), 331–336.

[2] According to Beuken, the existence of other dated prophecies in Jeremiah and Ezekiel demonstrates that the dates are original (Ibid., 25f). A chronistic report is "a type of brief report explicitly dated by regnal year and thus having the character of chronicle." See B. O. Long, *1 Kings with an Introduction to Historical Literature*, The Forms of Old Testament Literature, 9 (Grand Rapids: Eerdmans, 1984), 246.

[3] Beuken, *Haggai-Sacharja 1–8*, 331.

[4] H. W. Wolff makes a similar argument in his commentary on Haggai. Wolff refers to the final redactor of Haggai as "the Haggai chronicler." See Hans Walter Wolff, *Haggai: A Commentary* (Minneapolis: Augsburg Publishing House, 1988), 18. The main characteristics of a chronicle, according to Wolff, are "a highly official character" and a chronological structure (Ibid., 32).

[5] Beuken, *Haggai-Sacharja 1–8*, 331.

6 Peter R. Ackroyd, "The Book of Haggai and Zechariah I–VIII," *JJS* 3 (1952): 155–56.

7 Carol L. Meyers and Eric M. Meyers, *Haggai, Zechariah 1–8*, Anchor Bible Commentaries (Garden City, N.Y.: Doubleday, 1987), xliv–xlviii.

8 See the list of correspondences between Haggai and Zechariah 7–8 (Ibid., xlix).

9 There are eight chronological headings (Hag. 1:1, 15; 2:1, 10, 20; Zech. 1:1, 7; 7:1) but only seven dates. Two of the chronological headings refer to the same date, that is, December 18, 520 BCE (Hag. 2:10, 20). According to Carol and Eric Meyers, the arrangement of the other six dates (three dates preceding Hag. 2:10 and three dates following Hag. 2:20) causes the reader to focus on the central date (Ibid., xlvii).

10 David L. Petersen, *Haggai and Zechariah 1–8*, The Old Testament Library (Philadelphia: Westminster Press, 1984), 124.

11 Peter Marinkovic, "What does Zechariah 1–8 tell us about the Second Temple?" in *Second Temple Studies: 2. Temple Community in the Persian Period*, eds., Tamara C. Eskenazi and Kent H. Richards, JSOT Supplement Series 175 (Sheffield: JSOT Press, 1994), 22–33.

12 For example, Marinkovic translates Zech. 3:7c, "You will judge my community and be in charge of my farmsteads" (Ibid., 100).

13 In his commentary on Haggai, Petersen asks the following question: "Is this chronological ordering an artificial editorial technique, or does the substance of the prophetic words fit the surrounding narrative so as to create a book that evinces overall unity of purpose?" See Petersen, *Haggai*, 33.

14 Beuken, *Haggai-Sacharja 1–8*, 331–332.

15 Wolff, *Haggai*, 34. Wolff refers to the final editor of Haggai as "the Haggai chronicler."

16 Wolff detects three "growth rings" in the transmission of Haggai's prophetic tradition. The center is the prophetic proclamation delivered on five different occasions (1:4–11; 2:15–19; 2:3–9; 2:14; 2:21b–23). The inner ring is the scene-sketches in which a disciple "preserved not merely the prophetic words recorded, but also the history of their effect (1:12b–13) or the history that preceded them (2:11–13), as well as the opposition of Haggai's listeners (1:2)." The outer ring is the chronistic form of the text (Ibid., 18).

17 The editor also mentions Joshua and "the remnant of the people." However, as Wolff observes, Zerubbabel is always mentioned first.

[18] Petersen, *Haggai*, 32. Although Petersen does not define the form of Haggai as chronistic, he does acknowledge its similarity with the genre of the chronicles in the following statement: "The person who composed the book of Haggai has provided a narrative structured on the basis of chronological sequence. As literature, therefore, Haggai stands very near to a chronicle or historical narrative and less near to a prophetic collection as we know that genre from books such as Amos and Micah." (Ibid., 33).

[19] According to Lohfink, the following biblical texts are examples of this genre: Jer. 26 and 36, Jer. 37–41, 2 Kings 22–23, and to a lesser extent, the books of Ruth and Jonah. See N. Lohfink, "Die Gattung der 'Historischen Kurzgeschiche' in den letzten Jahren von Juda und in der Zeit des Babylonischen Exils," *ZAW* 90 (1978): 319–347. According to Petersen, this genre has the following characteristics. First, it takes the form of a short prose narrative. Second, examples of this genre tend to focus on an important person or persons. Third, it is marked by a chronological sequence of events. Fourth, the stories are made up of several different scenes. Fifth, dates regularly mark the boundaries between the individual scenes. Sixth; the scenes are often of unequal length. Finally, the accounts often have an apologetic focus. See Petersen, *Haggai*, 34–35.

[20] Meyers and Meyers, *Haggai*, 38.

[21] As Carol and Eric Meyers observe, Haggai and Zechariah 1–8 are unique among the prophetic books in their use of the regnal years of a foreign king. The book of Jeremiah employs the regnal years of Judean kings and the book of Ezekiel employs the years of captivity in Babylon. (Ibid., 5).

[22] As Carol and Eric Meyers rightly observed, the Persians had a different interpretation of these political actions: "The apparently magnanimous gesture of Darius in allowing the ancient Judean temple to be rebuilt was in Persian eyes part of an overarching plan to restore local governance in provincial territories. The temple in Jerusalem was, like all temples in the ancient world, an administrative institution. It functioned in political, economic and judicial matters as well as in strictly cultic or religious ones. Consequently, the restoration of a temple was a means of fostering local self-rule in a subunit of the Persian Empire." (Ibid., 37–38).

[23] Beuken, *Haggai-Sacharja 1–8*, 43–44.

[24] Beuken refers to this stylistic scheme as "ein Schema der Gegenseitigkeit des Verhaltens." Chronistic examples include 2 Chr. 12:5; 15:2; 24:20; 2 Chr. 15:2; 30:9.

[25] P. R. Ackroyd, "The Book of Haggai and Zechariah I–VIII," *JJS* 3 (1952): 2–3. Similarly, according to Beuken, the final redactor of Hag. 2:10–14 transformed the original prophecy of Haggai, which described the rejection of the syncretistic

population of Haggai's generation, into an anti-Samaritan polemic. See Beuken, *Haggai-Sacharja 1–8*, 72–73.

[26]   R. A. Mason, "The Purpose of the 'Editorial Framework' of the Book of Haggai," *VT* 27 (1977): 413–21.

[27]   Rex Mason, *Preaching the Tradition* (New York: Cambridge University Press, 1990), 191–95.

[28]   Mason acknowledges the anachronism of using the words "preachers" and "sermon" in this particular historical context but he continues: "By 'preachers' we must think of those who preserved, developed and taught the traditions which must have been becoming increasingly enshrined in Israel's 'Scriptures'. The activity of such tradents must have been both literary and rhetorical and have taken place in the study and the classroom as well as in more formally 'liturgical' settings." (Ibid., 2).

[29]   Petersen, *Haggai*, 35–36.

[30]   Michael Prokurat, "Haggai and Zechariah 1–8: A Form Critical Analysis" (Ph.D diss., Graduate Theological Union, 1988), 352–56.

[31]   Meyers and Meyers, *Haggai*, xlv.

[32]   There are many scholarly introductions to Mikhail Bakhtin and his distinctive approach to literary texts. Three books provide a helpful overview of Bakhtinian studies. *Mikhail Bakhtin* by Katerina Clark and Michael Holquist (Cambridge: Harvard University Press, 1984) introduces readers to the complexity of Bakhtin's thought from a biographical perspective. *Mikhail Bakhtin: Creation of a Prosaics* by Gary Saul Morson and Caryl Emerson (Stanford: Stanford University Press, 1990) focuses on Bakhtin's theories from a synchronic perspective rather than a diachronic one. Barbara Green, in her recent book *Mikhail Bakhtin and Biblical Scholarship: An Introduction* (Atlanta: The Society of Biblical Literature, 2000), has written an excellent introduction to Bakhtinian studies for biblical scholars. She also examines how other biblical scholars have applied Bakhtinian theory to the analysis of the biblical text.

[33]   According to Pam Morris: "The unifying concern of all the texts written by Bakhtin and/or Voloshinov and Medvedev is the nature of discourse.... All the texts insist upon the necessity of considering language not as words in the dictionary which have only meaning potential but as the actualized meaning of those words used in a specific utterance.... Thus discourse—the production of actualized meaning—can be studied adequately only as a communication event, as responsive interaction between at least two social beings." Pam Morris, "Introduction," in *The Bakhtin Reader: Selected Writings of Bakhtin, Medvedev, Voloshinov*, ed., Pam Morris (London: Edward Arnold, 1994), 4–5. Bakhtin discusses his understanding of the text as utterance in M. M. Bakhtin, "The Problem of Speech Genres," in *Speech Genres and Other Late Essays*,

ed. Caryl Emerson and Michael Holquist, trans. Vern W. McGee (Austin: University of Texas Press, 1986), 60–102.

34   Bakhtin, "Speech Genres," 91–102.

35   Martin Buss, "Understanding Communication," in *Encounter with the Text: Form and History in the Hebrew Bible*, ed. Martin J. Buss (Philadelphia: Fortress Press, 1979), 10.

36   Morson and Emerson summarize the Bakhtinian position as follows: "What genres of speech and literature do, in other words, is provide specific complexes of values, definitions of situation, *potentials* (not merely structures) for kinds of action.... We need genres to understand specific acts, Bakhtin argued, but in understanding genre we have not understood everything that is important about those acts or literary works. Genres provide the 'given,' but the work or act provides the 'created,' something new." Gary Saul Morson and Caryl Emerson, *Mikhail Bakhtin: Creation of a Prosaics* (Stanford: Stanford University Press, 1990), 89.

37   M. M. Bakhtin and P. N. Medvedev, *The Formal Method in Literary Scholarship*, trans. Albert J. Wehrle (Cambridge: Harvard University Press, 1985), 130–35.

38   Thus, according to Bakhtin and Medvedev: "The process of seeing and conceptualizing reality must not be severed from the process of embodying it in the forms of a particular genre. It would be naive to assume that the painter sees everything first and then shapes what he saw and puts it on the surface of his painting according to a certain technique. In real fact, seeing and representation merge.... The same is true in literature. The artist must learn to see reality with the eyes of the genre. A particular aspect of reality can only be understood in connection with the particular means of representing it." (Ibid., 134).

39   Morson and Emerson refer to the "form-shaping ideology" of a genre. By ideology, they mean a worldview. They summarize this Bakhtinian understanding of genre as follows: "Genres convey a vision of the world not by explicating a set of propositions but by developing concrete examples. Instead of specifying the characteristics of a worldview, as philosophical theories might, they allow the reader to view the world in a specific way.... In short, a genre, understood as a way of seeing, is best described neither as a 'form' (in the usual sense) nor as an 'ideology' (which could be paraphrased as a set of tenets) but as 'form-shaping ideology'—a specific kind of creative activity embodying a specific sense of experience." (Morson and Emerson, *Mikhail Bakhtin*, 282f).

40   M. M. Bakhtin, *The Dialogic Imagination*, ed. Michael Holquist, trans. Caryl Emerson and Michael Holquist (Austin: University of Texas Press, 1981), 84–258.

41   According to Bakhtin, each genre conveys a particular chronotope: "The chronotope in

literature has an intrinsic *generic* significance. It can even be said that it is precisely the chronotope that defines genre and generic distinctions." (Ibid., 84–85).

[42]   Thus, according to Michael Holquist: "At one extreme, chronotope has a relatively restricted set of applications that apply to literary texts conceived as single units. But chronotope may also be used as a means for studying the relation *between* any text and its times, and thus as a fundamental tool for a broader social and historical analysis." See Michael Holquist, *Dialogism: Bakhtin and his World* (London: Routledge, 1990), 113.

[43]   Bakhtin and Medvedev, *The Formal Method*, 135.

[44]   Fredric Jameson, *The Political Unconscious: Narrative as a Socially Symbolic Act* (Ithaca, N.Y.: Cornell University Press, 1981), 20, 76–79. See also Terry Eagleton, *Marxism and Literary Criticism* (Berkeley and Los Angeles: University of California Press, 1976), 16–19.

[45]   Michael Gardiner, *The Dialogics of Critique* (London: Routledge, 1992), 123–140. Ricoeur's theory of ideology is found in the following texts: Paul Ricoeur, *Lectures on Ideology and Utopia*, ed., George H. Taylor (New York: Columbia University Press, 1986); and "Ideology and Utopia," in *From Text to Action: Essays in Hermeneutics, II*, translated by Kathleen Blamey and John B. Thompson (Evanston, Illinois: Northwestern University Press, 1991), 308–324.

[46]   Unfortunately, as Gardiner observes, the "Bakhtin circle" did not delineate "in any systematic fashion what the term 'ideology' was meant to designate or how it was supposed to operate in the social world." (Gardiner, *Dialogics*, 59–60).

[47]   Ricoeur, "Ideology and Utopia," 308.

[48]   In his lecture on Clifford Geertz's theory of ideology, Ricoeur quotes Geertz who defines ideology as a cultural pattern which provides "a template or blueprint for the organization of social and psychological processes, much as genetic systems provide such a template for the organization of organic processes." (Ricoeur, *Lectures*, 257). See Clifford Geertz, *The Interpretation of Cultures* (New York: Basic Books, 1973), 216.

[49]   Ricoeur, "Ideology and Utopia," 315.

[50]   Terry Eagleton lists six strategies that are often used to distort reality: unifying, action-oriented, rationalizing, legitimating, universalizing, and naturalizing. See Terry Eagleton, *Ideology: an Introduction* (London: Verso, 1991), 45–61.

[51]   Ricoeur, "Ideology and Utopia," 319.

[52]　As Ricoeur observes, this tendency may explain why utopian discourse is usually associated with a particular literary genre: "writing becomes a substitute for acting."

[53]　Ricoeur quotes Erik Erikson who defines ideology as follows: "More generally...an ideological system is a coherent body of shared image, ideas, and ideals which...provides for the participants a coherent, if systematically simplified, over-all orientation in space and time, in means and ends." (Ricoeur, *Lectures*, 258). In other words, ideology performs the same function in social life as the chronotope in literary texts. See Erik Erikson, *Identity: Youth and Crisis* (New York: W. W. Norton, 1968), 189f.

[54]　M. M. Bakhtin, "From the Prehistory of Novelistic Discourse," *The Dialogic Imagin*ation, 53. In this essay, Bakhtin claims: "For any and every straightforward genre, any and every direct discourse—epic, tragic, lyric, philosophical—may and indeed must itself become the object of representation, the object of a parodic travestying 'mimicry.' It is as if such mimicry rips the word away from its object, disunifies the two, shows that a given straightforward generic word—epic or tragic—is one-sided, bounded, incapable of exhausting the object; the process of parodying forces us to experience those sides of the object that are not otherwise included in a given genre or a given style." (Ibid., 55).

[55]　M. M. Bakhtin, "Epic and Novel: Toward the Methodology for the Study of the Novel," in *The Dialogic Imagination*, 3–40.

[56]　Bakhtin, "Forms of Time and Chronotope," 167–206.

[57]　Morris, *The Bakhtin Reader*, 4.

[58]　According to Medvedev: "To understand an utterance means to understand it in its contemporary context and our own, if they do not coincide. It is necessary to understand the meaning of the utterance, the content of the act, and its historical reality, and to do so, moreover, in their concrete inner unity." (Bakhtin and Medvedev, *The Formal Method*, 121–122).

CHAPTER TWO
The Whole Utterance
of Haggai-Zechariah 1–8

In this chapter, we will examine the literary relation between Haggai and Zechariah 1–8 in order to determine the boundaries of the whole utterance. According to the "Bakhtin circle," an utterance is a communication event involving at least two social beings: a speaker/author and an audience/reader. The speaker/author of an utterance not only responds to previous utterances but also anticipates the response of a particular audience/reader. As an act of speech communication, an utterance must have clear-cut boundaries.[1] The audience/reader determines the literary boundaries of an utterance by observing "a change of speaking subjects, that is, a change of speakers."[2] In the case of complex literary texts, such as biblical texts, the composer "manifests his own individuality in his style, his world view, and in all aspects of the design of his work."[3] In other words, we can determine a change of speakers/authors and, consequently, the boundaries of a literary text, by differentiating changes in the structure, content, and style of a text. As we examine the literary relation between Haggai and Zechariah 1–8, we will discover many structural, thematic, and stylistic connections that demonstrate the literary unity of Haggai-Zechariah 1–8.

The Chronological Structure

The chronological structure that exists in both Haggai and Zechariah 1–8 is the most obvious literary connection between the two texts. Both texts consist of a sequence of dated prophetic sections. Dates are located at the beginning of each section.[4] Additionally, in both cases, these sections have been placed in chronological order.

In its present form, Haggai consists of four sections (Hag. 1:1–15a; 1:15b–2:9; 2:10–19; 2:20–23).[5] Each section begins with a date formula and a word event formula ("the word of Yahweh came"). The four sections are in chronological order. The first section is dated to the sixth month of the second year of King Darius, that is, August, 520 BCE (Hag. 1:1). The second section is dated to the seventh month of the same year, that is, October 520 BCE (Hag. 1:15b–2:1).[6] Both the third and fourth sections are dated to the ninth month, that is, December 520 BCE (Hag. 2:10, 20).

The first section of Haggai (Hag. 1:1–15a) is unusual in that it also concludes with a date formula (v. 15a). The presence of this date formula, at the end of the section, has led David Petersen to argue that Haggai actually consists of five dated sections (Hag. 1:1–11; 1:12–15; 2:1–9; 2:10–19; 2:20–23). In the second section (Hag. 1:12–15), the date formula concludes the unit instead of introducing it.[7] However, as other scholars have observed, these verses make better sense if they are read as the conclusion to vv. 1–11 rather than as a separate section.[8] For example, "the words of Haggai," mentioned in v. 12, must be the oracle found in vv. 4–11. In other words, according to 1:12–15, Zerubbabel, Joshua and "the remnant" obeyed the prophetic charge of 1:1–11. Moreover, Carol and Eric Meyers argue that the unusual placement of a date at the end of a unit "can be explained as a device to form an envelope with the date formula at the beginning of the book (1:1)."[9] Finally, Jer. 28 provides us with another example of a literary unit that begins and concludes with a date formula. Therefore, on the basis of these three considerations, I consider Hag. 1:1–15a to be a single literary unit.

Zechariah 1–8 consists of three sections (Zech. 1:1–6; 1:7–6:15; 7:1–8:23). Like Haggai, each section begins with a date and a word event formula. Moreover, like Haggai, these three dated sections have been placed in chronological order. The first section of Zechariah 1–8 is dated to the eighth month of the second year of King Darius, that is, October/November, 520 BCE (Zech. 1:1). The second section is dated to the eleventh month, that is, February 519 BCE (Zech. 1:7). The third section is dated to the ninth month of Darius' fourth year, that is, December, 518 BCE (Zech. 7:1).

The common use of a chronological structure in Haggai and Zechariah 1–8 is not coincidental. A closer examination of the chronological structure in Haggai and Zechariah 1–8 reveals evidence of a single editorial hand at work. This evidence suggests that Haggai and Zechariah 1–8 were originally a unified, whole utterance. First, the overlapping dates reinforce a thematic connection between the two prophetic texts. Second, the combination of Haggai's four dated sections and Zechariah's three sections creates seven sections. As we will discover, the number seven is a symbolically significant number in Zechariah 1–8.

According to the dates in Hag. 2:10, 20 and Zech. 1:1, the two prophets were contemporaries for at least a month, that is, between October/November and December 18, 520 BCE.[10] This chronological overlap is important because it establishes the beginning of Zechariah's prophetic ministry in the month prior to the founding of the temple on Dec. 18, 520 BCE. The editor of Zechariah 1–8 obviously considered this event to be a major milestone in the history of the community (Zech. 4:9 and 8:9). By dating Zech. 1:1–6 in the month prior to this event, the editor situates the prophet at the founding of the temple in December. According to Zech. 8:9, Zechariah was present "on the day" when "the foundation was laid for the rebuilding of the temple, the house of Yahweh Sebaoth." Moreover, this verse implies that at least one other prophet was also present. Haggai is the most obvious referent.

Zech. 1:6b also suggests that Zechariah was partly responsible for enabling this event to take place. According to Zech. 1:1–6, Zechariah was successful in persuading his audience to repent of their "evil ways and evil deeds." The editorial comment in v. 6b documents the audience's response. We can interpret Zech. 1.6b in one of two ways. On the one hand, we can interpret this verse as continuing the narrative description of past history. The verse describes the ancestors' response to the proclamation of the former prophets. On the other hand, we can interpret this verse to be an editorial comment that describes Zechariah's audience responding to Zechariah's message (contained in vv. 3–6a). Like many commentators, I consider the latter interpretation to make better sense of the Hebrew syntax and the literary context.[11] Consequently, Zech. 1:1–6 has a similar structure and message as Hag. 1:1–15a. Both passages contain the words of the prophet and an editorial comment describing the response of the audience. Just as Haggai was successful in persuading the people to rebuild the temple (Hag. 1:12–

15a), so Zechariah was successful in persuading the people to return to Yahweh (Zech. 1:6b). Therefore, the use of the date in Zech. 1:1 and the editorial comment in Zech. 1:6b create both a formal and a thematic connection with Haggai.

The curious omission of the day in Zech. 1:1, which distinguishes this date from all the other dates in Haggai and Zechariah 1–8, reinforces the thematic connection. The Syriac version includes the day as the first day of the eighth month. According to H. G. Mitchell, the Syriac version supports his claim that the day, in the Massoretic Text, "must have been lost in transmission."[12] However, as Baldwin observes, the Syriac version tends to "amplify and harmonize verses" and "the omission argues for its genuineness."[13] Moreover, Petitjean refers to other biblical texts in the Old Testament that omit the day (Num. 9:1; 1 Kings 6:38).[14] The omission of the day suggests that, unlike the other dates in Haggai and Zechariah 1–8, the date in Zech. 1:1 is an editorial addition. A possible explanation for this omission is the editorial concern to establish a chronological and thematic connection between Haggai and Zechariah 1–8. By omitting the day in Zech. 1:1, the editor of Haggai-Zechariah 1–8 emphasized a historical association between the two prophets. Haggai and Zechariah were contemporaries who were both responsible for motivating the leaders of the Judean community to restart the rebuilding of the temple. Eventually, according to the chronology established in Haggai-Zechariah 1–8, the foundation of the temple was laid on December 18, 520 BCE.[15]

The existence of seven dated sections in Haggai and Zechariah 1–8 provides further evidence that Haggai-Zechariah 1–8 is a unified, whole utterance. The combined use of dates in Haggai and Zechariah 1-8 creates seven sections. Moreover, there is a total of seven different dates: Aug. 29, 520 BCE (Hag. 1:1); Sept. 21, 520 BCE (Hag. 1:15); Oct. 17, 520 BCE (Hag. 2:1); Dec. 18, 520 BCE (Hag. 2:10, 20); Oct./Nov. 520 BCE (Zech. 1:1); Feb. 15, 520 BCE (Zech. 1:7); and Dec. 7, 518 BCE (Zech. 7:1). The number seven and multiples of seven are symbolic throughout the Hebrew Bible and are especially significant in Zechariah 1–8.[16] For example, in Zech. 1:12, "the messenger of Yahweh" announces the end of "seventy years" of judgment.[17] In Zech. 3:9, "a single stone with seven eyes" is placed before Joshua. Finally, in Zech. 4, Zechariah sees a vision of a lampstand with seven lamps (v. 2). Each lamp has seven lips.

Elsewhere in the prophetic canon of the Hebrew Bible, we can find examples of other prophetic texts being divided into seven sections. In two separate prophetic books, the editor has divided a collection of oracles against foreign nations into seven sections: Amos 1–2 and Ezek. 25–32. Amos 1–2 contains a collection of seven oracles against foreign nations that culminates with an eighth oracle against Israel.[18] Each oracle begins with the same identical formulaic introduction: "Thus says Yahweh, for three transgressions…and for four, I will not turn it back."[19] Similarly, the editor who was responsible for the structural arrangement of Ezekiel 25–32 was clearly fascinated with the number seven.[20] In this collection of oracles against foreign nations, the prophet addresses seven nations.[21] The seventh nation, Egypt, is addressed seven times[22] and the seventh oracle against Egypt refers to seven other nations. Moreover, the editor of Ezekiel 25–32 uses seven dates.[23] These two examples from prophetic literature demonstrate that editors of prophetic texts used a sevenfold structural pattern. Therefore, the existence of seven different dates and seven dated sections in Haggai-Zechariah 1–8 provides further evidence that the same editor composed Haggai-Zechariah 1–8 as a unified, whole utterance.

In conclusion, both Haggai and Zechariah 1–8 have a chronological structure. A closer examination reveals evidence that a single editor used the chronological structure to connect Haggai and Zechariah 1–8. The overlapping dates reinforce a thematic connection between the two texts. Both Haggai and Zechariah were present at the founding of the temple. In addition, the combined use of dates, in Haggai and Zechariah 1–8, creates seven sections, a symbolically significant total. These literary connections support my contention that the same editor composed Haggai-Zechariah 1–8 as a unified, whole utterance.

The Thematic Content

Haggai and Zechariah 1–8 share in common not only a chronological structure but also a thematic interest in the rebuilding of the Jerusalem temple. According to both texts, the rebuilding of the temple marks the beginning of a new era of blessing for a specific group within the Judean community. In addition, both Haggai and Zechariah 1–8 have a similar understanding of the temple's significance. Both texts understand the rebuilt temple to be not only the center of Yahweh's universal rule but also the basis for Joshua's and Zerubbabel's political authority. This common thematic emphasis on the Jerusalem temple supports my contention that the same editor composed Haggai-Zechariah 1–8 as a unified, whole utterance.

Both Haggai and Zechariah 1–8 place special emphasis upon the founding of the temple on December 18, 520 BCE (see Hag. 2:18; Zech. 4:9; 8:9). Both texts claim that this particular day marked the beginning of a new era of blessing and salvation for the survivors of the exile who had returned to Judah. Additionally, they both contrast this new era with the past when the community had been the object of God's judgment. Finally, both Haggai and Zechariah 1–8 state that the dawning of this new era of blessing depends upon the people obeying the prophetic word.

The first section of Haggai (Hag. 1:1–15a), which is dated to the period before the founding of the temple, describes the consequences of a ruined temple. Since the temple of Yahweh lies in ruins, Yahweh issues the following judgment:

> Therefore, the heavens above you have withheld the dew and the earth has withheld its produce. Moreover, I have called for drought on the land, on the hills, on the grain, on the new wine, on the oil, on what the ground produces, on human beings, on animals, and on all their labors. (verses 10–11)

Similarly, according to Hag. 2:15–19, Yahweh had punished the community, in the days preceding the founding of the temple, with the following judgment:

> Before a stone was placed upon a stone in Yahweh's temple, how did you fare? …I struck you and all the products of your hands with blight and mildew and hail. (verses 15–17)

This particular punishment (drought, blight, mildew and hail) is almost identical with one of the curses in Deut. 28:

> Yahweh will strike (you) with consumption, fever, inflammation, violent heat, drought, blight, and mildew; and they will pursue you until you perish. (v. 22)

According to Deut. 28, this curse and others will come upon those who "do not obey the voice of Yahweh, your God" (v. 15).

Rather than disobey the word of Yahweh, Haggai's audience, that is, Joshua, Zerubbabel and "the remnant of the people" (שְׁאֵרִית הָעָם), "obeyed the voice of Yahweh, their God" (Hag. 1:12). They began to rebuild the temple (1:15) and, subsequently, the foundation of the temple was laid on December 18, 520 BCE (2:18). On that day, Yahweh declared, through the prophet Haggai, "From this day on, I will bless you" (2:19). Because the people obeyed the prophetic summons to rebuild the temple, Yahweh declares the beginning of a new era of blessing.[24] Disobeying the voice of Yahweh results in curses; obeying that same voice results in blessing.

The second section of Haggai (Hag. 1:15b–2:9) describes the future prosperity of the new temple. Yahweh will subjugate the nations of the world and use their wealth to beautify the temple that is now being rebuilt. Consequently, "the latter glory of this house," that is, the glory of the Second Temple, "will be greater than the former," that is, the glory of the Solomonic Temple (see 2:3). Moreover, Yahweh declares his intention to establish *šālôm* "in this place" (2:9). The final comment of Hag. 2:9 is ambiguous because it is difficult to know the precise meaning of the phrase, וּבַמָּקוֹם הַזֶּה אֶתֵּן שָׁלוֹם. The phrase, "this place," can mean the city of Jerusalem or the actual temple. The preposition בְּ can mean "in" or "through." Moreover, שָׁלוֹם can mean peace (as in lack of war), prosperity, fertility, or all of the above.[25] Since the passage immediately preceding this verse links the future prosperity of the temple with Yahweh's subjugation of the nations, I consider this phrase to be referring primarily to the economic prosperity of the temple. This economic prosperity is due to the re-establishment of Yahweh's rule over the nations of the world.[26] As a consequence of Yahweh's suzerainty, the subservient nations will send tributes of silver and gold to Jerusalem. The Judean community will subsequently use this wealth to beautify the temple and make it as glorious as the former temple.

We find a similar emphasis on the founding of the temple in Zechariah 7–8. These two chapters also use many of the same words and phrases as Haggai to convey this particular emphasis. Like Carol and Eric Meyers, I consider these thematic and stylistic similarities between Haggai and Zechariah 7–8 to be the intentional design of the editor of Haggai-Zechariah 1–8.[27] By emphasizing the same themes in both Haggai and Zechariah 7–8, the editor creates an inclusio. The discovery of an inclusio in a text helps the reader determine the structural limits of a text.[28] Therefore, the discovery of an inclusio in Haggai and Zechariah 7–8 provides further evidence that Haggai-Zechariah 1–8 is a unified, whole utterance.

Like Haggai, Zechariah 7–8 contrasts the cursed era that preceded the founding of the temple with an era of blessing that followed December 18, 520 BCE. In addition, both Haggai and Zechariah 7–8 state that the dawning of this new era of blessing depends upon the obedience of the people.

Zechariah 7 describes the cursed era of the past. In the past, the people disobeyed the word of Yahweh as "the former prophets" proclaimed it (7:9–12). Consequently, Yahweh punished them by scattering the people among the nations and by desolating the land (7:13–14). Zechariah 8 describes the era of blessing that has now dawned on the Judean community. Whereas, in the past, Yahweh purposed to bring disaster on the people, Yahweh has "purposed in these days to do good to Jerusalem and to the house of Judah" (8:14–15).

The editor of Zechariah 7–8 also uses the same language as Haggai to express this contrast between the cursed era of the past and the blessed era of the present and future. First, in both Haggai and Zechariah 7–8, the people either did or did not hear (שמע) the words (דְּבָרִים) of the prophets whom Yahweh had sent (שׁלח). See Hag. 1:12; Zech. 7:12; 8:9. Second, both Haggai and Zechariah 7–8 state that a new era began on the day the foundation of the temple was laid (הַיּוֹם יֻסַּד הַהֵיכָל). See Hag. 2:18 and Zech. 8:9. Third, both Haggai and Zechariah 7–8 imply that the exiles, "the remnant," are the primary recipients of God's promise.[29] Thus, in Hag. 1:12–14 and 2:1–9, words of encouragement are directed to "the remnant of the people" (שְׁאֵרִית הָעָם). Similarly, in Zech. 8:6, 11–12, God assures "the remnant of this people" (שְׁאֵרִית הָעָם הַזֶּה) that, unlike their ancestors, they will be blessed rather than cursed. Finally, Haggai and Zechariah 7–8 use the same language of blessings and curses. Zechariah's description of the new era, in Zech. 8:12–13, is almost an exact reversal of Haggai's description of the old era. Whereas the vine yielded nothing in the former days (Hag. 2:19), it will now yield fruit (Zech. 8:12). Whereas the heavens withheld the dew and the earth withheld its produce in the former days (Hag. 1:10), the earth will now yield its produce and the heavens will now yield their dew (Zech. 8:12). Instead of being under the curse of God, Judah will now become the recipient of God's blessing (Hag. 2:19; Zech. 8:13).

In summary, both Haggai and Zechariah 1–8 emphasize the importance of the temple reconstruction project. More specifically, they both claim that the founding of the temple on December 18, 520 BCE marked the beginning of a new era of blessing for "the remnant." Within

Zechariah 1–8, this emphasis upon the founding of the temple is especially present in Zechariah 7–8. These two chapters form an inclusio with Haggai. The existence of such an inclusio provides further evidence that the same editor composed Haggai-Zechariah 1–8 as a unified, whole utterance.

Haggai and Zechariah 1–8 also share a common understanding of the temple's significance. Both texts consider the temple in Jerusalem to be the place where Yahweh dwells as king. In other words, they understand the temple to be the center of Yahweh's universal rule. This shared understanding of the temple provides further evidence that a single editorial hand is at work in Haggai-Zechariah 1–8.

Both Haggai and Zechariah 1–8 refer to the temple as "the house of Yahweh Sebaoth" (בֵּית־יהוה צְבָאוֹת).[30] The occurrences of the divine title, Yahweh Sebaoth, are "disproportionately frequent" in Haggai and Zechariah 1–8.[31] The title occurs in the message formula ("thus says Yahweh Sebaoth") as well as in the prophetic utterance formula ("oracle of Yahweh Sebaoth").[32] Alongside these prophetic formulas, which establish the divine authority of the prophetic word, the title is also used in reference to the temple,[33] the prophetic commission,[34] and the wrath of Yahweh.[35] As many scholars have observed, this title is a royal title.[36] Elsewhere in the Old Testament, it designates Yahweh as the heavenly king who reigns supreme in the divine council.[37] As the heavenly king, Yahweh Sebaoth "is enthroned upon the cherubim" in the temple.[38]

Both Haggai and Zechariah 1–8 claim that Yahweh Sebaoth dwells in the rebuilt temple of Jerusalem. Thus, in Hag. 2:5, Yahweh encourages the people to rebuild the temple because "my spirit abides in your midst" (רוּחִי עֹמֶדֶת בְּתוֹכְכֶם). Zechariah 1–8 uses the same preposition (בְּתוֹךְ) to refer to Yahweh's presence in the rebuilt temple (Zech. 2:9, 14–15 and 8:3). Zech. 8:3 is significant because, in this verse, the prophet predicts that Yahweh will return "to Zion," that is, the temple mount. The temple mount is later described as "the mountain of Yahweh Sebaoth." The prophet also states that Yahweh "will dwell in the midst of (בְּתוֹךְ) Jerusalem." By preserving and using this language, the composer draws upon the mythological connotations associated with the temple as the palace of Yahweh Sebaoth, which we find elsewhere in the Old Testament.[39]

We find further evidence that Zechariah 1–8 understands the temple to be the specific abode of Yahweh in Zech. 2:5–9 and 2:10–17. In these two texts, the composer draws upon the Priestly tradition of the

Pentateuch and of Ezekiel. In Zech. 2:9, Yahweh promises to be "glory in the midst of" Jerusalem and, in Zech. 2:14–15, Yahweh promises Jerusalem, "I will dwell in your midst." The reference to Yahweh's "glory" (כָּבוֹד), in Zech. 2:9, is reminiscent of priestly descriptions of God's presence in the tabernacle.[40] Similarly, as Carol and Eric Meyers observe, "For Ezekiel, the Glory is a necessary presence in the temple; without it, the temple does not enjoy its proper sacred status."[41] Yahweh's promise to "dwell in the midst of" (שָׁכַן בְּתוֹךְ) Jerusalem is identical with priestly descriptions of Yahweh's presence in the tabernacle.[42] Just as Yahweh's glory dwelt in the tabernacle in the midst of the community, so Haggai and Zechariah 1–8 claim that Yahweh Sebaoth will dwell in the rebuilt temple in the midst of Jerusalem.

Both Haggai and Zechariah 1–8 portray Yahweh Sebaoth as the universal ruler. Yahweh Sebaoth reigns supreme on earth as well as in heaven. Thus, according to Hag. 2:6–7 and 2:21–22, Yahweh Sebaoth will shake the heavens and the earth in order to overthrow the thrones of earthly kingdoms. The nations of the world will acknowledge Yahweh's rule by sending a tribute of silver and gold to Yahweh's temple in Jerusalem (see 2:7–8). Similarly, the visions of Zechariah clearly portray Yahweh Sebaoth as the universal ruler. For example, the first and last visions portray Yahweh as "the lord of all the earth" (אֲדוֹן כָּל־הָאָרֶץ), who dispatches envoys throughout the whole earth (Zech. 1:7–17; 6:1–8). The second vision (2:1–4) depicts, in symbolic form, the destruction of Judah's enemies.[43] The oracular interlude of Zech. 2:10–17 describes Yahweh's subjugation of the nations (vv. 8–9) as well as the nations' acknowledgment of Yahweh's suzerainty (v. 11). Finally, according to Zech. 8:22, "many peoples and strong nations" will acknowledge Yahweh's universal rule by seeking Yahweh Sebaoth in Jerusalem.

In summary, both Haggai and Zechariah 1–8 understand the temple to be the center of Yahweh's universal rule. As the heavenly king, Yahweh Sebaoth dwells "in the midst of" Jerusalem (Hag. 2:5; Zech. 2:14–15; 8:3), in "the house of Yahweh Sebaoth" (Hag. 1:14; Zech 8:9). Since Yahweh dwells in the rebuilt temple of Jerusalem, the subjugated nations of the world will acknowledge Yahweh's universal rule by sending their wealth to Jerusalem in order to beautify the temple (Hag. 2:6–9) and by coming to Jerusalem in order to seek Yahweh Sebaoth (Zech. 8:20–23). This common understanding of the temple is further evidence that the same editor composed Haggai-Zechariah 1–8 as a unified, whole utterance.

Haggai and Zechariah 1–8 also share a common understanding of the political authority of Joshua and Zerubbabel. Both Haggai and Zechariah 1–8 portray Joshua and Zerubbabel as sharing political power in Judah. In addition, both Haggai and Zechariah 1–8 contend that their political authority depends upon their actions toward the temple. Finally, both Haggai and Zechariah 1–8 assign messianic status to Zerubbabel on the basis of his leadership role in rebuilding the temple.

The first two sections of Haggai (1:1–15a; 1:15b–2:9) are addressed to both Joshua and Zerubbabel. According to these two sections, Joshua and Zerubbabel, as the two leaders of Judah, are equally responsible for rebuilding the temple. These two sections address Joshua and Zerubbabel in their official roles as the high priest (הַכֹּהֵן הַגָּדוֹל) and the governor of Judah (פַּחַת יְהוּדָה). By addressing them together, the editor implies that these two individuals shared political power in Judah.

In its present form, the oracle in Hag. 1:4–11 is addressed to Zerubbabel and Joshua (see v. 1).[44] In this section, the prophet criticizes Joshua and Zerubbabel for their neglect of the temple and the lack of progress on its rebuilding. As soon as Joshua and Zerubbabel "obey the voice of Yahweh" (v. 12), however, Yahweh not only assures them of his supportive presence (v. 13) but also "stirs up" the spirits of Joshua and Zerubbabel so that they came and worked on "the house of Yahweh Sebaoth" (v. 14).[45]

The oracle in Hag. 2:2–9 encourages Joshua and Zerubbabel to be strong and to rebuild the temple (v. 4). Certain individuals within the Judean community were denigrating the new temple (v. 3). These individuals were complaining that the new temple would never be as beautiful or as meaningful as the former temple. Since Joshua and Zerubbabel were the leaders of the reconstruction project, this complaint also cast doubts on their political authority. Yahweh encourages Joshua and Zerubbabel to complete the rebuilding of the temple by assuring them of his supportive presence (vv. 4–5) and by promising to use the wealth of the subjugated nations to beautify the new temple (vv. 6–9).

Significantly, according to Haggai, Yahweh designates Zerubbabel to be his chosen servant, that is, Yahweh's messiah, on December 18, 520 BCE.[46] Hag. 2:18–19 had already stated that this day, when the foundations of the temple had been laid, marked the beginning of a new era of blessing. According to Hag. 2:20–23, it was on this day that Yahweh also declares his intention to make Zerubbabel his royal representative on earth. In other words, the prophet designates

Zerubbabel to be the messiah on the same day that he founded the temple.

Zechariah 1–8 shares and develops Haggai's understanding of Zerubbabel's and Joshua's political roles. First, Zechariah 1–8 portrays Joshua and Zerubbabel as sharing political power. Although they are not explicitly named in either text, Zech. 4 and Zech. 6:9–15 imply that Zerubbabel and Joshua are the two divinely ordained leaders of Judah. In Zech. 4, the prophet sees a vision of a lampstand with seven lamps beside which stand two olive trees (vv. 1–3). According to the interpretation in vv. 10b and 14, the seven lamps represent "the eyes of Yahweh which range through all the earth" and the two olive trees represent "the sons of oil who stand beside the lord of the whole earth."[47] Although Joshua and Zerubbabel are not explicitly named, the literary context implies that they are the two sons of oil. Zech. 4:6b–10a celebrates Zerubbabel's achievements as the builder of the temple and, in Zech. 3, Yahweh promises Joshua that he has direct access "among these who are standing" in the divine council of Yahweh (v. 7b). This description of Joshua and Zerubbabel as two olive trees portrays them as sharing political authority in both the heavenly realm and the earthly realm.

We find a similar portrayal of a diarchy, involving Joshua and Zerubbabel, in Zech. 6:9–15. In this passage, Joshua is crowned as the symbol of a future political establishment. In the future, an individual named "Branch," who will build the temple of Yahweh, will rule on his throne beside a "priest." The priest and Branch will be in a harmonious relationship with each other (see vv. 12–13). Again, the text does not explicitly name Joshua and Zerubbabel. However, since Zech. 6:11 identifies Joshua as "the high priest," the "priest" in question must be Joshua. Similarly, since Zech. 4:9 has already stated that Zerubbabel will rebuild the temple, "Branch" must be Zerubbabel. Therefore, Zech. 6:9–15, like Zech. 4, portrays Joshua and Zerubbabel as sharing political authority in Judah and understand that shared authority to be divinely ordained.

Second, like Haggai, Zechariah 1–8 designates Zerubbabel as the messiah on the basis of his role in rebuilding the temple. Zech. 4:6b–10a assures Zerubbabel that he will complete the rebuilding project which he had started: "The hands of Zerubbabel laid the foundation of this house and his hands will also complete it" (v. 9). As we have already observed, Zech. 6:9–15 assigns a messianic title, "Branch," as well as royal authority, to the one who will rebuild the temple of Yahweh.[48] Since Zech. 4:9 has already stated that Zerubbabel will rebuild the temple, this person called Branch must be Zerubbabel.[49] In other words, Zech. 6:9–15 ascribes messianic status to Zerubbabel on the basis of his work on the temple and, therefore, this passage resembles Hag. 2:20–23.

Third, Zechariah 1–8 also develops the implications of Haggai's understanding of Joshua's political role. As we have already observed, Haggai implies that Joshua's political authority depends upon his role in the rebuilding of the temple. A similar understanding of Joshua's political authority is found in Zech. 3:7. In this verse, Yahweh promises Joshua direct access to the divine council, "if you render judgment in my house and administer my courts."[50] Joshua's political authority is dependent upon his administrative work in the temple of Yahweh.

In summary, both Haggai and Zechariah 1–8 designate Joshua and Zerubbabel as the divinely ordained leaders of the Judean community. In both texts, the basis for their political authority is their work in the temple. In addition, both Haggai and Zechariah 1–8 portray Zerubbabel as Yahweh's messiah. This similar understanding of Joshua's and Zerubbabel's political roles provides further evidence of a single editorial perspective. Therefore, Haggai and Zechariah 1–8 are a unified, whole utterance.

In conclusion, Haggai and Zechariah 1–8 share a common thematic interest in the rebuilding of the Jerusalem temple. Both Haggai and Zechariah 1–8 understand the rebuilding of the temple to mark the beginning of a new era of blessing for the remnant, the survivors of the exile who had returned to Judah. In addition, both Haggai and Zechariah 1–8 understand the rebuilt temple to be the center of Yahweh's universal rule as well as the basis for Joshua's and Zerubbabel's political authority. This shared thematic interest provides further evidence that the same editor composed Haggai-Zechariah 1–8 as a unified, whole utterance.

The Prophetic Style

Haggai and Zechariah 1–8 also exhibit a similar prophetic style. Bakhtin defines style as being "the selection of the lexical, phraseological, and grammatical resources of the language."[51] In this section, I will concentrate on the selection of particular prophetic formulas in Haggai and Zechariah 1–8. In both Haggai and Zechariah 1–8, the composer makes extensive use of the word event formula and the message formula. The use of these two formulas provides further evidence that the same editor composed Haggai-Zechariah 1–8 as a unified, whole utterance.

As we have already observed, each section of Haggai and Zechariah 1–8 begins with a date and a word event formula. Apart from slight variations in the latter half of the formula, which specifies the recipient of the divine word, all seven occurrences are very similar (see Hag. 1:1; 2:1; 2:10; 2:20; Zech. 1:1; 1:7; 7:1). Besides the seven occurrences of the formula in the introductions to each section of Haggai and Zechariah 1–8, we find seven other occurrences (Hag. 1:3; Zech. 4:8; 6:9; 7:4; 7:8; 8:1; 8:18). Although they exhibit slightly more variations in wording, these latter examples of the formula provide further evidence that one editor is responsible for composing Haggai and Zechariah 1–8. First, the use of the formula in Zechariah 7–8 creates a structural inclusio with Haggai. Second, in Zech. 4:8 and 6:9, the formula introduces prophetic oracles that contain the same themes that we find in Haggai.

In both Haggai and Zechariah 7–8, the word event formula is repeated five times (Hag. 1:1, 3; 2:1, 10, 20; Zech. 7:1, 4, 8; 8:1, 18). The use of five formulas in Zechariah 7–8 parallels the usage in Haggai. Thus, Zech. 7:1 introduces the last dated section of Zechariah 1–8 just as Hag. 1:1 introduces the first dated section of Haggai. Like Hag. 1:2, Zech. 7:2–3 defines the stimulus for the oracles that follow. According to Hag. 1:2, the people were arguing that it was not the appropriate time to rebuild the temple. In his prophetic response (Hag. 1:3–11), Haggai disputes this argument. Zech. 7:2–3 contains a question about the appropriate length of time to continue mourning the destruction of Jerusalem in the fifth month. Zechariah provides the prophetic response in the oracles that follow (Zech. 7:4–8:23). In both Hag. 1:3 and Zech. 7:4, the word event formula introduces the prophetic response. The remaining occurrences of the formula in Zech. 7:8, 8:1 and 8:18 parallel the section headings of Hag. 1:15b–2:1, 2:10 and 2:20.

The use of the word event formula to create a parallel structure to Haggai seems to be an intentional design on the part of the editor of Zechariah 7–8. For example, the use of the formula in 7:8 interrupts the prophetic argument that begins in 7:5–7 and continues in 7:9ff. Zech. 7:9–10 contains a quotation from "the words which Yahweh proclaimed by the agency of (בְּיַד) the former prophets" (v. 7). The most likely explanation for this interruption is a deliberate attempt on the part of the editor to create a parallel structure to Haggai. Moreover, in Zech. 7:7, the preposition בְּיַד is used in connection with the prophetic proclamation of the divine word just as it is used in the word event formula of Hag. 1:1, 3 and 2:1. This parallel usage of the word event formula in Haggai and Zechariah 7–8 creates a structural inclusio. The existence of this inclusio provides further evidence that Haggai-Zechariah 1–8 is a unified, whole utterance.

The word event formula is also used in Zech. 4:8 and 6:9. These two verses introduce prophetic material that contains the same characters and the same themes that we find in Haggai. Zech. 4:8 introduces an oracle in which Yahweh states that just as Zerubbabel laid the foundation of the temple so he will complete the temple reconstruction (v. 9a). This statement expands upon the chronistic report of Hag. 1:1–15a which claims that Zerubbabel (along with Joshua and "the remnant") "came and worked on the house of Yahweh Sebaoth" (v. 14). Similarly, Zech. 6:9 introduces a series of oracles which mention Joshua son of Jehozadak, the high priest (v. 11) and "a man called Branch...who will build the temple of Yahweh" (v. 12). As we have already observed, this individual called Branch must be Zerubbabel. As Zech. 6:13 implies, the title Branch is a messianic appellation (see Jer. 23:5). In other words, Zech. 6:9–15 ascribes messianic status to Zerubbabel and, therefore, this passage resembles Hag. 2:20–23. Thus, in both Zech. 4:8 and 6:9, the editor of Zechariah 1–8 uses a word event formula to introduce oracles that refer to and expand upon the oracular material in Haggai.

Haggai and Zechariah 1–8 are also similar in their use of the message formula. The wording of the formula is identical in both books: "thus says Yahweh Sebaoth" (כֹּה אָמַר יהוה צְבָאוֹת).[52] As I have already observed, the occurrences of the divine title, Yahweh Sebaoth, are "disproportionately frequent" in Haggai and Zechariah 1-8.[53] The consistent and frequent use of this title in the message formula is significant in its demonstration of a stylistic coherence within Haggai and Zechariah 1-8.

In summary, Haggai and Zechariah 1–8 display a similar prophetic style. Both Haggai and Zechariah 1–8 consistently use the same two prophetic formulas: the word event formula and the message formula. As we will discover in the next section, the consistent use of these two prophetic formulas distinguishes Haggai-Zechariah 1–8 from its canonical context. The similarities they demonstrate provide further evidence that the same editor composed Haggai-Zechariah 1–8 as a unified, whole utterance.

The Canonical Context

Let me conclude this chapter by briefly comparing Haggai-Zechariah 1–8 with the books that comprise its canonical context.[54] The canonical literature surrounding Haggai-Zechariah 1–8 exhibits different structural, thematic, and stylistic characteristics, and these variations imply that Haggai-Zechariah 1–8 was originally an independent literary utterance. In this section, therefore, I will argue that "a change of speakers" delineates Haggai-Zechariah 1–8 from its canonical context.

First, the use of a chronological structure distinguishes Haggai-Zechariah 1–8 from its canonical context. No other book in the Twelve Prophets uses such a form to structure the text. Moreover, in contrast to Haggai-Zechariah 1–8, we do not find any dates in Zechariah 9–14. Rather than use a chronological structure, Zechariah 9–14 is divided into two main sections (9:1–11:17 and 12:1–14:21). Each section begins with the same three words: מַשָּׂא דְּבַר־יהוה (9:1 and 12:1). Malachi begins in a similar way (Mal. 1:1). As David Petersen observes of Haggai, "No other prophetic book evinces such a distinctive chronological ordering of a prophetic activity."[55] Moreover, unlike Jeremiah and Ezekiel, which also use dates, Haggai-Zechariah 1–8 is unusual in its use of a Persian royal chronology. In contrast, Jeremiah and Ezekiel use the regnal years of Judean kings to date their prophetic material.

Haggai-Zechariah 1–8 is also distinctive in its interest in the rebuilding of the temple and the political roles of Joshua and Zerubbabel. These two themes are absent in both Zephaniah, which precedes Haggai, and Zechariah 9–14. These two themes separate Haggai-Zechariah 1–8 from its canonical context and unify it as a single work.

Finally, Haggai-Zechariah 1–8 is distinctive in its consistent and frequent use of the word event formula and the message formula. Although these two formulas are employed in Zephaniah and Zechariah 9–14, their occurrences in these latter works are occasional only. For example, the word event formula occurs only once in Zephaniah (1:1). It does not occur at all in Zechariah 9–14. The message formula does occur in Zechariah 11:4. However, the wording of this particular formula is different from that found in Zechariah 1–8. Therefore, the high concentration of the word event formula and the message formula in Haggai-Zechariah 1–8 can only be attributed to the style and agenda of one particular editor.

In conclusion, Haggai-Zechariah 1–8 is the work of a single editor. This editor composed Haggai-Zechariah 1–8 as a unified, whole utterance. We have come to this conclusion by examining the structural, thematic and stylistic connections between Haggai and Zechariah 1–8. Of these three comparative categories, the chronological structure is the most patent, and it deserves further comment. In the following chapters, we will suggest reasons why the editor of Haggai-Zechariah 1–8 employed such a distinctive structure.

NOTES

[1]   M. M. Bakhtin, "The Problem of Speech Genres," in *Speech Genres and Other Late Essays* (Austin: University of Texas Press, 1986), 71.

[2]   Ibid.

[3]   Ibid., 75.

[4]   Like Beuken, I see no reason for doubting the authenticity of the dates in Haggai and Zechariah 1–8. See Beuken, *Haggai-Sacharja 1–8*, 25f. The only exception, in my opinion, is the date in Zech. 1:1. As we will discover, there is some evidence that this date is an editorial creation.

[5]   According to Wolff, the pre-chronistic form of Haggai consisted of five "scenes" (1:1–14; 1:15a and 2:15–19; 1:15b–2:9; 2:10–14; 2:20–23). The date in 1:15a was originally connected with the oracle now located in 2:15–19. However, the "Haggai-chronicler" reinterpreted the oracle of 2:15–19 by placing it after 2:10–14. The day of blessing, mentioned in the 2:15ff, is no longer associated with the rebuilding effort, as it was in the original "scene-sketch" (1:12–14), but is now associated with the refusal to let "the unclean" participate in the rebuilding (2:10–14). See Wolff, *Haggai*, 57–68.

[6]   The words, "in the second year of King Darius," in 1:15b can either be read with 1:15a or 2:1. As Carol and Eric Meyers observe, the phrase "may have been intended to do double duty" or "haplography may have caused the loss of one year phrase." See Meyers and Meyers, *Haggai*, 37.

[7]   Petersen, *Haggai*, 32.

[8]   Beuken, *Haggai-Sacharja 1–8*, 31–33; Meyers and Meyers, *Haggai*, 36.

[9]   Meyers and Meyers, *Haggai*, 36. Carol and Eric Meyers continue: "The ordering of the chronological information in 1:15 repeats, in reverse order, the information provided at the beginning of the chapter: 1:1 gives year, month, day; and 1:15 has day, month, year."

[10]   The author of Ezra also assumes that the two prophets were contemporaries whose primary task was to urge the people to rebuild the temple (Ezra 5:1).

[11]   See Petersen, *Haggai*, 128; Meyers and Meyers, *Haggai*, 96. According to Petitjean, v. 6b is an editorial addition but it represents a cultic confession that was used by both generations. See Albert Petitjean, *Les Oracles du Proto-Zacharie* (Paris: Gabalda, 1969), 49–52.

[12]   H. G. Mitchell, J. M. P. Smith, J. A. Bewer, *Haggai, Zechariah, Malachi and Jonah*, International Critical Commentaries (Edinburgh: T. & T. Clark, 1912), 109.

[13]   Joyce G. Baldwin, *Haggai, Zechariah, Malachi*, Tyndale Old Testament Commentaries (Leicester: Inter-Varsity Press, 1972), 87.

[14]   Petitjean, *Oracles*, 5.

[15]   According to Carol and Eric Meyers, the editor omitted the day in order to create a literary connection between Haggai and Zechariah 1–8: "The specific reasons or literary procedures behind the day's omission, if we assume it to be intentional, cannot be more than speculative. But its absence is surely a sign of the overriding concern to link the prophecies of Haggai and Zechariah so that their message became complementary parts of one larger whole." See Meyers and Meyers, *Haggai*, 90–91 and Petersen, *Haggai*, 128.

[16]   Joel F. Drinkard, "Numbers." In *Harper's Bible Dictionary*, ed., Paul J. Achtemeier (San Francisco: Harper Collins, 1985), 711–712. See Gen. 1:1–2:4; Lev. 25:2–7, 8–55; Exod. 24:1, 9; Jer. 25:12; Dan. 9:2.

[17]   On the basis of biblical and extrabiblical evidence, David Petersen argues that the "seventy years" was "a literary convention by which seventy years was the standard length for a period in which a nation suffers degradation because of divine displeasure" (Petersen, *Haggai*, 149). For biblical examples of this literary convention, see Isa. 23:15; Jer. 25:11; and Jer. 29:10.

[18]   The oracles are in the following order: Damascus (1:3–5), Gaza (1:6–8), Tyre (1:9–10), Edom (1:11–12), Ammon (1:13–15), Moab (2:1–3) and Judah (2:4–5). Each nation is threatened with a judgment of fire.

[19]   As Anderson and Freedman observe: "The numerical pattern 'three…four' also points to the symbolic total seven…. Although Amos makes only a single charge against each of the nations in this final reckoning, the sum is seven…. Thus the numerical pattern is more than a stereotype for a string of prophecies directed at each nation individually. It points as well to the total of seven nations, and their seven acts of rebellion against the suzerainty of the God of heaven and earth." See Francis I. Anderson and David Noel Freedman, *Amos*, The Anchor Bible (New York: Doubleday, 1989), 207.

[20]   Ronald M. Hals, *Ezekiel*, Forms of Old Testament Literature (Grand Rapids: Eerdmans, 1989), 178.

21   The seven nations are as follows: Ammon (25:1–7), Moab (25:8–11), Edom (25:12–14), Philistia (25:15–17), Tyre (26:1–28:19), Sidon (28:20–26) and Egypt (29:1–32:32). As Hals observes, the list of seven nations probably stems from the Deuteronomic tradition that seven nations of Canaan had to be defeated before Israel could take possession of the land. See Deut. 7:1. (Ibid., 180).

22   Ezek. 29:1–16; 29:17–21; 30:1–19; 30:20–26; 31:1–18; 32:1–16; and 32:17–32.

23   Ezek. 26:1; 29:1; 29:17; 30:20; 31:1; 32:1; and 32:17.

24   According to Deut. 28:1–2, "all these blessings" (כָּל־הַבְּרָכוֹת הָאֵלֶּה) will come upon the people "if you truly obey the voice of Yahweh your God."

25   See Petersen, *Haggai*, 70; Wolff, *Haggai*, 83f; Meyers and Meyers, *Haggai*, 55 and 75f. The ancient translators obviously had some trouble understanding this phrase as well because the LXX includes the following clause immediately after v. 9b: καὶ εἰρήνην ψυχῆς εἰς περιποίοιν παντὶ τῷ κτίζοντι τοῦ ἀναστῆσαι τὸν ναὸν τοῦτον. This particular translator interprets *šālôm* as being "peace of mind" for those who built the temple.

26   Thus, according to Carol and Eric Meyers: "This eschatological vision accords Yahweh the position of king. It is his House that is to be exalted with treasures, and Yahweh will give his blessings from there. The temple is a symbol of divine kingship, and no political king shares Yahweh's rule." See Meyers and Meyers, *Haggai*, 75–76.

27   Ibid., xlix and lx.

28   James Muilenburg, "Form Criticism and Beyond," *JBL* 88 (1969): 9.

29   According to H. W. Wolff: "שְׁאֵרִית ('remnant') is a term which is applied to the exiles as bearers of the promise. It becomes the title to salvation for the people who survived. It is widely used in exilic prophecy (cf. Isa. 46:3; Jer. 23:3; Mic. 2:12; 4:7; Zeph. 3:13 and frequently). The term is applied first of all to the people "who had escaped from the sword" at the deportation of 597 and 587 (2 Kings 19:31; Ezra 9:14; 2 Chron. 36:20) and later to homecomers from the gola (Neh. 7:71; cf. Mic. 7:18; Jer. 44:28; Zech. 8:6, 11f)." See Wolff, *Haggai*, 51–52.

30   Hag. 1:14; Zech. 7:3; 8:9. See also the reference to "the mountain of Yahweh Sebaoth" in Zech. 8:3.

31   According to Meyers and Meyers, "Haggai constitutes only about .2 percent of the Hebrew Bible, yet it contains 5 percent of the number of appearances of the title—namely fourteen occurrences. Similarly, Zechariah 1–8, which represents about .6 percent of the Hebrew Bible, includes forty-four occurrences of the title, or 15 percent of the total." (Meyers and Meyers, *Haggai*, 18). See also Tryggve N. D. Mettinger, *In Search of God: The Meaning and Message of the Everlasting Names* (Philadelphia: Fortress Press, 1988), 152.

32 For example, see Hag. 1:2, 5, 7, 9; Zech. 1:3, 4, 14, 16, 17.

33 The temple is called "the house of Yahweh Sebaoth" (בֵּית־יהוה צְבָאוֹת) in Hag.
    1:14; Zech. 7:3; and 8:9. Zion is called "the mountain of Yahweh Sebaoth" (צְבָאוֹת
    הַר־יהוה) in Zech. 8:3. Finally, Zech. 8:21–22 refer to "many peoples" coming to
    Jerusalem (presumably the temple. see 7:2–3) in order "to entreat the favor of
    Yahweh" and "to seek Yahweh Sebaoth" (לְבַקֵּשׁ אֶת־יהוה צְבָאוֹת).

34 See Zech. 2:13, 15; 4:9; 6:15; 7:12.

35 See Zech. 1:6, 12.

36 See Mettinger, *In Search of God*, 123–157; F. M. Cross, *Canaanite Myth and
    Hebrew Epic* (Cambridge, MA: Harvard University Press, 1973), 91–111; Ben C.
    Ollenburger, *Zion the City of the Great King*, JSOT Supplement Series 41
    (Sheffield: JSOT Press, 1987), 37f.

37 C. L. Seow summarizes this conception of Yahweh Sebaoth as follows: Yahweh
    Sebaoth "was perceived as the divine warrior who, having fought and won
    cosmogonic battles, had gained ascendency in the divine council as the supreme
    deity, the king over all the heavenly hosts." See C. L. Seow, *Myth, Drama, and the
    Politics of David's Dance*, Harvard Semitic Monographs (Atlanta: Scholars Press,
    1989), 13. Ps. 24 provides an excellent biblical example of this conception of
    Yahweh.

38 Thus, according to Mettinger: "The nucleus of the Zion-Sabaoth theology is the
    concept of God as the heavenly King who thrones upon the cherubim and who is
    invisibly present in his Temple." See T. N. D. Mettinger, *The Dethronement of
    Sabaoth: Studies in the Shem and Kabod Theologies*, trans. F. H. Cryer (Lund:
    CWK Cleerup, 1982), 37. See 2 Sam. 6:2; Isa. 6.

39 For example, see Joel 4:17; Isa. 2:2–3; and Ps. 48:2–3.

40 See Exod. 29:42–46; 40:34–35; Lev. 9:5–6, 23; Num. 14:10; 16:19.

41 Meyers and Meyers, *Haggai*, 157. In Ezek. 8–11, the prophet sees a vision of
    Yahweh's "glory" abandoning the temple (e.g., Ezek. 10:18–19; 11:22–23) and, in
    Ezek. 40–48, the prophet sees a vision of Yahweh's "glory" returning to the temple
    (e.g., Ezek. 43:2–5; 44:4).

42 See Exod. 25:8; 29:45; Lev. 16:16; 26:11–12; Num. 35:34. See also 1 Kings 6:13
    and Ezek. 43:7. On the basis of these biblical parallels to Zech. 2:14, Petersen
    concludes: "Given this particular linguistic background, it is difficult to gainsay the
    ritual implications of this formulation, that Yahweh's presence will dwell in the
    temple" (Petersen, *Haggai*, 180).

43 I understand the number four, as in four horns and four blacksmiths, to symbolize
    the four corners of the earth, that is, the entire earth. Thus, just as Yahweh
    dispatches four chariots to patrol the entire earth in the last vision (6:1–8), so

Yahweh declares his intention to subjugate the entire earth in the second vision (2:1–4).

44 According to Wolff, the "Haggai-chronicler" transformed the original "scene-sketch" of 1:4–11, 12b–13, which described how Haggai brought his people to "fear God," into a chronistic report about the beginning of the temple's reconstruction. By adding 1:1–3, 12a, 14, the "Haggai-chronicler" answers the questions: Who? (Zerubbabel, Joshua, and "the remnant") When? (August 29, 520 BCE) Why? (Yahweh "stirs up" the spirits of Zerubbabel, Joshua and "the remnant") How? (by the agency of the prophet Haggai). See Wolff, *Haggai*, 54–55.

45 Usually, the phrase, "Yahweh stirs up the spirit," is used in reference to the actions of kings. See Jer. 51:11; 1 Chron. 5:26; 2 Chron. 21:16; 36:22; Ezra 1:1.

46 The term "servant" is used as a royal title in 2 Sam. 7:5; Ps. 132:10 and Isa. 37:35. The simile, "like a signet ring," is another royal image (see Jer. 22:24). See Petersen, *Haggai*, 103f.

47 Many commentators translate and interpret the phrase, "sons of oil" (בְנֵי־הַיִּצְהָר), to mean "anointed ones." For example, see Baldwin, *Haggai*, 124; H. G. Mitchell, *Haggai*, 165; R. L. Smith, *Micah-Malachi*, Word Biblical Commentary (Waco: Word Books, 1984), 205. However, in the Hebrew Bible, the word יִצְהָר is never used to refer to anointing oil. The word שֶׁמֶן is usually used for anointing oil (see 1 Sam. 10:1; 16:1; 2 Kings 9:3; Lev. 8:30). As Petersen observes, the word יִצְהָר "is regularly used in a stereotypical list ("grain, wine, oil") to indicate the natural and bountiful harvest of Syria-Palestine.... The primary connotation of the noun remains, however, fertility." See Petersen, *Haggai*, 230. The following texts exemplify this meaning of יִצְהָר : Hos. 2:10; Joel 2:19, 24; Jer. 31:12; Deut. 7:13; and Hag. 1:11.

48 As Zech. 6:13 implies, the title Branch is a messianic appellation (see Jer. 23:5).

49 See Petersen, *Haggai*, 276; Baldwin, *Haggai*, 134; Mitchell, *Haggai*, 185ff. In contrast, other scholars argue that Zech. 6:12 is referring to a future Davidic ruler who, unlike Zerubbabel, will not be subservient to the Persians. See Meyers and Meyers, *Haggai*, 356f and Janet E. Tollington, *Tradition and Innovation in Haggai and Zechariah 1–8*, JSOT Supplement Series (Sheffield: JSOT Press, 1993), 172.

50 The interpretation of Zech. 3:7 is difficult because of syntactical ambiguity: where does the apodosis of this conditional blessing begin? According to Carol and Eric Meyers, the shift from אִם to גַם marks the beginning of the apodosis and, therefore, they translate this verse as follows: "If you walk in my ways and if you keep my service, then you will render judgment in my House and you will administer my courts; I will give you access to those who are standing here." See Meyers and Meyers, *Haggai*, 194. However, on the basis of normal syntax (the adverb גַם usually means "in addition, moreover" and "does not regularly occur at the beginning of the apodosis of a conditional clause") and similar content ("all the first four cola in Zech. 3:7 raise the issue of responsibility over areas of action"), David

Petersen argues that the apodosis does not begin until the final cola of the verse. See Petersen, *Haggai*, 203–206 and Beuken, *Haggai-Sacharja 1–8*, 293.

[51]   M. M. Bakhtin, "Speech Genres," 60.

[52]   For example, see Hag. 1:5, 7; 2:6; Zech. 1:3, 4, 14, 17.

[53]   Meyers and Meyers, *Haggai*, 18.

[54]   For more detailed discussions on the historical-critical distinction between Zechariah 1–8 and Zechariah 9–11, 12–14, see B. S. Childs, *Introduction to the Old Testament as Scripture* (Philadelphia: Fortress, 1979), 479–487; O. Eissfeldt, *The Old Testament: An Introduction* (Oxford: Basil Blackwell, 1965), 435–440; Mitchell, *Haggai*, 232–259.

[55]   Petersen, *Haggai*, 32–33.

CHAPTER THREE
The Babylonian Chronicles

We can only determine the uniqueness of Haggai-Zechariah 1–8 by comparing it with other ancient Near Eastern chronicles. Before we can analyze the distinctive use of the chronistic form in Haggai-Zechariah 1–8, we must first define the generic characteristics of the chronicles. In this chapter, therefore, we will analyze the chronistic genre as it is exemplified in a group of texts known as the Babylonian chronicles.

John van Seters defines the generic characteristics of an ancient Near Eastern chronicle as follows: "A chronicle is a narration of political or religious events in chronological order and is closely dated to the years of a king's reign."[1] Unfortunately, the only extant examples of this genre are the Babylonian chronicles.

Apparently, the genre of the chronicles also existed in ancient Israel. The two sources used by the Deuteronomistic historian to compose the Book of Kings, "the book of the annual actions of the kings of Israel" and "the book of the annual actions of the kings of Judah," were probably chronicles. The historian refers to these two sources throughout 1 and 2 Kings (e.g., 1 Kings 14:19, 29; 15:7, 23, 31). In the next chapter, we will examine the biblical evidence of 1 and 2 Kings to determine whether these two sources were Israelite examples of the chronistic genre. However, since these two books no longer exist, we must rely upon the Babylonian chronicles to provide the primary evidence of this particular ancient Near Eastern genre.

Kirk Grayson classifies twenty-four Babylonian texts as chronicles.[2] However, in this analysis of the genre, we will only examine the following fourteen texts: the seven chronicles of the Neo-Babylonian Chronicle Series;[3] the Esarhaddon Chronicle; the Shamash-shuma-ukin Chronicle; the

Akitu Chronicle; the Religious Chronicle; the Chronicle of the Early Kings; Chronicle P; and the Eclectic Chronicle.[4] All these chronicles were composed in Babylon prior to Haggai-Zechariah 1–8. In other words, they were composed before the end of the fifth century BCE.

We have not included the six chronicles of the Late Babylonian Chronicle Series in this analysis because these chronicles were written later, i.e., in the late Persian period and the Hellenistic period. We have not included the so-called Synchronistic History because this particular text originated in Assyria rather than in Babylon. The Dynastic Chronicle has not been included because, as Grayson observes, it "defies precise classification as either chronicle or king list" (p. 40). Finally, we have not included the remaining two texts, in Grayson's list, because of their unique content. As Grayson observes, the Weidner Chronicle "is unique…in comparison with other Babylonian chronicles" because it contains direct speech of divine beings and is, therefore, more mythological (p. 43). The Chronicle of Market Prices "is unique among ancient Mesopotamian chronicles in that it is concerned with prices of commodities at various periods of time in Babylonian history" (p. 60).

As a genre, the fourteen Babylonian chronicles, listed above, share a similar perspective on time and space. They all exhibit the same chronotope. According to Bakhtin, "it is precisely the chronotope that defines genre and generic distinctions."[5] Therefore, in the first section of this chapter, we will analyze the generic chronotope of the Babylonian chronicles.

The literary representation of time and space is organically related to the time and place in which the chronotope was developed. Consequently, the chronotope provides insights about the social and historical setting of a genre. Therefore, in the second section, we will reconstruct the socio-historical setting of the Babylonian chronicles.

A chronotope also performs a particular socio-political function within this setting. A chronotope either preserves the socio-political order (ideological function) or subverts it (utopian function). Therefore, in the third section, we will conclude this chapter by examining the socio-political function of the chronistic chronotope.

The Chronotope

In his essay, "Forms of Time and of the Chronotope in the Novel," Bakhtin distinguishes various novelistic genres according to how each genre conveys its view of time (*chronos*) and of space (*topos*). Each genre prescribes a particular temporal and spatial context for the materialization of actions and events. In this section, we will analyze the chronotope of the Babylonian chronicles by examining the chronicles' conceptualization of time, of space, and of the human actor. As we begin this analysis, let us realize that isolating characteristics of a generic chronotope from its textual embodiment is artificial. Nonetheless, for the purpose of this analysis, we must isolate these characteristics in order to identify the distinctiveness of the genre.[6] A proper analysis requires that these characteristics be not only isolated but also compartmentalized despite the fact that this is an artificial dissection of the text.

The actions of the king

The chronotope of the chronicles provides a temporal and spatial context for the actions of kings.[7] The actions upon which the Babylonian chronicles focus are military actions. The main emphasis of the Babylonian chronicles is to narrate the wars of the Babylonian kings. A common refrain that we find in all the chronicles of the Neo-Babylonian Chronicle Series is the phrase "the king mustered his army and marched." For example, in Chronicle 3, we read: "The tenth year of Nabopolassar: In the month Iyyar he mustered the army of Akkad and marched along the bank of the Euphrates" (line 1, ABC p. 91).[8] Another common refrain is the phrase "PN did battle against...." For example, in Chronicle 1, we read: "The second year of Merodach-baladan (II): Humban-nikash (I), king of Elam, did battle against Sargon (II), king of Assyria" (i.33f, p. 73).[9] According to the chronotopic perspective of the Babylonian chronicles, the king's primary responsibility was to raise an army and lead it into battle.

The Babylonian chronicles also document the wars of foreign kings. For example, Chronicle 1 narrates the campaigns of Assyrian and Elamite kings. Similarly, Chronicle 7 narrates the campaigns of Cyrus II of Persia. These chronicles document these wars because they ultimately affected the royal succession in Babylon.[10] Babylonian kings were overthrown by the military actions of the foreign kings.

The Babylonian chronicles also describe how the military activity of kings affected cultic activity in the region. According to these chronicles, the wars of the kings resulted in the capture or return of cultic images.[11] For example, according to Chronicle 1 iii.2–3, "the Elamites had come and carried off the gods and inhabitants of Uruk" (ABC, p. 79). Later, the chronicle documents the return of the gods: "On the third day of the month Tammuz the gods of Uruk went from [Ela]m into Uruk" (iii.28–29, p. 81).

The first action of Nabopolassar, upon ascending the throne of Babylon, was to return to Susa the city's divine images (Chronicle 2 lines 16–17, p. 88).[12] Interestingly, within these chronicles, the movement of divine images is often placed in parallel to the military movement of kings and their armies. The chronicles employ the same language to describe both the movement of kings and the movement of divine images. Just as the kings "march" (*alāku*) to war and then return "to Babylon," so the gods also "march" (*alāku*) to Babylon.[13]

The wars of the kings also caused interruptions in the celebration of the Akitu festival, the most important cultic event of the Babylonian year.[14] According to Chronicles 14, 16 and 22, Babylon could not celebrate the Akitu festival because the Assyrian army had brought the captured image of Marduk to Assyria after subjugating Babylon.[15] Military disorder in Babylonia also resulted in the non-celebration of the festival. For example, according to Chronicle 16, the Akitu festival did not take place because of "insurrections in Assyria and Akkad" (lines 17–19, p. 132). Similarly, Chronicle 17 explains the non-celebration of the festival by referring to the "belligerence" of the Arameans (iii.6–9, p. 137).

In summary, the Babylonian chronicles document the actions of kings. They primarily emphasize the military activity of Babylonian kings; the kings raise an army and march to battle. However, the chronicles also document the effect that these wars had on cultic activity in the region. As a consequence of the military actions of kings, cultic images were captured or returned and the Akitu festival was either neglected or celebrated.

The temporal perspective

The chronicles visualize the military actions of the king from the temporal perspective of the Babylonian royal succession.[16] The movement of time is associated with the succession of kings. Time progresses as each new king ascends the throne of Babylon.

The Neo-Babylonian Chronicle Series establish a temporal sequence whereby not only the duration of each reign but also each year within that reign is used to date all actions and events. The king's regnal years are the means by which time is measured. At the beginning of each new reign, a new system of numbering the years begins. Moreover, the documentation of each reign begins and ends in a similar way: "PN ascended the throne in Babylon" and "N years was PN king in Babylon." We find a concise example of the use of these formulas in Chronicle 1 i.12–15:

For fourteen years Nabu-nasir ruled Babylon. (Nabu)-nadin-(zeri), his son, ascended the throne in Babylon. The second year: (Nabu)-nadin-(zeri) was killed in a rebellion. For two years (Nabu)-nadin-(zeri) ruled Babylon (ABC, p. 72).

In order to maintain a consistent chronology, the chronicles even mention the length of time that there was no king in Babylon.[17] This is significant because it demonstrates that the chronicles are primarily interested in the continuation of the royal succession and not in the reign of any individual king.

The temporal perspective of the royal succession is also evident in the chronicles' use of a common terminology to describe each king's reign. Within Chronicles 3–6, each king in the royal succession marches to war and then returns to Babylon. The same words and formulas are consistently used to describe royal activity. For example, King Nabopolassar and his two successors, Nebuchadnezzar and Neriglissar, all "mustered" (*dekû*) the Babylonian army, "marched" (*alāku*) to war, and then "returned" (*târu*) to Babylon.[18]

Within the overarching perspective of the Babylonian royal succession, the chronicles also refer to the Assyrian and the Elamite royal successions. However, apart from the time when an Assyrian king sat on the throne of Babylon, the chronicles always date the accession of Assyrian and Elamite kings to the reign of a Babylonian king. Thus, Tiglath-pileser III ascended the throne of Assyria in the third year of Nabu-nasir (Chronicle 1 i.1–2, p. 70), and Humbannikash I ascended the throne of Elam in the fifth year of Nabu-nasir (Chronicle 1 i.9–10, p. 71). The Babylonian chronicles include this synchronistic information because these Assyrian and Elamite kings ultimately impacted the Babylonian royal succession. The military actions of these foreign kings resulted in the overthrow and replacement of Babylonian kings.[19]

We can discern the temporal perspective of the royal succession in other Babylonian chronicles. For example, although the Esarhaddon Chronicle (Chronicle 14) records the events of this Assyrian king's reign, lines 31–37 demonstrate that the chronicle is written from the perspective of the Babylonian royal succession and not the Assyrian royal succession. Ashurbanipal may succeed Esarhaddon and ascend the throne in Assyria (line 34), but the chronicle documents the events that follow according to the regnal years of Shamash-shuma-ukin, the new king of Babylon (lines 35–44, p. 127f). The Akitu Chronicle (Chronicle 16) also envisages time in terms of the Babylonian royal succession. This particular chronicle records and dates the interruptions of the Akitu festival by the reigns of five successive kings, beginning with Sennacherib and continuing with Esarhaddon, Shamash-shum-ukin, Kandalanu, and Nabopolassar (p. 131f). Finally, Chronicle 20 documents the actions of a series of kings beginning with Sargon of Akkad and concluding with Agum III (p. 152–156).

In summary, the Babylonian chronicles conceive time from the perspective of the Babylonian royal succession. These chronicles not only narrate the actions of the king in chronological order, according to the years of a king's reign, but also place each king's reign within a sequence of successive kings.

The spatial perspective

An examination of the chronotope must examine the spatial perspective of the genre as well as its temporal perspective. The Babylonian chronicles visualize the actions of the king from the spatial perspective of the royal city of Babylon. The worldview contained in the chronicles has as its basic geographical point of reference the city of Babylon. This geographic centrality is primarily due to the city's unique status as the location of the royal accession, rule, and authority.

According to the spatial perspective of the chronicles, the king rules in Babylon. A king could not be a Babylonian king in any other city. A voluntary or enforced absence from Babylon, for a long period, meant the loss of the throne. For example, after being defeated by the Assyrians, King Merodach-baladan II "fled to Elam" and, subsequently, Sargon II "ascended the throne in Babylon" (Chronicle 1 ii.1–5, p. 75). Similarly, Bel-ibni's reign ended as soon as he was "led away to Assyria" (Chronicle 1 ii.26–31, p. 77). Thus, it is no coincidence that in Chronicle 7, the narration of the Persian victory over Nabonidus occurs after the fourfold repetition of the phrases, "the king (Nabonidus) was in Tema" and "the king did not come to Babylon in the month Nisan" (p. 106–108).[20] By means of repetition, the composer of the chronicle implies that Nabonidus lost his throne, in part, because he was absent from Babylon. Therefore, according to the spatial perspective of the chronicles, the continuation of the royal succession is intricately connected with, if not dependent upon, the king's presence in the royal city of Babylon.

The chronicles also exhibit the spatial perspective of the chronicles through the documentation of royal activity. As the geographical center of power, authority, and rule, Babylon is the site to which Babylonian kings must return after a military campaign. Thus, in the Neo-Babylonian Chronicle Series, most campaigns conclude with a reference to the king and his army returning "to Babylon" or "to his land" with booty in hand.[21] For example, after describing a successful campaign in the tenth year of King Nabopolassar, Chronicle 3 concludes:

> They (the army of Akkad) inflicted a major defeat upon them (the army of Assyria) and drove them (back) to the Zab River. They captured their chariots and horses and plundered them extensively. They took many [...] with them across the Tigris and brought (them) into Babylon (lines 13–15, p. 92).

Similarly, Chronicle 20 B obverse 8–12 concludes its account of Hammurapi's war against Rim-Sin I, king of Ur, as follows: "(Hammurapi) captured Ur and Larsa (and) took their property to Babylon" (p. 155).

The chronicles also describe the wars of foreign kings from the perspective of the city of Babylon. According to the spatial perspective of the chronicles, these foreign wars ultimately affected the city of Babylon. For example, Chronicle 22 iv.1–6 documents the war of the Assyrian king, Tukulti-Ninurta I, who "destroyed the wall of Babylon (and) [pu]t the Babylonians to the sword" (p. 175). As we have seen, the wars of foreign kings also affected the royal succession *in Babylon*. For example, according to Chronicle 1, Sargon II of Assyria invaded Akkad, deposed Merodach-baladan II of Babylon, and subsequently, ascended the throne *in Babylon* (Chronicle 1 ii.1–5, p. 75). Similarly, Chronicle 7 records two military campaigns of the Persian king, Cyrus II (ii.1–4, 15–18, p. 106f). The chronicle documents these wars because the army of Cyrus eventually invaded Akkad, deposed Nabonidus from the throne of Babylon and "entered Babylon" in triumph (iii.12–16, p. 109f).

The thematic concern to document the occasions when military activity interrupted the celebration of the Akitu festival is another means by which the chronicles exhibit the spatial perspective. This recurrent etiology presupposes the spatial perspective of the royal city because the festival could not be celebrated if the king was not present *in Babylon*. For example, according to Chronicle 7, the Akitu festival could not be celebrated during the reign of Nabonidus because Nabonidus remained in Tema and "did not come to Babylon" (Chronicle 7 ii.5–6, p. 106). According to the Esarhaddon Chronicle (Chronicle 14), the Akitu festival was not celebrated for twenty years because the cultic image of Marduk had been brought to Assyria (Chronicle 14 lines 32–33, p. 127). These twenty years coincided with the period of time when there was no king *in Babylon*. As soon as a king ascended the throne *in Babylon*, however, Marduk returned to Babylon and the city celebrated the Akitu festival.[22]

In summary, the Babylonian chronicles visualize space from the perspective of the royal city of Babylon. As the dwelling place of the king, Babylon is the location of royal rule and authority, the primary beneficiary of a successful military campaign, and the setting for the celebration of the Akitu festival.

The royal image

The ultimate goal of a Bakhtinian analysis of a chronotope is to discern the generic portrayal of the human image. As we might expect, the main protagonist in the chronicles is the ever-changing occupant of the royal throne. Consequently, the human image in the chronicles is a royal one. The particularity of the person of the king is unimportant. The proper execution of the royal office is paramount. Within the temporal confines of the royal succession and the spatial confines of the city of Babylon, the Babylonian chronicles compare each king with an image of an ideal king. The Babylonian chronicles portray this ideal king as a warrior who protects and enriches the city of Babylon.

According to the Babylonian chronicles, the primary responsibility of the king is to guarantee the safety of Babylon by protecting or by extending the national borders. The chronicles contrast kings who fulfilled this obligation with those kings who destroyed and impoverished Babylon. Occasionally, the chronicles explicitly condemn kings for their military actions against Babylon. Chronicle 20 contains two examples of such an explicit judgment. In the account of King Sargon's reign, the chronicle concludes:

> He (Sargon) dug up the dirt of the pit of Babylon and made a counterpart of Babylon next to Agade. Because of the wrong he had done the great lord Marduk became angry and wiped out his people by famine. They (his subjects) rebelled against him from east to west and he (Marduk) afflicted [him] with insomnia (Chronicle 20 A lines 18–23, p. 153f).

Digging up dirt from a city is an idiom for the destruction of a city.[23] Because Sargon destroyed Babylon, Marduk "became angry" and punished him. Similarly, in the same chronicle, Marduk punishes king Shulgi because "he had criminal tendencies and took away the property of Esagil and Babylon as booty" (Chronicle 20 A lines 28–30, ABC, 154). Both Sargon and Shulgi compared unfavorably with the chronistic image of the ideal king. Instead of protecting the city, they weakened and impoverished Babylon.

The composer of Chronicle 20 contrasts the "sinful" actions of Sargon and Shulgi with the military success of Hammurapi. In contrast to Sargon and Shulgi, Hammurapi fought a successful war against a neighboring city-state and brought booty "to Babylon:"

> Hammurapi, king of Babylon, mustered his army and marched against Rim-Sin (I), king of Ur. He captured Ur and Larsa (and) took their property to Babylon. He brought [*Rim-S*]*in* (I) in a ... to Babylon (Chronicle 20 B Obverse lines 8–12, p. 155).

By extending the borders and, consequently, enriching Babylon through warfare, Hammurapi fulfilled the expectations of the chroniclers.[24]

We find a similar contrast in Chronicle 22. This particular chronicle contrasts an Assyrian king with a Babylonian king. The Assyrian king impoverished Babylon and was punished. The Babylonian king enriched Babylon by means of military success. Chronicle 22 ii.1–iii.22 records the reign of King Kurigalzu II of Babylon. On two occasions, the chronicle mentions the enrichment of Babylon through the military success of the king.[25] In other words, the chronicle clearly associates the military victories of Kurigalzu with the resulting prosperity brought to the city of Babylon.

In contrast to the prosperous reign of Kurigalzu, the reign of Tukulti-Ninurta I of Assyria brought disaster to Babylon:

> He (Tukulti-Ninurta) destroyed the wall of Babylon (and) [pu]t the Babylonians to the sword. He took out the property of Esagil and Babylon amid the booty. He removed the great lord Marduk [from] his [dais] and sent (him) to Assyria (Chronicle 22 iv.4–6, p. 175f).

A few lines later, the chronicle records the subsequent death of this king "who had carried out criminal designs on Babylon" (Chronicle 22 iv.8–11, p. 176). Because of his "criminal designs on Babylon," Tukulti-Ninurta lost his throne. The stated contrast between Kurigalzu and Tukulti-Ninurta indicates an underlying chronistic image of the ideal king. An ideal king protects and enriches Babylon.

Chronicle 1 implicitly indicts another Assyrian king because of his actions toward the city of Babylon. According to this chronicle, the Assyrian army destroyed Babylon in the fourth year of King Mushezib-Marduk of Babylon (Chronicle 1 iii.19–24, p. 80f). Although it is not actually stated, we know that King Sennacherib of Assyria was responsible for this demise.[26] The chronicle continues with a record of events in the eighth year after Babylon's destruction (Chronicle 1 iii.28–38, p. 81f). In this year,

"Sennacherib, king of Assyria, was killed by his son in a rebellion." By not recording the events of the intervening eight years, the chronicle clearly connects Sennacherib's death with his "capture" of Babylon; the implication is that a causal relationship exists between the desecration of the royal city and the personal and political death of the offender. [27]

I have already mentioned the chronistic concern to narrate the military actions of foreign kings. In Chronicle 1, Assyrian and Elamite kings are the military agents of change. The Babylonian kings, by contrast, are passive agents because they are impotent at preventing military incursions into Akkad. Subsequently, they are unable to prevent the impoverishment of Babylon and other Babylonian cities. For example, the chronistic record of Nabu-nasir's third year does not contain any information about the Babylonian king but rather records an Assyrian invasion of Akkad:

> [*The third year of Nabu-nasir,*] king of Babylon: Tiglath-pileser (III) ascended the throne in Assyria. In that same year [the king of Assyria] went down to Akkad, plundered Rabbilu and Hamranu, and abducted the gods of Shapazzu (Chronicle 1 i.1–5, Grayson's italics, ABC, 70f).

In Chronicle 1, the Babylonian kings are ineffectual. They cannot prevent foreign kings from ravaging their kingdom.[28] This portrayal of royal passivity is an implicit condemnation of those kings.

In contrast to the ineffective Babylonian kings of Chronicle 1, the Babylonian kings of Chronicles 2–6 are portrayed more positively. Chronicles 2–6 portray these latter kings as active agents. These kings "muster" the troops, "march" to war, and enrich Babylon with foreign booty. A well-known example is the chronistic account of Nebuchadnezzar's capture of Jerusalem in 597 BCE:

> The seventh year: In the month Kislev the king of Akkad mustered his army and marched to Hattu. He encamped against the city of Judah and on the second day of the month Adar he captured the city (and) seized (its) king. A king of his own choice he appointed in the city (and) taking the vast tribute he brought it into Babylon (Chronicle 5 Reverse lines 11–13, p. 102).

Nebuchadnezzar is one example of an effective Babylonian king who protects and enriches Babylon. Such is the image of the ideal king in the Babylonian chronicles.[29]

Just as the chronicles compare kings according to their effectiveness in protecting and enriching Babylon, so too they compare kings on the basis of their cultic participation in the Akitu festival. On the one hand, the chronicles associate military weakness with the royal neglect of the Akitu festival. On the other hand, the chronicles associate military strength with royal participation in the festival.

Chronicle 1, Chronicle 14, and Chronicle 16 all refer to the twenty years that Marduk was exiled in Assyria, during which time the Akitu festival was not celebrated.[30] These twenty years correspond to a period when there was no king in Babylon and Babylon was ruled by the Assyrian kings, Sennacherib and Esarhaddon. In other words, this period corresponds to a low-point in Babylonian military and political history. However, as soon as a king ascends the Babylonian throne and celebrates the Akitu festival, the chronicle records a military victory. Thus, we read in Chronicle 14:

> The accession year of Shamash-shuma-ukin: In the month Iyyar Bel and the gods of [Akkad] went out from Baltil (Ashur) and on the twenty-fifth day of the month Iyyar [they entered] Babylon. Nabu and the gods of Borsippa [went] to Babylon. In that same year Kirbitu was taken (and) its king cap[tured] (Chronicle 14 lines 35–38, p. 127). [31]

This passage clearly places the responsibilities of the Babylonian king within the temporal context of the royal succession and the spatial context of the city of Babylon. By celebrating the Akitu festival in Babylon, the king guarantees his own succession and achieves military success.[32]

In contrast to Shamash-shuma-ukin who secured his rule and guaranteed military success by celebrating the Akitu festival, Nabonidus lost his throne because he neglected the festival. According to Chronicle 7, Nabonidus neglected the festival with the result that Cyrus defeated Nabonidus in battle. For five years in a row, Nabonidus was absent from Babylon and the Akitu festival was not celebrated. Subsequently, the chronicle records the defeat of Nabonidus and the victorious entrance of Cyrus into Babylon (Chronicle 7 iii.12–18, p. 109f).[33]

In summary, the Babylonian chronicles portray the king as a warrior who protects and enriches the city of Babylon. Within the confines of the temporal perspective and spatial perspective, the chronicles contrast kings who destroyed and impoverished Babylon with kings who enriched it by military conquest. The chronicles also contrast kings who celebrated the Akitu festival with kings who did not. Royal participation in the festival is associated with military strength. Royal neglect of the festival is associated with military weakness.

In conclusion, all the Babylonian chronicles share a similar chronotopic perspective. All these chronicles describe the actions of the king from the temporal perspective of the Babylonian royal succession and the spatial perspective of the royal palace of Babylon. Consequently, all these chronicles portray an image of the ideal king. The ideal king, according to these chronicles, protects and enriches the city of Babylon.

The Socio-Historical Context

From a literary representation of the world (time, space and the human actor), we must progress to the socio-historical setting of the text. A chronotope is organically related to the time and the place in which it was created. According to the Bakhtin Circle, "(t)he conceptualization of reality develops and generates in the process of ideological social discourse."[34] A literary chronotope reflects the worldview of a particular social group at a particular point in history as they interact and communicate with other social groups. Therefore, in this section, we will reconstruct the social discourse that generated the chronotopic worldview of the Babylonian chronicles. First, we will identify the original participants (the addresser and the addressee) in the discourse. We will then reconstruct the historical situation from which the chronicles emerged. If the previous section enabled us to "see" through the lens of the chronicles, this section will enable us to "hear" the voices of the discourse.

The addresser

In his portrait of the ancient Mesopotamian civilization, A. Leo Oppenheim suggests that temple scribes composed the chronicles. All the Mesopotamian city temples had scribes whose primary responsibility it was to administer the business of the temple. These scribes kept records of the income and the payments of the temple organization.[35] As Oppenheim observes, temple scribes also collected and copied older texts:

> The names as well as deeds, crimes, and victories of famous rulers seem to have been kept alive through some oral tradition that must have centered in sanctuaries rather than in palaces. The interest of the palace in tradition was by nature short-lived and geared to matters of immediate concern, but the scholars, administrators, and experts living in the temple were prone to keep stories alive that enhanced the importance of the sanctuary or record, in lamentations, its destruction. From such a body of written and unwritten stories must come all the proverbial sayings, the king lists and the chronicles and, above all, the references in the omen collections to the famous kings of old.[36]

In contrast to the palace scribes who composed the royal inscriptions that celebrated the military and/or building achievements of the present king, the temple scribes maintained records of past kings who did or did not respect the temple and its cult.

On the basis of our prior analysis of the chronistic chronotope, we can advance four arguments in support of Oppenheim's suggestion that the temple scribes of Esagil were the composers of the Babylonian chronicles. First, the chronotopic worldview of the chronicles is similar to the mythic-cultic worldview of the temple scribes of Esagil who organized the Akitu festival. Second, the chronicles display a particular interest in the fate of Esagil and its treasures. Third, the composers of the chronicles used sources that were composed by temple scribes. Finally, unlike the Assyrian annals, the Babylonian chronicles were more critical toward the monarchy. This critical stance suggests that the composers of the chronicles were temple scribes rather than palace scribes.

The vast majority of the chronicles refer to the celebration or non-celebration of the Akitu festival. For example, the major concern of the Akitu Chronicle and the Religious Chronicle is to explain interruptions in the annual celebration of the festival. Moreover, as we observed in our analysis of the chronotope, the chronicles associate the military success of kings with royal participation in the Akitu festival. If we examine the main themes of the Akitu festival, as it was celebrated in Babylon, we will discover that the chronotopic worldview of the chronicles and the mythic-cultic worldview of the Akitu festival share a similar perspective on time, space and the responsibilities of the king. These similarities suggest that the composers of the chronicles belonged to the social group that organized the festival, that is, the temple scribes of Esagil.

The Akitu festival was the most important cultic event of the Babylonian year.[37] The festival was originally an agricultural festival that either celebrated or ensured the barley harvest.[38] In Babylon, this agricultural festival gradually merged with the New Year festival (*zagmukku*), celebrated in the first twelve days of Nisan.[39] Various cultic ceremonies took place during these twelve days. The most important ceremonies were the recitation of the Enuma Elish, the arrival of Nabu into Babylon, the ritual humiliation of the king, the procession of the gods to the Akitu temple, a cultic drama symbolizing Marduk's victory over Tiamat, and a sacred marriage. Instead of explaining all these ceremonies according to a single, unified interpretation, J. A. Black considers these ceremonies to be "a complex accretion, over a long period, of a number, probably at least half a dozen, different elements from different rites and cults."[40] Thus, Black claims that, over a long period of time, the Akitu festival came to be associated with the following six themes:

> (1) an attempt to celebrate or ensure the success of the spring harvest or barley (the "cultic picnic"),
> (2) a patronal festival of the city-god, Marduk, including his enthronement ("taking Bel by the hand"), including (3) symbolic representation of certain episodes in the Epic of Creation,
> (4) the marking of the calendrical aspect of the New Year,
> (5) the affirmation of the king as high priest of Marduk, owing his kingship to the god: but *not* as substitute for or representative of the god, and
> (6) the reception and enthronement of the god Nabû.[41]

For the purpose of this study, we will examine the second, third, and fifth themes of the festival. As we will discover, these three themes display a similar chronotopic perspective as the Babylonian chronicles.

First, the Akitu festival was "the patronal festival of the city-god of Babylon, Marduk." As such, the festival affirmed not only the divine kingship of Marduk but also the special status of Babylon as the dwelling place of Marduk. In the various prayers of the Akitu ritual, the priest addressed Marduk (Bel) as the divine king who dwelt in Babylon. For example, on the second day of Nisan, the *šešgallu*-priest prayed the following prayer:

> O Bel, who has no equal when angry, O Bel, excellent king, lord of the countries... O Bel, your dwelling is the city of Babylon, your tiara is the (neighboring) city of Borsippa.... Grant mercy to your city, Babylon! Turn your face to the temple Esagil, your house! Establish the "liberty" of the people of Babylon, your subordinates.[42]

In this prayer, the priest repeatedly emphasized the special relationship between Marduk and Babylon in order to remind Marduk of his responsibility to protect the city. This understanding of Babylon as a royal city in need of protection from the divine king is similar to the spatial perspective of the chronicles. Just as Marduk is expected to dwell in the royal capital city of Babylon and establish "liberty" for his people, so the human king of Babylon, according to the chronotopic perspective of the chronicles, is expected to follow Marduk's example.

Second, the Akitu festival also included the "symbolic representation of certain episodes in the Epic of Creation." The Babylonian Creation Epic, the Enuma Elish, was the cult-myth of the Akitu festival. During the festival, the

Epic was recited on the fourth day of Nisan.[43] In addition, certain episodes of the Epic were symbolically reenacted on other days of the festival. For example, according to W. G. Lambert, a cultic drama, symbolizing Marduk's victory over Tiamat (as recounted in the Epic), was performed in the Akitu temple on the tenth day of Nisan.[44] Black claims that the two assemblies of the cultic images, on the eighth and the eleventh days, were "symbolic representations of the two divine assemblies described respectively in the 3rd and 4th, and 6th tablets of the Epic."[45]

As the cult-myth of the festival, the Enuma Elish provided a mythological etiology of Marduk's status as the king of the gods and of Babylon's status as his royal dwelling place. According to Jacobsen, the Enuma Elish is:

> a mythopoeic adumbration of Babylon's and Marduk's rise to rulership over a united Babylonia, but projected back to mythical times and made universal.... It is a story of world origins and world ordering.[46]

The gods proclaimed Marduk as the heavenly king because he was the divine warrior who had defeated Tiamat (Tablet IV). Upon establishing order in the cosmos, Marduk's first demand, as the divine king, was that the gods build him a city. This city was to become Marduk's dwelling place and the permanent site for the divine assembly. Marduk designated the name of this city to be Babylon (Tablet V). The Epic concludes with the construction of Babylon and the acknowledgment, by the divine assembly, of Marduk's permanent rule over heaven and earth (Tablet VI).

The Enuma Elish not only reinforces Babylon's status as a royal city but also establishes a mythical origin for the Babylonian royal succession. As Jacobsen observes, the Enuma Elish portrays the world as "a well-run paternalistic monarchy with permanent king, capital, parliament, and royal palace in Babylon."[47] This is also the worldview of the chronicles. The movement of time is associated with the succession of kings. Like Marduk, the kings of Babylon receive this status because they are responsible for maintaining order. Just as Marduk established his rule as a consequence of his victory over Tiamat, so the Babylonian kings ensure the royal succession by means of military conquest. In other words, the temporal perspective of the chronicles is the same as the worldview of the Enuma Elish.

Third, the Akitu festival was "the affirmation of the king as high priest of Marduk." The king played a central role in the celebration of the Akitu festival. In particular, the king played a central role in three ceremonies: the entrance of Nabu into Babylon on the fourth day of Nisan, the ritual humiliation of the king on the fifth day, and the procession of the gods on the eighth day.

On the fourth day of Nisan, the king travels to Borsippa to fetch the statue of Nabu. The chronicles refer to this ceremony with the words, "Nabu came (or did not come) to Babylon (for the procession of Bel)."[48] On the following day, the king enters Esagil and is ritually humiliated. The *šešgallu*-priest removes the royal insignia (scepter, ring, and sword), strikes the king on the cheek, and forces the king to kneel before Marduk. In this position, the king makes the following confession:

> I have not sinned, Lord of the lands, I have not been negligent of your godhead. I
> have not destroyed Babylon, I have not ordered her to be dispersed. I have not
> made Esagil quake, I have not forgotten its rites. I have not struck the privileged
> citizens in the faces, I have not humiliated them. I have paid attention to Babylon,
> I have not destroyed her walls.[49]

In response, the *šešgallu*-priest assures the king: "He (Marduk) will destroy your enemies, defeat your adversaries."[50] Finally, on the eighth day, the king "took Bel by the hand" and initiated the procession of the gods through the streets of Babylon. The chronicles refer to this ceremony with the phrases, "RN took Bel by the hand" and "Bel went out (or did not go out)."[51]

These ceremonies affirm the king's role as the high priest of Marduk. As high priest, the king has a cultic responsibility to ensure the performance of certain rituals in Babylon as well as a military responsibility to protect Babylon. These are also the responsibilities of the ideal king in the chronicles. According to the chronicles, the ideal king ensures the survival and prosperity of Babylon by celebrating the Akitu festival in Babylon.

In summary, the chronotopic worldview of the chronicles is similar to the mythic-cultic worldview of the Akitu festival. As the patronal festival of Marduk, the Akitu festival affirms Babylon's status as a royal dwelling place. As the cult-myth of the festival, the Enuma Elish establishes a mythical etiology for the Babylonian royal succession. As the high priest of Marduk, the king is called upon to protect the city and to celebrate the Akitu festival. These similarities suggest that the composers of the chronicles belonged to the social group that organized the Akitu festival, that is, the temple scribes of Esagil.

Second, apart from the obvious interest in the celebration of the Akitu festival, the chronicles also display a particular interest in the fate of Esagil and its cultic treasures. For example, three chronicles document the return of the cultic image of Marduk to its original home in Babylon after a twenty-year exile in Assyria during the reigns of Sennacherib and Esarhaddon.[52] The Shamash-shuma-ukin Chronicle not only records the return of "the former bed" of Marduk to Babylon but also documents the building of a new "chariot" of Marduk (Chronicle 15 lines 4–5, p. 129). The Chronicle of Early Kings describes the "criminal tendencies" of Shulgi who "took away the property of Esagil and Babylon as booty" (Chronicle 20 A lines 28–30, p. 154). As we have already observed, Chronicle P contrasts Kurigalzu II, who built "a canopy of pure gold for Marduk," with Tukulti-Ninurta I, who plundered Esagil. (Chronicle 22 iii.8 and iv.5–6, p. 174, 176). Finally, the Eclectic Chronicle documents how Eriba-Marduk "set up the[*thro*]*ne* of Bel in Esagil and Ezida" (Chronicle 24 Reverse line 14, p. 183). In summary, the particular interest in the fate of Esagil and its treasures is further evidence that the temple scribes of Esagil composed the Babylonian chronicles.

Third, the composers of the chronicles used sources that were composed by temple scribes. One such source is the so-called "astronomical diaries." Astronomical diaries are:

> records of various phenomena, each text recording the events of half a specified year. The diaries are divided into sections, each section covering the almost day-to-day events of one month. Most of the phenomena recorded are of an astronomical or meteorological nature but at the end of each section there are statements about market prices, the height of a river, and matters of historical interest (ABC, p. 13).

The purpose of these diaries was "to provide accurate observation both for calendrical use and for prediction of the future by astrology."[53] On the basis of a number of factors—phraseology, typology, content, and chronology— Grayson argues that these diaries were used as sources for the Babylonian Chronicle Series (ABC, 174). Since the observation and documentation of unusual phenomena, for the purpose of omen predictions, probably occurred in the temple,[54] temple scribes probably composed these diaries.

The form and content of the Religious Chronicle suggest that an omen source, possibly the astronomical diaries, also underlie this particular chronicle. The Religious Chronicle documents not only interruptions of the Akitu festival but also mysterious events such as the appearance of wild animals in the city precincts. These mysterious events, however, are closely connected with interruptions of the festival. The documentation of a mysterious event is immediately followed by the news that the festival had not been celebrated.[55] The form of the chronicle implies that the two themes are interrelated. The formal relationship between these two themes parallels the relationship between the protasis of an omen and its apodosis.[56] In other words, the form of the Religious Chronicle is similar to, and is probably derived from, an omen collection.

In his introduction to the Chronicle of Early Kings (Chronicle 20), Grayson claims that this particular chronicler used two primary sources to compose the chronicle: the omen collections and the Weidner Chronicle.[57] All the information about Sargon and Naram-Sin is found in either the apodoses of the omen collections or in the Weidner Chronicle.[58] The use of omens as a literary source for the Chronicle of Early Kings is further evidence that temple scribes composed the chronicles. The use of the Weidner Chronicle suggests the same conclusion. The sole concern of this particular text is to document the success or failure of various kings in providing fish offerings for Esagil. As Grayson says, "The text, therefore, is a blatant piece of propaganda written as an admonition to future monarchs to pay heed to Babylon and its cult."[59] Consequently, the temple scribes of Esagil must have written it. The copying and preservation of this text also must have occurred in the temple. Therefore, the use of the Weidner Chronicle as a literary source for the Chronicle of Early Kings supports the likelihood that the temple scribes of Esagil developed the chronistic chronotope. In summary, the sources underlying the Babylonian chronicles were texts that must have been written and copied by temple scribes. The use of these sources is further evidence that the temple scribes of Esagil composed the chronicles.

One of the unusual characteristics of the Babylonian chronicles is their documentation of Babylonian military defeats. In stark contrast, the annals of Assyrian kings record only Assyrian military victories. While it is unlikely that a palace scribe would consistently record the failures of past kings, it is certainly possible that a Babylonian temple scribe would document the reigns of kings with special reference to their positive or negative actions toward Esagil. The Weidner Chronicle is a clear example of such a text.

The difference between the Assyrian annals (written by palace scribes) and the Babylonian chronicles (written by temple scribes) is due, in part, to the relative independence of the Babylonian temple from the royal palace. The political independence of the Babylonian temple, as compared with the Assyrian temple, is illustrated by differences in the cultic role of the king and the architecture of the temple.

In contrast to the Assyrian kings who had an important cultic role, Babylonian kings had a limited cultic role. Thus, according to Oppenheim:

The essential fact concerning the Assyrian king is that he was the high priest of the god Aššur. As such, he performed sacrifices and was in a position to influence both temple and cult. The Babylonian king was admitted into the cella of Marduk but once a year, and then only after having put aside his royal insignia.[60]

Significantly, the cultic role of the Babylonian king does not demonstrate his power but instead emphasizes his subservience to the city and to the temple.

Babylonian temple architecture also differed from Assyrian architecture; these differences again symbolically illustrate the extent of the king's influence in the ritual sphere. In Assyria, temple and palace formed a single fortified urban unit.[61] In Babylon and other Babylonian cities, the temple was clearly separated from the palace.[62] The architectural and the political separation of temple and palace in Babylon correspond to a limited cultic role for the king. This logistical and political distance explains why temple scribes were able to be critical of kings.

In summary, the temple scribes of Esagil composed the Babylonian chronicles. Consequently, the chronotopic perspective of the chronicles is similar to the mythic-cultic worldview of the Akitu festival, which was organized by the temple scribes. The thematic interest in the fate of Esagil and its treasures as well as the use of sources that must have been composed and copied in the temple support the conclusion that the temple scribes of Esagil composed the Babylonian chronicles. These temple scribes composed the chronicles in order to maintain a record of past kings who did or did not respect the temple and its important status in Babylonian society.

The addressee

Having identified the social group that authored the chronistic chronotope, let us now identify those whom they were addressing in the Babylonian chronicles. As the temple scribes composed the chronicles, they had a particular audience in mind. According to Bakhtin, each genre "has its own typical conception of the addressee."[63] The content of the Babylonian chronicles, with its emphasis on the military actions of the Babylonian kings, suggests that the kings themselves were the intended audience.

We can confirm this argument by examining royal inscriptions in which the kings apparently addressed the temple scribes of Esagil. In these inscriptions, the kings seek the political support of Esagil by claiming to be a particular type of king. The royal image that we find in the inscriptions is identical with the royal image that we find in the chronistic chronotope. In other words, the Babylonian chronicles and the royal inscriptions represent the two "voices" of the social discourse that underlies the chronistic chronotope. The chronicles represent the "voice" of the temple scribes as they addressed the kings and the inscriptions represent the "voice" of the kings as they addressed and responded to Esagil.[64]

We will begin by examining two inscriptions of Sennacherib in which Sennacherib refers to the destruction of Babylon in 689 BCE. Both inscriptions are primarily concerned to commemorate the building activity of Sennacherib. In the Bavian Inscription, Sennacherib describes the building of a canal that he built "for the good of Nineveh" (ARAB II, p. 153, paragraph 342). According to this inscription, Babylon was obliterated in the same year that this canal was opened. Sennacherib takes great delight in describing the fall of Babylon (p. 152, paragraph 341). Sennacherib also refers to Babylon's destruction in another building inscription. This second inscription commemorates the building of the Akitu temple outside the city walls of Assur. In this inscription, Sennacherib describes how Babylon was destroyed, its gods smashed, and its dust removed (ARAB, p. 185, paragraph 438). In each inscription, Sennacherib seeks political support from the inhabitants of either Nineveh or Assur. Thus, in the first text, Sennacherib contrasts his destruction of Babylon with his "building up" of Nineveh.[65] In the second text, Sennacherib claims that his destruction of Babylon demonstrates both the superiority of the Assyrian god, Assur, and the preeminence of the Assyrian city of Assur. Sennacherib justifies his destruction of Babylon by claiming that he was acting out of pious regard for the god, Assur, and out of duty to the city of Assur.[66]

The inscriptions of Esarhaddon provide another theological interpretation of Babylon's destruction. According to Esarhaddon, Marduk commanded "a former king" to destroy Babylon in order to punish Babylonian wickedness (ARAB, p. 242f, paragraph 642). Interestingly, Esarhaddon does not mention Sennacherib's military involvement in carrying out Marduk's punishment of Babylon. According to Cogan, this theological explanation for Babylon's destruction is of Babylonian origin. As evidence, Cogan refers to the inscriptions of Merodach-baladan and Nabonidus.[67] Further evidence for the Babylonian origin of this particular theological explanation is a bilingual composition that refers to the Elamite destruction of Babylon in the twelfth century BCE.[68] All these texts blame the destruction of the city on Babylonian wickedness during the reign of a former king. By employing this "apologia," Esarhaddon "sought to appease and win back Babylonia to the camp of Assyria."[69]

Esarhaddon's inscriptions support his political agenda by emphasizing his own role in rebuilding Esagil and Babylon. In contrast to Sennacherib, who took great pride in being known as the destroyer of Babylon, Esarhaddon refers to himself, in numerous inscriptions, as "the restorer of Esagil and Babylon."[70] While Esarhaddon portrays Sennacharib as the divinely appointed destroyer of Babylon, he depicts himself as the divinely appointed restorer of Babylon. Therefore, when "the merciful Marduk" resolves to restore Babylon after eleven years instead of the allotted seventy-year punishment,[71] Marduk commands Esarhaddon to accomplish this restoration. (ARAB, p. 243, paragraph 643). According to his royal inscriptions, Esarhaddon claims that he was commissioned by Marduk to restore Babylon and Esagil in the first year of his reign (p. 243, paragraph 645). However, as Cogan observes, this date is obviously a "pseudo-date." In these inscriptions, Esarhaddon insists that he was concerned about Marduk's city from the beginning of his reign.[72]

Esarhaddon's inscriptions also emphasize his role in reviving the economy of the city. In particular, Esarhaddon re-established the temple offerings (ARAB, p. 244, paragraph 646); released enslaved citizens of Babylon (p. 244, paragraph 646); protected the agricultural holdings of the city (p. 213, paragraph 535);[73] and restored the city's *kidinnûtu* status (p. 253, paragraph 659E).[74] All these actions were designed to reactivate the support of both the temple priesthood of Esagil and the free citizens of the city.

We find a similar political agenda underlying the Babylon-Borsippa dedicatory texts of Ashurbanipal. On Cylinder P[1], for example, Ashurbanipal explicitly refers to the exile of Marduk in Assyria. The underlying assumption is the Babylonian "apologia" for Babylon's destruction; Marduk deserted Babylon "in the reign of a former king" because he was angry at his city.[75] Ashurbanipal continues by emphasizing that it was during his own reign that Marduk returned to Babylon "amid rejoicing." Finally, Ashurbanipal insists that he provided "regular offerings" for Esagil, completed the temple rebuilding, and restored the agricultural holdings of the city (ARAB, p. 372, paragraph 962).

The Babylonian-oriented inscriptions of Esarhaddon and Ashurbanipal reflect Assyrian attempts to gain political support from both the priests of Esagil and the citizens of Babylon. By listening carefully to these ideological statements of the Assyrian kings, we can reconstruct the political agenda of the temple scribes of Esagil. For example, as we have seen, the Babylonian "apologia" for the destruction of Babylon, used by these Assyrian kings, is borrowed from the temple scribes of Esagil. The restoration of the temple and the return of Marduk are obviously major concerns of the temple scribes as is the economic situation of the temple. In their inscriptions, Esarhaddon and Ashurbanipal claim to live up to the expectations of the temple organization in order to gain their political support. Therefore, by listening to the "voices" of the Assyrian kings, we can also hear the muted "voice" of Esagil.

The "voice" of Esagil becomes louder when we turn to two royal inscriptions from a later period. In both inscriptions, the royal "author" contrasts himself with one or more previous kings. Whereas the previous king(s) had angered Marduk by neglecting the cult of Esagil and by impoverishing the city of Babylon, the present king claims to be an obedient servant of Marduk.

An inscription of Nabonidus provides a summary of Babylonian history from the reign of Sennacherib (704–681 BCE) to the reign of Nabonidus (555–536 BCE).[76] This inscription contrasts kings who destroyed temples and neglected cultic rites with kings who respected the gods and maintained temple worship.[77] The first column of the inscription describes the destruction of Babylon by Sennacherib. Even after almost one hundred and fifty years, this calamitous event is still being remembered as a traumatic event in the collective consciousness of the Babylonians. Even though Sennacherib was carrying out "the wrathful will" of Marduk against the wicked inhabitants of Babylon, he himself was an evil king because "with evil intentions against Babylon he let its sanctuaries fall in disrepair, disturbed the(ir) foundation outlines and let the cultic rites fall into oblivion." Subsequently, when Marduk "remembered (again) Esagila and Babylon, his princely residence," Marduk punished Sennacherib by causing his own son to murder him (ANET, p. 309).

In contrast to Sennacherib, Nabonidus claims to be a king "who always, daily (and) without interruption, is interested in the maintenance of the temples Esagila and Ezida" (p. 310). Accordingly, with great pride, Nabonidus mentions his silver plating of various rooms in the temple and he claims to be "a caretaker who brings large gifts to the great gods" (p. 310f). Nabonidus' most recent pious act was to restore, at Marduk's command, the temple of Sin in Harran (Ehulhul).[78]

Like Esarhaddon and Assurbanipal before him, Nabonidus sought the political support of both the temple administration of Esagil and the citizens of Babylon.[79] More specifically, Nabonidus sought political support for his restoration of Ehulhul in Harran. Apparently, Nabonidus' political authority in Babylon was precarious at the time that this inscription was composed. In the inscription, Nabonidus justifies his overthrow of Labashi-Marduk by insisting that he is "the real executor of the wills of Nebuchadnezzar and Neriglissar" rather than Labashi-Marduk who "sat down on the royal throne against the intentions of the gods" (p. 309). As evidence, Nabonidus claims that Nebuchadnezzar, his illustrious predecessor on the throne of Babylon, appeared to him in a dream to assure him of success (p. 310). In addition, Nabonidus makes a vow to Marduk that if Marduk gives him a long life and reign, he will take care of the sanctuaries (p. 310). Nabonidus claims that he had fulfilled this vow in Babylon and other Babylonian cities. He concludes his inscription with an account of his restoration of Ehulhul. This latter action, Nabonidus insists, was ordered by Marduk himself and had a precedent in the actions of Ashurbanipal (p. 311).

In spite of Nabonidus' insistence that he was carrying out the will of Marduk and was following the example of his illustrious royal predecessors, Nabonidus' restoration of Ehulhul was obviously not approved by either the temple priesthood of Esagil or the citizens of Babylon. The disapproval of Babylon is obvious in other texts of the period. For example, in an inscription from Harran, Nabonidus bitterly complains about the opposition of Babylonian citizens to his plan to restore Ehulhul.[80] Additionally, the so-called "Verse Account of Nabonidus" refers to his restoration of Ehulhul as one of the sins of Nabonidus (ANET, p. 313).

Let me conclude this reconstruction of the audience of the Babylonian chronicles by examining one final inscription, the Cyrus Cylinder.[81] In this inscription, Cyrus contrasts himself with Nabonidus. Whereas Nabonidus performed sacrilegious acts against Esagil and tormented the citizens of Babylon with corvée work,[82] Cyrus:

> strove for peace in Babylon and in all his (Marduk's) (other) sacred cities. As to the inhabitants of Babylon, [who] against the will of the gods [had/were..., I abolished] the corvée (lit., yoke) which was against their (social) standing. I brought relief to their dilapidated housing, putting (thus) an end to their (main) complaints. Marduk, the great lord, was well pleased with my deeds and sent friendly blessings to myself, Cyrus, the king who worships him, to Cambyses, my son, the offspring of [my] loins, as well as to all my troops, and we all [praised] his great [godhead] joyously, standing before him in peace (ANET, p. 316).

In addition, Cyrus claims to have repaired the other ruined sanctuaries of Babylonian and Assyrian cities. Cyrus also "resettled upon the command of Marduk, the great lord, all the gods of Sumer and Akkad whom Nabonidus had brought into Babylon to the anger of the lord of the gods, unharmed, in their (former) chapels" (p. 316). Interestingly, the inscription, according to a Yale fragment of the Cylinder, concludes with a reference to Ashurbanipal.

In other words, like Nabonidus, Cyrus contrasts himself with an evil king who disregarded the cult of Marduk and impoverished the city of Babylon (i.e., Sennacherib or Nabonidus) as well as presenting himself as "a restorer of what was right in the tradition of an earlier, venerated predecessor" (i.e., Ashurbanipal).[83]

In the Cyrus Cylinder, we can observe Cyrus following in the political tradition of Esarhaddon, Ashurbanipal and, for that matter, Nabonidus. Like these other kings, Cyrus seeks political support from both the priesthood of Esagil and the citizens of Babylon by claiming to have performed both cultic and economic actions that benefited the city and the temple. For example, Cyrus claims that he restored the preeminence of the Marduk cult and reestablished the *kidinnûtu* status of Babylon.

By examining the inscriptions of Esarhaddon, Assurbanipal, Nabonidus, and Cyrus, we can detect the political agenda and the "voice" of the temple scribes of Esagil whom these kings were courting. This agenda is comprised of the following assumptions directed toward the king; all these assumptions presuppose the preeminence of the city of Babylon and the cult of Esagil. First, Esagil expects the king to patronize the cult of Esagil by the reconstruction of temple buildings, the refurbishment of temple furniture, and the performance of certain cultic functions. Second, Esagil also expects the king to maintain the economic health and commerce of the city and temple. Third, Esagil judges and compares individual kings to their predecessors on the basis of their fulfillment of these first two assumptions.

We can corroborate these political assumptions by examining two non-chronistic texts that are clearly propagandistic compositions of Esagil; the Weidner Chronicle and the Persian Verse Account.[84] In his introduction to the Weidner Chronicle, Grayson observes:

> In so far as the text is preserved, it is exclusively concerned with the importance of the city Babylon and its patron deity, Marduk, and in particular with the provision of fish for Marduk's temple Esagil. In fact the whole point of the narrative is to illustrate that those rulers who neglected or insulted Marduk or failed to provide fish offerings for the temple Esagil had an unhappy end while those who did concern themselves with these matters fared well.... The text, therefore, is a blatant piece of propaganda written as an admonition to future monarchs to pay heed to Babylon and its cult.[85]

In a similar manner, the Persian Verse Account contrasts the reign of Nabonidus with the beginning of the reign of Cyrus. Among the "sins" of Nabonidus are the confiscation of (Babylonian?) property, the building of an "abomination, a work of unholiness" (the temple of Ehulhul in Harran), the building of a palace in Tema like the royal palace in Babylon, and the cessation of "important ritual observances" (ANET, p. 313f). In contrast, Cyrus "declared a state of peace" for the inhabitants of Babylon, increased the regular offerings for Marduk, repaired the city of Babylon, and returned the cultic images to their rightful temples (p. 314f). Interestingly, a major "sin," according to both the Weidner Chronicle and the Persian Verse Account, is the building of a rival city to Babylon.[86]

Like the preceding royal inscriptions, these two texts from Esagil judge and compare individual kings with their predecessors on the basis of their fulfillment of the following political assumptions. First, Esagil expects the king to patronize the cult of Esagil by the reconstruction of temple buildings, the refurbishment of temple furniture, and the performance of certain cultic functions. Second, Esagil also expects the king to maintain the economic health and commerce of the city and temple. These political assumptions correspond to the royal image of the chronistic chronotope. As we have already seen, the Babylonian chronicles portray the ideal king as a warrior who protects and enriches the city of Babylon.

In summary, the addressees of the Babylonian chronicles were the Babylonian kings. By examining the royal inscriptions of these kings, we can partially reconstruct the social discourse between the palace and Esagil. These inscriptions represent the royal response to the temple scribes of Esagil. In these inscriptions, the kings seek the political support of Esagil by claiming to be the ideal king as he is portrayed in the chronicles.

The situation

Every type of discourse arises out of a particular historical situation. As Voloshinov explains:

> In life, verbal discourse is clearly not self-sufficient. It arises out of an extraverbal pragmatic situation and maintains the closest possible connection with that situation.[87]

Accordingly, the social discourse between Esagil and the palace must have arisen out of a particular type of historical situation. As we will discover, the chronicles were written at different times. However, all the chronicles, in whatever period they were written, reflect a similar pragmatic situation. All the chronicles reflect a situation in which the political and economic prerogatives of Babylon and Esagil had recently been threatened by the military actions of certain individual kings.

Let me begin with the Neo-Babylonian Chronicle Series. This series of seven extant chronicles documents a period of history from the reign of Nabu-nasir (747–734 BCE) to the Persian overthrow of Nabonidus in 539 BCE. Although it is possible that all seven chronicles were written at the same time, it is more likely that each chronicle was written shortly after the last year documented. Therefore, a temple scribe probably composed Chronicle 1 in the 660s BCE whereas another temple scribe composed Chronicle 7 in the 530s BCE.[88] In other words, the *terminus a quo* for Chronicle 1 is 669 BCE and the *terminus a quo* for Chronicle 7, if not the whole series, is 539 BCE. As the chronicles and the royal inscriptions demonstrate, these two dates—669 and 539 BCE—were two critical years in the social consciousness of the temple scribes of Esagil. The year 669 BCE marked the end of a twenty-year period when the Akitu festival could not be celebrated in Babylon. Similarly, 539 BCE marked the end of the reign of Nabonidus who, for at least five years in a row, was absent from Babylon and did not celebrate the Akitu festival in Babylon.

Both the chronicles and the royal inscriptions, examined previously, indicate that the twenty-year period, commencing with the sack of Babylon by Sennacherib in 689 BCE, was a critical period in the social consciousness of the temple scribes of Esagil. Babylon's destruction is mentioned in the inscriptions of Sennacherib and Esarhaddon as well as in the inscriptions of Nabonidus a hundred years later. Chronicle 1 of the Neo-Babylonian Series, Chronicle 14 (Esarhaddon Chronicle), and Chronicle 16 (Akitu Chronicle) also document this twenty-year period. As Grayson observes, these twenty years (689–669 BCE) were a critical period in Babylonian history:

> The temple of Esagil was sacked and the statue of the god Marduk carried off to Assyria. Marduk's statue remained in Assyria during the rest of Sennacherib's reign and all through Esarhaddon's reign—a total of twenty years in which the Akitu festival could not be celebrated. This was indeed a dark moment in Babylonian history.[89]

Let us now examine Chronicle 1 in more detail so that we might comprehend the severity of this historical crisis.

The historical crisis of 689–669 BCE is clearly a major concern of the composer of Chronicle 1. Because this chronicle concludes with a description of the return of Marduk to Babylon from Assyria in the accession year of Shamash-shuma-ukin (669 BCE), we are certain that the end to twenty years of crisis was noteworthy for the chronicler. What is surprising about this particular chronicle is the absence of any reference to the capture of Marduk in 689 BCE. The chronistic record of Sennacherib's destruction of Babylon is exceedingly terse: "On the first day of the month Kislev the city (i.e., Babylon) was captured" (Chronicle 1 iii.22, ABC, p. 80). We do not find any reference to the Assyrian abduction of Marduk. Using Jamesonian terminology, the text exhibits a literary "contradiction."[90] The text does not explain how or why Marduk came to be in Assyria. This extreme minimalization is also present in Chronicle 14 and Chronicle 16. Both chronicles refer to the twenty-year period of 689–669 BCE and to the return of Marduk in 669 BCE, but they do not mention Marduk's capture in 689 BCE.[91]

While the scribes cannot deny the absence of Marduk or the cessation in the Akitu festival, they seem intentionally to omit any acknowledgment that a huge rift has occurred in the reality of their time and space. Having built a worldview on the premise that Babylon is the dwelling place of Marduk, the scribes are unable to admit or to explain Marduk's abduction and Babylon's destruction. Instead, their initial response is one of silence. This internal literary contradiction, according to Jameson's theory, is clear evidence of a tear in the fabric of social reality.

As we observed in the previous section, the destruction of Babylon in 689 BCE was also a major concern in the royal inscriptions. Within these inscriptions, we find three different interpretations of this traumatic event. Sennacherib claimed that Babylon's destruction demonstrated the superiority of Assyria and the Assyrian gods. In contrast, Esarhaddon justified Babylon's destruction by claiming that it was the result of Babylonian wickedness. A century later, Nabonidus argued that Sennacherib's destruction of Babylon was itself a sinful act. All these inscriptions demonstrate that the destruction of Babylon in 689 BCE was a critical event in the social consciousness of Esagil in need of explanation.

In summary, Chronicle 1 was, most likely, written at the end of and in response to the historical crisis of 689–669 BCE. The destruction of Babylon was a calamity, socially, economically and politically. Faced with the inexplicable, the temple scribes sought to craft a literary response to this disastrous situation. This response took the form of a chronicle that minimalizes Babylon's destruction by placing it in the context of a historical sweep of events.

As the inscriptions of Nabonidus and Cyrus and the Persian Verse Account indicate, the temple scribes faced another crisis during the reign of Nabonidus (556–539 BCE). All these texts demonstrate that the temple scribes of Esagil opposed Nabonidus because of his apparent neglect of

Babylon and the worship of Marduk in Esagil. The temple scribes were especially critical of two actions of Nabonidus: the building of Ehulhul in Harran and the establishment of a royal residence in Tema. According to the perspective of Esagil, the building of Ehulhul threatened the cultic supremacy of Babylon just as the king's presence in Tema threatened the political supremacy of Babylon. The establishment of a rival cultic center in Harran and a rival political center in Tema also threatened the economic supremacy of Babylon. Ehulhul, rather than Esagil, benefited from the king's cultic offerings and Tema, rather than Babylon, benefited from the presence of a large royal establishment. Finally, Nabonidus' presence in Tema rather than in Babylon also meant that the Babylonian Akitu festival, which depended on the king's participation, could not be celebrated.

The Nabonidus Chronicle (Chronicle 7) confirms the impression left by Nabonidus' own inscriptions and the Persian Verse Account that the temple establishment of Esagil opposed Nabonidus. This particular chronicle records not only the consistent absence of Nabonidus from Babylon but also the eventual defeat of Nabonidus by Cyrus. In contrast to Cyrus whose military victories are celebrated, Nabonidus' military accomplishments are minimalized. In other words, like the Cyrus Cylinder and the Persian Verse Account, the Nabonidus Chronicle contrasts the ineffectual reign of Nabonidus with the successful reign of Cyrus.

In summary, the Nabonidus Chronicle confirms the impression left by other contemporary texts that the reign of Nabonidus was a period of crisis for the temple scribes of Esagil. Nabonidus' decisions to rebuild Ehulhul and to dwell in Tema threatened the cultic, political and economic prerogatives of Babylon. The temple scribes wrote the chronicle in response to this crisis.

Compared to the first and last chronicles in the Neo-Babylonian Chronicle Series, the remaining five chronicles reflect a period of political and economic stability in Babylon. According to these latter chronicles, Nabopolassar, Nebuchadnezzar, and Neriglissar not only maintained the security of Babylon but also enriched the city with foreign booty. However, the crisis of 689–669 BCE underlies these latter chronicles as much as Chronicle 1. Like a painful memory that refuses to go away, so the memory of the years when there was no king in Babylon has influenced the chronistic record of Chronicles 2–6. These five chronicles provide the positive image of the king that contrasts with the negative image found in Chronicle 1. Unlike the Babylonian kings of Chronicle 1, the kings described in Chronicles 2–6 (Nabopolassar, Nebuchadnezzar, and Neriglissar) protected and enriched the city of Babylon.

In summary, the discourse that underlies the Neo-Babylonian Chronicle Series arose out of a crisis situation for the temple scribes of Esagil. The temple scribes wrote these chronicles at a time when the political and economic prerogatives of Esagil had been threatened by the actions of certain individual kings. The actions of two kings, in particular, were deemed especially damaging. In 689 BCE, King Sennacherib destroyed Babylon and captured the cultic image of Marduk. In 539 BCE, the Persian king Cyrus defeated Nabonidus and, thus, concludes another painful period for Esagil. During his reign, Nabonidus had threatened the political and economic privileges of Babylon by establishing a rival cultic center in Harran and a rival political center in Tema. Therefore, the temple scribes of Esagil wrote the Neo-Babylonian Chronicle Series in the context of a discourse between Esagil and the royal palace that took place between the two traumatic years of 689 BCE and 539 BCE.

Let us now examine the other Babylonian chronicles to see if they reflect a similar type of situation. Both the Esarhaddon Chronicle (Chronicle 14) and the Akitu Chronicle (Chronicle 16) document the twenty-year period of 689–669 BCE. The Akitu Chronicle and the Shamash-shuma-ukin Chronicle (Chronicle 15) also document the period immediately following 669 BCE. According to these latter chronicles, the period immediately following 669 BCE was characterized by a military struggle between Babylon and Assyria. This struggle often resulted in the non-celebration of the Akitu festival.[92] In other words, these three chronicles were written at approximately the same time as the Neo-Babylonian Chronicle Series. Moreover, like the Neo-Babylonian Chronicle Series, these chronicles reflect a situation in which the military actions of foreign kings threatened the political and economic life of Esagil.

The temple scribes of Esagil wrote, at least, one more extant chronicle at approximately the same time as the Neo-Babylonian Chronicle Series. According to Grayson, the Eclectic Chronicle (Chronicle 24) may have concluded with the reign of Sennacherib.[93] Unfortunately, the concluding sections of Chronicle 24 are either badly preserved or missing altogether. However, the text does seem to include a reference to Tiglath-pileser III (745–727 BCE) and his successor, Shalmaneser V (727–722 BCE). It is certainly possible that the missing sections at the end of the chronicle contained an account of Sennacherib's reign (705–681 BCE). Consequently, the temple scribes of Esagil must have written Chronicle 24 either during or shortly after Sennacherib's reign.

According to Grayson, the complete text of Chronicle 24 may have covered a period beginning with the Isin II dynasty (c. 1156 BCE) and concluding with the destruction of Babylon in 689 BCE. As Grayson observes, this is:

> a period which stretches from the end of the first "dark" period of Babylonian history (Kassite domination) to the beginning of the second "dark" period (complete control by Assyria).[94]

If Grayson's hypothesis is correct, then Chronicle 24 reflects a similar situation as the other chronicles that we have already examined.

As we have seen, eleven chronicles out of the fourteen that we have examined were composed in the seventh and sixth centuries BCE. The remaining three chronicles were, most likely, written at a much earlier date. Using the last recorded year as a clue, the *terminus a quo* for each of these three chronicles is as follows: 942 BCE for the Religious Chronicle (Chronicle 17);[95] 1450 BCE for the Chronicle of Early Kings (Chronicle 20);[96] and 1157 BCE for Chronicle P (Chronicle 22).[97] Whatever the actual composition dates, all three chronicles document different periods when the political and economic prerogatives of Babylon had been threatened by the military actions of certain individual kings. In other words, these three chronicles, by their content, reflect a similar crisis situation as the other eleven chronicles.

Like the Akitu Chronicle, the Religious Chronicle documents interruptions in the celebration of the Akitu festival. According to the Religious Chronicle, the main reason why the Akitu festival could not be celebrated was because the king was unable to stop Aramean attacks on Babylon (for example, see Chronicle 17 iii.4–10, ABC, p. 137). This chronicle also documents mysterious events such as the appearance of wild animals within the city of Babylon (iii.3-4, p. 137). This emphasis on interruptions of the Akitu festival and the occurrences of mysterious events within Babylon portrays Babylonian society as one that is filled with political and religious insecurity. In other words, the Religious Chronicle reflects another crisis situation for the temple scribes of Esagil.

As the name suggests, the Chronicle of Early Kings documents an early period of Babylonian history. Significantly, this chronicle begins with the reign of Sargon of Akkad (c. 2334–2279 BCE). Just as the Persian Verse Account condemns Nabonidus for establishing a rival political center to Babylon in Tema, so the Chronicle of Early Kings condemns Sargon because he destroyed Babylon and "made a counterpart of Babylon next to

Agade" (Chronicle 20 A lines 18–19, p. 153f). This chronicle also documents the reign of Shulgi who "took away the property of Esagil and Babylon as booty" (A lines 28–30, p. 154). Thus, again, the content of a chronicle reflects a period of crisis for Babylon when the military actions of individual kings threatened the political and economic prerogatives of the temple and city.

Finally, Chronicle P (Chronicle 22) reflects another crisis for Babylonian society when it documents Babylon's destruction during the reign of Tukulti-Ninurta I (c. 1234–1197 BCE).[98] Just as Sennacherib's destruction of Babylon in 689 BCE resulted in the capture of Marduk and a twenty-year exile in Assyria, so Tukulti-Ninurta's destruction of Babylon resulted in an at least six-year exile (Chronicle 22 iv.12, p. 176). In other words, Chronicle 22, like most of the other chronicles, documents a period of political weakness for Babylon during which the political and economic prerogatives of the city had been eroded by the military actions of certain individual kings.

According to John van Seters, the Chronicle of Early Kings, Chronicle P and the Eclectic Chronicle are actually a series of chronicles just like the Neo-Babylonian Chronicle Series. Moreover, he argues that these three chronicles were written in the Neo-Babylonian period in order to provide a chronistic account of Babylonian history prior to the Neo-Babylonian period.[99] If van Seters is correct in his hypothesis, then it is possible that all three chronicles were written sometime after Sennacherib's destruction of Babylon in 689 BCE. Consequently, the account of Sargon's destruction of Babylon in Chronicle 20 and the account of Tukulti-Ninurta's destruction of Babylon in Chronicle 22 can be read as a foreshadowing of Sennacherib's destruction. Therefore, these three chronicles were written at the same time and in response to the same historical crisis as Chronicle 1, Chronicle 14 and Chronicle 15. On the basis of similar terminology, van Seters also argues that the Religious Chronicle was written at approximately the same time as the Akitu Chronicle.[100] In other words, if van Seters is correct, then all fourteen chronicles were composed after and in response to Babylon's destruction in 689 BCE.

In summary, all fourteen Babylonian chronicles, in whatever period they were written, reflect a similar pragmatic situation. All the chronicles reflect a situation in which the political and economic prerogatives of Babylon and Esagil had recently been eroded by the military actions of certain individual kings. More specifically, most, if not all, of the chronicles were composed after Sennacherib's destruction of Babylon in 689 BCE. This traumatic event was the archetypal situation that provoked the discourse between Esagil and the palace.

In conclusion, the chronotope of the Babylonian chronicles was generated in the context of a socio-historical discourse between the temple of Esagil and the palace of the Babylonian kings. The temple scribes of Esagil composed the chronicles for the Babylonian kings. The temple scribes wrote the chronicles at a time when the military actions of certain individual kings threatened the political and economic prerogatives of Esagil and Babylon. Sennacherib's destruction of Babylon in 689 BCE was the archetypal situation that provoked the discourse between Esagil and the palace.

The Socio-Political Function

A Bakhtinian analysis of a genre concludes with an examination of the socio-political function of the chronotope. As the worldview of a particular social group in a particular historical setting, a chronotope either preserves the socio-political order (ideological function) or subverts it (utopian function). Therefore, we will conclude this chapter by examining the socio-political function of the chronistic chronotope. We will argue that the chronotope of the Babylonian chronicles performed an ideological function within the social discourse between Esagil and the royal palace that followed the destruction of Babylon in 689 BCE.

We will explore the ideological function of the chronistic chronotope by applying Paul Ricoeur's analysis of ideology to this discussion.[101] According to Ricoeur's "regressive method" which "attempts to dig under the surface of the apparent meaning to the more fundamental meanings,"[102] ideological discourse operates at three levels. On the surface level, ideology "distorts" reality. It provides a false "picture" of real social life. Ideology distorts reality because, on the second level, it "legitimates" the political authority of a particular social group. At its deepest level, however, ideology "integrates" a social group. It preserves the group's social "identity."

As ideology, at its deepest level, the chronistic chronotope is an attempt to "preserve" the social order of Esagil in the years that followed the destruction of Babylon in 689 BCE. Ultimately, preservation of this social order is dependent upon the cooperation of the palace. By composing texts that "chronicle" the reigns of both "good" and "bad" kings, the temple scribes seek to "persuade" the kings to patronize the cult of Esagil and to maintain the economic health and commerce of the city and temple.[103]

At the deepest or "integrative" level of the ideological discourse, the chronistic chronotope preserves the "identity" of a social group by providing a symbolic "template" or "blueprint" for the organization of socio-political life.[104] As Ricoeur observes, this "blueprint" supports the integration of a social group in time and space.[105] Such "blueprints" are especially necessary during periods of socio-psychological crisis when the group's identity is threatened.[106] The years following the destruction of Babylon in 689 BCE were years of crisis for the scribes of Esagil. The chronistic chronotope preserved the identity of this social group by providing such an orientation in space and time.

The Babylonian royal succession provides the temporal orientation. By placing the destruction of Babylon in the context of a succession of kings, the temple scribes of Esagil not only remind the kings that they were obligated to protect the city but also soften the socio-psychological impact of the city's destruction in 689 BCE. The chronotope diverts blame away from the temple complex and toward the palace while, at the same time, implying that this time of crisis is only a temporary setback that will soon be overcome with the cooperation of the palace.[107]

The chronotope affirms not only the enduring prestige of the city through time but also the central importance of the city in space. The chronicles refuse to acknowledge any other geographic center to the Babylonian world, even when Babylon itself lies in ruins. In this obdurate contention that Babylon alone is the center of royal authority, the scribes of Esagil demonstrate an unmistakable egocentrism. Though this contention may be unrealistic, it serves to preserve the desired reality of the temple scribes.

The chronistic chronotope also functioned on the second or "legitimating" level. As Ricoeur observes, "ideology preserves reality, but it also wants to conserve what exists and is therefore already a resistance."[108] In the case of the chronistic chronotope, the temple scribes sought to "conserve" their political authority. The chronistic chronotope is an attempt to "fill up the credibility gap" when the temple's claim to authority was undermined by the palace's belief in that authority.[109] Sometimes, the palace was unable to acknowledge the temple's claim to authority because of other political priorities. For example, the absence of King Nabonidus from Babylon was probably due to legitimate political and/or economic reasons.[110]

The temple scribes support their appeal to legitimacy on the basis of the "tradition" of the ideal king.[111] The chronistic image of the ideal king challenges the royal audience of the chronicles to respect the authority of

Esagil. The ideal king is like Hammurapi, Shamash-shuma-ukin, and Nebuchadnezzar. He celebrates the Akitu festival, protects the borders, and enriches the city. The consequences of not following the examples of these illustrious predecessors are dire. Like Sargon, Sennacherib, and Nabonidus, a disobedient king eventually loses his throne and, possibly, his life.

In the social discourse between the temple and the palace, the chronistic interest in the celebration of the Akitu festival performs a legitimating function. As we have seen, one of the characteristics of the ideal king is regular participation in the Akitu festival. By celebrating the Akitu festival, the king acknowledges the authority of Esagil and the preeminence of Babylon. Seen in this light, the ritual humiliation of the king takes on a political significance. For at least twelve days of the year, Esagil reigns supreme and the king is subservient.

In order to preserve the social identity of the temple scribes and to legitimate the political power of Esagil, the chronistic chronotope "distorts" reality. More specifically, the chronotope distorts the representation of time, of space, and of the royal actor.

The chronotope distorts the representation of time in two ways. First, the chronotope deconstructs the period of Assyrian political ascendancy by superimposing a Babylonian royal chronology upon this time. For example, although Assyrian kings perform most of the actions in Chronicle 1, these actions are dated to the reigns of Babylonian kings. Second, the chronotope implicitly judges individual kings by intentionally omitting chronological information. For example, Chronicle 22 documents the political downfall of Tukulti-Ninurta I immediately after recording his destruction of Babylon.[112]

The chronotope also distorts the representation of space. All the chronicles affirm the importance of Babylon as the dwelling place of the king and as the seat of power. However, the political reality differed substantially at various points in time, most especially in the years that followed the destruction of Babylon in 689 BCE. By dating all events to the royal succession of Babylon, the chronicles maintain the fiction that the standard of Babylonian rule is eternal, and the location of that rule is Babylon.

Finally, the chronicles give a distorted representation of the king. By selectively recording royal actions and their consequences, the chronicles imply a portrait of the ideal king. This image is ideal because it conforms to the political agenda of Esagil. Moreover, no monarch could fulfill all its expectations since, as in the case of Nabonidus, other political and military priorities interfered with the king's cultic responsibilities.

In summary, the chronotope of the Babylonian chronicles performs an ideological function in the socio-historical discourse between Esagil and the palace. In the years that followed the destruction of Babylon in 689 BCE, the temple scribes of Esagil sought to "preserve" the social order of Esagil. These temple scribes composed the chronicles in order to "persuade" the kings to patronize the cult of Esagil and to maintain the economic health and commerce of the city and temple.

In conclusion, all the Babylonian chronicles display a similar chronotopic perspective. All the chronicles describe the actions of the king from the temporal perspective of the Babylonian royal succession and the spatial perspective of the city of Babylon. Consequently, the Babylonian chronicles portray an image of the ideal king. The ideal king, according to these chronicles, protects and enriches the city of Babylon. The literary chronotope is organically related to a particular socio-historical context. The temple scribes of Esagil developed the chronistic chronotope in the context of a social discourse between the temple and the palace during the years of crisis that followed the destruction of Babylon in 689 BCE. In this socio-historical context, the temple scribes composed the chronicles in order to preserve and legitimate the socio-political order of Esagil.

NOTES

[1] John van Seters, *In Search of History* (New Haven: Yale University Press, 1983), 80.

[2] A. Kirk Grayson, *Assyrian and Babylonian Chronicles*, Texts from Cuneiform Sources (Locust Valley, N.Y.: J. J. Augustin, 1975). Grayson also includes a number of Assyrian and Babylonian fragments that he claims to be chronicle fragments.

[3] Although we no longer have the complete series, the Babylonian Chronicle Series originally contained a chronicle for each king of Babylon from 747 BCE to the mid-3rd century BCE. According to Grayson, we can divide this series of chronicles into two sub-divisions, the "Neo-Babylonian Chronicle Series" and the "Late Babylonian Chronicle Series," the dividing point being the Persian capture of Babylon in 539 BCE (Ibid., 8f). In this study, I will focus on the texts of the "Neo-Babylonian Chronicle Series."

[4] According to Grayson's classification, these texts are numbered as follows: the Babylonian Chronicle Series (Chronicles 1–13); the Esarhaddon and Shamash-shuma-ukin Chronicles (Chronicles 14 and 15); the Akitu Chronicle (Chronicle 16); the Religious Chronicle (Chronicle 17); the Chronicle of the Early Kings (Chronicle 20); Chronicle P (Chronicle 22); and the Eclectic Chronicle (Chronicle 24).

5   M. M. Bakhtin, "Forms of Time and of the Chronotope in the Novel," in *The Dialogic Imagination*, ed., Michael Holquist, trans., Caryl Emerson and Michael Holquist (Austin: University of Texas Press, 1981), 85.

6   Thus, according to Morson and Emerson: "The form-shaping ideology of any reasonably complex genre is never reducible to a set of rules, nor is it wholly transcribable in any other way. Here as elsewhere, the proper use of transcriptions, as analytic tools, is either to point in the direction where real vision lies or to recoup for abstract analysis as much of the genre's wisdom as can be captured. So long as one does not confuse transcribed propositions for the essence of the genre, they can be helpful. In this sense they are like sets of linguistic rules, which may be quite useful even if language is not ultimately a matter of rules." (Gary Saul Morson and Caryl Emerson, *Mikhail Bakhtin: Creation of a Prosaics* [Stanford: Stanford University Press, 1990], 283).

7   In his definition of the genre, van Seters refers to the content of the Babylonian chronicles as "a narration of political or religious events" (van Seters, *In Search of History*, 80). However, this definition requires some clarification and specification. The chronicles narrate specifically the military and cultic activity of kings. The chronicles emphasize the king's role as a military commander and as the royal celebrant of the Akitu festival.

8   In this chronicle alone, the refrain is repeated in lines 16, 32, 38, 53, 58, and 76. This refrain is also found in other chronicles. See Chronicle 15 lines 7–8 (ABC, 129) and Chronicle 20 B r.8–9, 14–15 (Ibid., 155).

9   See also i.7f; ii.2; iii.4, 17f (Ibid., 71, 75, 79f). This refrain is also found in other chronicles. See Chronicle 20 B r.4 and Chronicle 22 iii.11f, 14, 21 (Ibid., 156, 174f).

10 For example, Chronicle 1i.19–23 concludes its report on a military campaign of Tiglath-pileser III with his accession to the Babylonian throne. Similarly, Chronicle 7 narrates the wars of Cyrus because these wars ultimately resulted in the overthrow of Nabonidus and the beginning of Persian rule over Babylon (Ibid., 72 and 110).

11 According to Miller and Roberts: "The practice of carrying off divine images is attested in cuneiform sources at least as early as the Old Babylonian period, and it continued down to the end of the Neo-Babylonian state and beyond. Part of the motivation behind such action was clearly economic...but one need not look far to find another, more theological motivation. The capture of the enemy's gods was seen, by the conquering power, as clear evidence for the superiority of the victor's gods." (Patrick D. Miller and J. J. M. Roberts, *The Hand of the Lord* [Baltimore: The Johns Hopkins University Press, 1977], 10).

12 See Chronicle 1 i.3–5; ii.4'–5'; iii.1, 44f; iv.17f; Chronicle 3 lines 7–9 (Ibid., 71, 76, 79, 82, 84, 91).

13 For example, see Chronicle 2 lines 18–22 and Chronicle 7 ii.5f, 10f, 19f. (Ibid., 88f, 106–108).

[14] For example, see Chronicle 22 iv.12f (Ibid., 176); Chronicle 16 lines 17–19 (Ibid., 132).

[15] Chronicle 14 lines 31–37 (Ibid., 127); Chronicle 16 lines 1–8 (Ibid., 131); Chronicle 22 iv.12–13 (Ibid., 176).

[16] According to van Seters' definition of the genre, the Babylonian chronicles are "in chronological order" and are "closely dated to the years of a king's reign." (van Seters, *In Search of History*, 80). However, once again, this definition requires some clarification and specification. The chronological order of the chronicles is based specifically upon a succession of Babylonian kings and not just the years of a single king's reign.

[17] For example, see Chronicle 1 iii.28 and Chronicle 2 line 14 (Ibid., 81, 88).

[18] For example, see Chronicle 3, line 1, 8–9: "The tenth year of Nabopolassar: In the month Iyyar he mustered the army of Akkad and marched along the bank of the Euphrates. In the month Elul the king of Akkad and his army returned...to Babylon." (Ibid., 91). Chronicle 5 Obverse lines 15–16, 20: "The first year of Nebuchadnezzar (II): In the month Sivan he mustered his army and marched to Hattu. In the month Shebat he marched away and [returned] to Bab[ylon]" (Ibid., 100). Chronicle 6 lines 3f, 26f: "Neriglissar mustered his army and marched to Hume. In the month Adar the king of Akkad went home" (Ibid., 103f).

[19] For example, Chronicle 1 i.19–23 records Tiglath-pileser's victory over Nabu-mukin-zeri and his subsequent accession on the throne of Babylon (Ibid., 72). Chronicle 1 ii.21–23 records how Sennacherib overthrew Merodach-baladan and placed Bel-ibni on the throne of Babylon (Ibid., 77).

[20] Chronicle 7 ii.5f; ii.10f; ii.19; ii.23.

[21] Among the booty brought to Babylon were the cultic images of defeated cities. According to the chronicles, a victorious army would often "abduct" the gods of a defeated city and bring these captured images to their own capital city. For example, in Chronicle 3 lines 6–9, we read: "In the month Ab the king of Akkad (and) his army went upstream to Mane, Sahiri, and Balihu. He plundered them, sacked them extensively, (and) abducted their gods. In the month Elul the king of Akkad and his army returned and on his way he took (the people of) Hindanu and its gods to Babylon" (Ibid., 91).

[22] According to Chronicle 1, Shamash-shuma-ukin ascended the throne "in Babylon" and, subsequently, Marduk returned and "entered Babylon." See Chronicle 1 iv.33–36 (Ibid., 86).

[23] In his commentary on these lines, Grayson refers to parallel accounts in Assyrian records in which the Assyrian king boasts of having set up a mound of dust from a conquered city by his own city. For example, Sennacherib states that he removed dust from the conquered city of Babylon and placed it in the Akitu Temple of Assur. See D.

D. Luckenbill, *Ancient Records of Assyria and Babylonia*, vol. 2 (Chicago: University of Chicago Press, 1927), 185, paragraph 439.

[24]   A similar contrast is found in the so-called Weidner Chronicle (Chronicle 19). In fact, the same negative judgments of Sargon and Shulgi are also found in the Weidner Chronicle (lines 52, 64f; Ibid., 149f).

[25]   Thus, in ii.9–12, a defeated enemy is quoted as saying: "We did not know, Kurigalzu, that you [had *conquered*] all peoples. We had no rival among people. Now you... [...]. We have set out, sought the place where you are and [*brought*] gifts." (Ibid., 173). A few lines later (iii.7–9), we read: "Silver, gold, precious sto[nes, ... I brought. I [*made*] a canopy of pure gold for Marduk my lord. I...Babylon and Borsippa upon/over me. [...]" (Ibid., 174). Although the exact meaning of these lines is uncertain, the enrichment of Babylon is certainly implied.

[26]   Chronicle 1 iii.22f records the transportation of Mushezib-Marduk to Assyria. Since the chronicle had previously stated that Sennacherib was the king of Assyria during this period of time (ii.19ff), Sennacherib must have been the Assyrian king who led the assault on Babylon.

[27]   A royal inscription of Nabonidus explicitly claims that Sennacherib was killed as punishment for his "evil intentions" against Babylon (ANET, 309).

[28]   The only exception is Merodach-baladan II. Unlike the other Babylonian kings, he apparently defended Akkad and Babylon against Assyrian attacks. According to the chronicle, there was constant warfare between Assyria and Babylon for the first ten years of Merodach-baladan's reign. (Chronicle 1 i.41–42; ABC, 75). It was not until his twelfth year that Sargon II successfully invaded Akkad and deposed Merodach-baladan (Chronicle 1 ii.1–5; Ibid).

[29]   A similar contrast between an ineffective king and a successful king can be observed in Chronicle 7. Like the Babylonian kings of Chronicle 1, Nabonidus is portrayed as passive. For five years, Nabonidus does nothing but remain in Tema and stay away from Babylon. During this time, Cyrus is the successful king who "musters" his army and defeats his enemies. While Nabonidus remained in Tema in Nabonidus' ninth year, "Cyrus (II), king of Parsu, mustered his army and crossed the Tigris below Arbail. In the month Iyyar [he marched] to Ly[dia]. He defeated its king, took its possessions, (and) stationed his own garrison (there)." (Grayson's italics. Chronicle 7 ii.15–17; Ibid., 107). The chronicle continues with an account of Nabonidus' defeat at the hands of Cyrus.

[30]   Chronicle 1 iv.34–36 (Ibid., 86); Chronicle 14 lines 31–37 (Ibid., 127); Chronicle 16 lines 1–8 (Ibid., 131).

[31]   Line 37 ("Nabu and the gods of Borsippa [went] to Babylon") must be a reference to the Akitu festival because it is an obvious contrast with lines 32b–33 ("the Akitu festival did not take place. Nabu did not come from Borsippa for the procession of Bel").

32 A similar chronotopic expression is found in Chronicle 1 ii.5, 1'–2' (ii.5 is found in both copy A and copy B of the chronicle; ii.1'–2' is only found in copy B): "Sargon (II) ascended the throne in Babylon. The thirteenth year: Sargon (II) took Bel's hand. He (also) captured Dur-Yakin" (Ibid., 75).

33 For another example, see Chronicle 24 Reverse lines 9–14 (Ibid., 182f).

34 Bakhtin and Medvedev, *The Formal Method*, 135.

35 See Wolfram von Soden, *The Ancient Orient: An Introduction to the Study of the Ancient Near East*, trans. D. G. Schley (Grand Rapids: Wm B. Eerdmans, 1994), 70–71.

36 A. Leo Oppenheim, *Ancient Mesopotamia: Portrait of a Dead Civilization*, revised ed., completed by Erica Reiner (Chicago: University of Chicago Press, 1964, 1977), 150–151.

37 The Akitu festival was celebrated elsewhere in Mesopotamia. I will focus on the Babylonian festival.

38 Jacob Klein, "Akitu," *The Anchor Bible Dictionary*, volume 1, ed. David Noel Freedman (New York: Doubleday, 1992), 138. In Ur, the festival was celebrated twice a year; in the beginning of barley sowing season and in the beginning of the barley harvest. In other words, the festival both ensured and celebrated the barley harvest. See J. A. Black, "The New Year Ceremonies in Ancient Babylon: 'Taking Bel by the hand' and a Cultic Picnic," *Religion* 11 (1981): 49.

39 Klein, "Akitu," 138.

40 Black, "The New Year Ceremonies," 49. J. A. Black distinguishes between the "Unity theory" and the "Conglomerate theory." The Unity theory of H. Frankfort interprets all the ceremonies in terms of a single unifying theme, i.e., a celebration of Marduk's triumph over chaos. See *Kingship and the God* (Chicago: University of Chicago Press, 1948), 313–33. On the other hand, the Conglomerate theory of S. A. Pallis provides a historical interpretation of the variety of ceremonies, i.e., various ceremonies were added over a long period of time. See *The Babylonian Akîtu Festival* (Copenhagen: Bianco Lunos Bostrykkes, 1926). I concur with Black who considers the "Conglomerate approach as, methodologically, the correct way to go about analyzing the New Year ceremonies" (Black, 49).

41 Ibid., 56.

42 ANET, 331.

43 According to the Akitu ritual text, the high priest recites the Epic "to the god Bel" on the fourth day (Ibid., 332).

44 W. G. Lambert, "The Great Battle of the Mesopotamian Religious Year: The Conflict in

the Akitu House," *Iraq* 25 (1963): 189-190. According to Lambert, Marduk's victory was symbolized by placing Marduk's statue on a dais. However, Jacobsen claims that this act rather symbolized the establishment of Marduk's abode on the body of Tiamat. Marduk's victory is symbolized by the statue's boat ride to the Akitu temple. See Thorkild Jacobsen, "Religious Drama in Ancient Mesopotamia," in *Unity and Diversity: Essays on the History, Literature, and Religion of the Ancient Near East,* eds. Hans Goedicke and J. J. M. Roberts (Baltimore: The Johns Hopkins University Press, 1975), 73.

[45]   Black, "The New Year Ceremonies," 50.

[46]   T. Jacobsen, *The Treasures of Darkness: A History of Mesopotamian Religion* (New Haven: Yale University Press, 1976), 191. Jacobsen claims that Tiamat is symbolic of the "Sealand" (*mat tâmti*) who was Babylon's chief opponent in the second millenium BCE (Ibid., 189f).

[47]   Ibid., 191.

[48]   For example, see Chronicle 7 iii.5 (ABC, 109): "[N]abu [came] from Borsippa for the procession of Bel."

[49]   Black, "The New Year Ceremonies," 44.

[50]   Ibid., 45. See also ANET, 334.

[51]   For example, see Chronicle 5 Obverse line 14 (ABC, 100); Chronicle 7 iii.5 (Ibid., 109). According to Frankfort, the procession "represented the victorious army of the gods who, on the eve of Creation, went out against Tiamat and destroyed her forces." (Frankfort, *Kingship*, 327).

[52]   Chronicle 1 iv.34–36 (ABC, 86); Chronicle 14 lines 35f (Ibid., 127); Chronicle 16 lines 5–7 (Ibid., 131).

[53]   A. Kirk Grayson, "Histories and Historians: Assyria and Babylonia," *Orientalia* 49 (1980): 175.

[54]   Oppenheim, *Ancient Mesopotamia*, 210f.

[55]   For example, see Chronicle 17 iii.3–6: "In the month Iyyar a deer, which no one had seen [enter] the city (Babylon) was seen in Bab-beliya ("Gate of My Lord") and killed. In the month Nisan, in the seventh year, the Arameans were belligerent so that the king could not come up to Babylon. Neither did Nabu come nor Bel [come out]." (ABC, 137). See also Chronicle 17 iii.11–15.

[56]   Grayson recognizes the similarity between the "bizarre phenomena" of the chronicle and the protases of omens. However, according to Grayson, the chronicle does not contain any apodoses and the phenomena are unique to the chronicle ("no omen protases known...are exactly like those found in the chronicle") (Ibid., 37). In my

opinion, the mysterious events "function" as the protases and interruptions of the Akitu festival "function" as the apodoses. The chronicle is not an omen text but the form of omens clearly influenced the composition of the chronicle.

57 Ibid., 46f. Grayson gives four reasons why he thinks that the chronicle is secondary to the omens: omens appeared as early as the Old Babylonian period; the omen collections are more detailed that the chronicle; the phrase "in the reign of Ishtar" (Chronicle 20 A line 1; Ibid., 152) is a characteristic phrase of omen literature but not of chronistic literature; it is unlikely that the compiler of the omen collections would invent protases to match the information derived from the chronicle.

58 For example, see Chronicle 20 A lines 20–23 (Ibid., 154) is also found in Chronicle 19 (Weidner Chronicle) line 52 (Ibid., 149).

59 Ibid., 43f.

60 Oppenheim, *Ancient Mesopotamia*, 99.

61 Ibid., 130–132. Oppenheim hypothesizes about this architectural arrangement: "Can it be taken to express the role of the king as high priest in the cult of the nation's main deity? We find this fusion in all the capitals of Assyria, and the pertinent ritual texts show us convincingly the cultic importance of the king and high priest" (Ibid., 132).

62 Ibid., 133.

63 Bakhtin, "Speech Genres," 95.

64 In other studies, these inscriptions have been analyzed in order to understand the political and theological significance of the capture and return of cultic images. For example, see Morton Cogan, *Imperialism and Religion: Assyria, Judah and Israel in the Eighth and Seventh Centuries BCE*, SBL Monograph Series, volume 19 (Missoula: Scholars Press, 1974), 9–41; Patrick D. Miller and J. J. M. Roberts, *The Hand of the Lord: A Reassessment of the "Ark Narrative" of 1 Samuel*, The Johns Hopkins Near Eastern Studies (Baltimore: The Johns Hopkins University Press, 1977), 14–16.

65 Nineveh is "enlarged" (ARAB, 149. Paragraph 332); Babylon is destroyed "from top to bottom" (Ibid., 152. Paragraph 341). Sennacherib renovates the canals of Nineveh (Ibid., 149. Paragraph 332); Sennacherib floods Babylon (Ibid., 152. Paragraph 341). In other words, Nineveh is raised high and Babylon is brought low.

66 A similar concern to stress the superiority of the Assyrian god Assur at the expense of the Babylonian city-god, Marduk, is found in the ritual commentary text KAR 143. In this unusual text, various ceremonies of the Akitu festival are reinterpreted to represent Marduk being put on trial for rebelling against Assur. Most scholars now consider this ritual text to be Assyrian anti-Babylonian propaganda from the time of Sennacherib. See W. von Soden, "Gibt es ein Zeugnis dafür, dass die Babylonier an Wiederauferstehung Marduks geglaubt haben?" *ZA* 51 (1955): 130–166; "Ein neues

Bruchstück des assyrischen Kommentar zum Marduk-Ordeal." *ZA* 52 (1957): 224–234; Jacobsen, "Religious Drama," 73f.

[67]   M. Cogan, *Imperialism and Religion*, 12f.

[68]   W. G. Lambert, "Enmeduranki and Related Matters," *JCS* 21 (1967): 126–138; Miller and Roberts, *The Hand of the Lord*, 13.

[69]   Cogan, *Imperialism and Religion*, 12. According to Cogan, the Babylonian "priesthood and/or party" insisted that the Assyrians accepted this theological interpretation "as part of its price for rapprochement." Cogan also observes, "it was in Assyrian self-interest to accede to such Babylonian rationalizations, inasmuch as they legitimized the Assyrian conquest" (Ibid., 13).

[70]   For example, see Prism S (ARAB, 203. Paragraph 507); The Senjirli Stele (Ibid., 225. Paragraph 576).

[71]   As Luckenbill observes, "The Babylonian numeral 70, turned upside down or reversed, becomes 11, just as our printed 9, turned upside down, becomes 6." (Ibid., 242. Paragraph 639).

[72]   Mordechai Cogan, "The Chronicler's Use of Chronology as Illuminated by Neo-Assyrian Royal Inscriptions," in *Empirical Models of Biblical Criticism*, ed., Jeffrey H. Tigay (Philadelphia: University of Pennsylvania Press, 1985), 200f.

[73]   For example, on Prism A, Esarhaddon boasts: "(I am he) who overwhelmed the land of Bît-Dakkuri, which is in Chaldea, Babylon's enemy, who captured Shamash-ibni, its king, a felon, outlaw, who did not fear the name of the lord of lords, (and) who forcibly seized the fields of the inhabitants (lit., sons) of Babylon and Borsippa. Because I was the one who knew the fear of Bêl and Nabû I returned those fields once more to the inhabitants of Babylon and Borsippa" (ARAB, 213. Paragraph 535).

[74]   Ibid., 253. Paragraph 659E. According to Oppenheim, the *kidinnûtu* status involved "freedom from *corvée* work, freedom from military service (or perhaps from certain types of military service), as well as a tax exemption" (Oppenheim, *Ancient Mesopotamia*, 120).

[75]   In Cylinder P^1, Ashurbanipal states that Marduk "took up his abode in the presence of the father, his begetter, in Assyria." As Miller and Roberts observe, this interpretation "moves toward" Sennacherib's interpretation (Miller and Roberts, *The Hand of the Lord*, 15). In another inscription, however, Ashurbanipal prays to Marduk, "Give thought to Babylon which thou didst destroy in the anger of thy heart" (ARAB, 381. Paragraph 988).

[76]   The basalt stela from Istanbul. C.f., Stephen Langdon, *Die Neubabylonischen Königsinschriften* (Leipzig: J. C. Hinrich, 1912), 53–57, 270–289; ANET, 308–311.

[77]   Langdon, *Die Neubabylonischen Königsinschriften*, 53f.

[78] Ibid., 311. Column x. The inscription subsequently documents the return of Sin to "his place."

[79] Significantly, Nabonidus mentions Ashurbanipal in the inscription (Ibid.).

[80] ANET, 3rd ed., 562f.

[81] Ibid., 315f.

[82] Among the sacrilegious acts are the removal of cultic images and the building of a replica of Esagil (Ibid., 315).

[83] A. Kuhrt, "The Cyrus Cylinder and Acheamenid Imperial Policy." *JSOT* 25 (1983): 92.

[84] ABC, 43–45, 145–151; ANET, 312–315; Sidney Smith, *Babylonian Historical Texts* (London: Methuen & Co., 1924), 27–97.

[85] ABC, 43f. In a footnote, Grayson mentions an inscription of Nebuchadnezzar II in which the king boasts about providing fish for Esagil. See Langdon, *Die Neubabylonischen Königsinschriften*, 154–157.

[86] Chronicle 19 line 51 (ABC, 149); ANET, 313. According to Kuhrt, the inhabitants of Babylon would look upon the building of Tema and Ehulhul as eroding their "cherished privileges" (Kuhrt, "The Cyrus Cylinder," 90).

[87] Pam Morris (ed.), *The Bakhtin Reader* (London: Edward Arnold, 1994), 162.

[88] Chronicle 1 concludes in the accession year of Shamash-shuma-ukin (669 BCE) and Chronicle 7 concludes in the accession year of Cyrus (539 BCE).

[89] ABC, 35.

[90] According to Fredric Jameson, a literary contradiction ("aporia" or "antinomy") is a "logical scandal or double bind...which cannot be unknotted by the operation of pure thought, and which must therefore generate a whole more properly narrative apparatus—the text itself—to square its circles and to dispel, through narrative movement, its intolerable closure." Jameson insists that the antinomy is just "the symptomatic expression and conceptual reflex of...a social contradiction." See Fredric Jameson, *The Political Unconscious: Narrative as a Socially Symbolic Act* (Ithaca, NY: Cornell University Press, 1981), 82f.

[91] Chronicle 14 lines 31–36 (ABC, 127) and Chronicle 16 lines 1–7 (Ibid., 131).

[92] See Chronicle 15 lines 6–22; Chronicle 16 lines 9–27 (Ibid., 129–132).

[93] Ibid., 35, footnote 57.

[94] Ibid., 64.

[95] Ibid., 38.

[96] Ibid., 45. Since this chronicle uses an omen collection as a source, it was probably written later than 1450 BCE.

[97] Ibid., 56. Grayson suggests the reign of Adad-nerari III (810–783 BCE) as the *terminus ad quem* for Chronicle 22.

[98] Chronicle 22 iv.1–6 (Ibid., 175–176).

[99] van Seters, *In Search of History*, 84–88.

[100] Ibid., 89.

[101] Paul Ricoeur, *Lectures on Ideology and Utopia*, ed., George H. Taylor (New York: Columbia University Press, 1986); "Ideology and Utopia," in *From Text to Action: Essays in Hermeneutics, II*, translated by Kathleen Blamey and John B. Thompson (Evanston, Illinois: Northwestern University Press, 1991), 308–324.

[102] Ricoeur, *Lectures*, 327.

[103] As Ricoeur observes, ideology uses "rhetorical" devices in order to distort, legitimate, and integrate (Ibid., 317).

[104] Ricoeur, *Lectures*, 257. Ricoeur borrows the terms, "template" and "blueprint" from Geertz's anthropological analysis of ideology. See Clifford Geertz, *The Interpretation of Cultures* (London: Hutchinson, 1973).

[105] Ricoeur, *Lectures*, 261. In his lecture on Geertz, Ricoeur quotes Eric Erikson: "More generally…an ideological system is a coherent body of shared images, ideas, and ideals which…provides for the participants a coherent, if systematically simplified, over-all orientation in space and time, in means and ends." (Ibid., 258). See Eric Erikson, *Identity: Youth and Crisis* (New York: W. W. Norton, 1968), 189f.

[106] Ricoeur, *Lectures*, 261. See Geertz, *The Interpretation of Cultures*, 287f.

[107] The ideological strategy of minimalizing the events of 689 BCE is especially obvious in Chronicle 1. See Chronicle 1 iii.22 (ABC, 80).

[108] Ricouer, *Lectures*, 266.

[109] According to Ricoeur, the legitimating function of ideology is to "fill up the credibility gap" between a "claim" to authority and the "belief" in that authority: "If this is the case, could we not say that the main function of a system of ideology is to reinforce the belief in the legitimacy of the given systems of authority in such a way that it meets the

claim to legitimacy? Ideology would be the system of justification capable of filling up the gap of political overvalue." ("Ideology and Utopia," 315).

[110] R. P. Dougherty suggests the following reasons for Nabonidus' stay in Tema: the influence of military strategy, the demands of political expediency, the incentive of commercial interests, the stimulus of religious zeal, and the sway of personal inclination. See R. P. Dougherty, *Nabonidus and Belshazzar: A Study of the Closing Events of the Neo-Babylonian Empire* (New Haven: Yale University Press, 1929), 138–60. See also A. Kuhrt, "Nabonidus and the Babylonian Priesthood," in *Pagan Priests: Religion and Power in the Ancient World*, eds. Mary Beard and John North (Ithaca, N.Y.: Cornell University Press, 1990), 117–55.

[111] In contrast to "reason" (legal authority) and "charisma" (charismatic authority). See Ricoeur's discussion of Weber's three types of "legitimate domination" (Ricoeur, *Lectures*, 198–215).

[112] Chronicle 22 iv.3–11 (ABC, 175f).

CHAPTER FOUR
The Chronistic Genre in Ancient Israel

The existence of a particular genre in Babylon does not necessarily mean that the genre existed in ancient Israel. The composer of Haggai-Zechariah 1–8 would have modeled this text on Israelite chronicles rather than Babylonian chronicles. In this chapter, we will examine the biblical evidence to determine whether the chronistic genre also existed in ancient Israel. Specifically, we will examine 1 and 2 Kings to determine whether the Deuteronomistic composer (Dtr) had access to Israelite chronicles.

Dtr mentions two sources that he or she used to compose 1 and 2 Kings: "the book of the annual actions of the kings of Israel" (יִשְׂרָאֵל סֵפֶר דִּבְרֵי הַיָּמִים לְמַלְכֵי) and "the book of the annual actions of the kings of Judah" (סֵפֶר דִּבְרֵי הַיָּמִים לְמַלְכֵי יְהוּדָה).[1] In this chapter, we will argue that these two sources were Israelite and Judean chronicles. We will defend this supposition on the basis of the following evidence: the names of the sources, the Deuteronomistic editorial comments about the content of these sources, the regnal formulas, and the use of chronistic reports.

The Names of the Sources

The names that Dtr gives to these sources provide the first indication that these sources were Israelite chronicles. Both sources are labeled "books" (סֵפֶר). Elsewhere in the Hebrew Bible, סֵפֶר is used for letters (2 Sam. 11:14, 15; 1 Kings 21:8ff; 2 Kings 5:5ff), legal documents (Deut. 24:1; Jer. 32:11), the book of the law/covenant (2 Kings 23:2; Deut. 28:61), and collections of prophecies (Jer. 25:13; Nahum 1:1). The construct chain that follows סֵפֶר provides further information about the exact nature of these two literary documents. סֵפֶר is in construct with דִּבְרֵי ("deeds" or "actions"). The genitive is adjectival. Specifically, it is a topical genitive. The books contained information about the actions being described. The end of the construct chain records whose actions are being described in these books. These books contained information about the actions of "the kings of Judah" (לְמַלְכֵי יְהוּדָה) or the actions of "the kings of Israel" (לְמַלְכֵי יִשְׂרָאֵל). The use of the plural form indicates that these books described the actions of a succession of kings and not just one king. Moreover, the construct chain also reveals that these actions were the annual deeds of the kings. The phrase הַיָּמִים דִּבְרֵי is similar to the phrase דְּבַר יוֹם . This latter phrase refers to the daily duties or daily assignments of priests (Exod. 5:13, 19; 16:4; Lev. 23:37; 1 Kings 8:59; 2 Kings 25:30). Once we take into consideration that the plural form of יוֹם can be translated "year," we can then translate דִּבְרֵי הַיָּמִים "the annual actions."[2] A literal translation of the names of these sources would then be "the book of the annual actions of the kings of Israel/Judah."

The fact that these sources contained information about the annual duties of a succession of kings is significant for identifying the genre of these sources. We have already seen how the Babylonian chronicles are structured by the Babylonian royal succession. The chronicles documented the reigns of a series of kings rather than the reign of one particular king. Moreover, we have also demonstrated how the Babylonian chronicles are primarily interested in describing royal activity.[3] The chronicles date each action of the king to a particular year in the king's reign. On the basis of the names given to these ancient Israelite books, we can assume a similar structure and content for the "the book of the annual actions of the kings of Israel/Judah." According to the names given to these books by Dtr, these two sources, like the Babylonian chronicles, contained a record of the royal activity of a series of kings.

The Content of the Sources

Dtr not only names these sources but also refers to the general information contained within these sources. For example, in 1 Kings, we find the following editorial comments:

> The rest of the actions of Jeroboam, how he fought and how he reigned, are written in the book of the annual actions of the kings of Israel. (1 Kings 14:19)

The rest of the actions of Rehoboam and all that he did, are they not written in the book of the annual actions of the kings of Judah. (1 Kings 14:29)

1 Kings 14:29 provides the basic form of these editorial comments.[4] In most cases, we find a reference to the "actions" (דְּבְרֵי) of a particular king and "all that he did" (כָּל־אֲשֶׁר עָשָׂה). In other examples, we find references to the king's "fighting" (נִלְחַם) or to "his might" (גְּבוּרָתוֹ). For example, see 1Kings 14:19, 15:23, 16:5, 27, 12:46, 2 Kings 10:34, 13:12, 14:28, 20:20. In 1 Kings 15:23, Dtr claims that "the book of the annual actions of the kings of Judah" contained a record of the cities that King Asa "built" (בנה). Similarly, "the book of the annual actions of the kings of Israel" apparently contained a record of King Ahab's ivory house (1 Kings 22:39). Moreover, on two occasions, Dtr claims that the Israelite source contained an account of a "conspiracy" (קֶשֶׁר) to seize the throne (1 Kings 16:20 and 2 Kings 15:15). We find examples of such accounts in 2 Kings 12:19–21, 14:18–20, 15:10–11, 25–26, 30–31, and 21:23–25. These editorial comments provide further evidence that these two books were the Israelite and Judean equivalents of the Babylonian chronicles. These two sources evidently described royal activity, especially military activity. As we have already seen, the Babylonian chronicles display a similar interest in the actions of kings.[5] Moreover, like the Babylonian chronicles, these two Israelite sources also documented actions that resulted in a change in the royal succession, such as conspiracies and coups.[6]

The Regnal Formulas

In 1 and 2 Kings, Dtr frames the accounts of each king's reign with similar introductions and conclusions. Apart from minor variations, the same regnal formulas are repeated for most of the kings that succeeded Rehoboam of Judah and Jeroboam I of Israel (1 Kings 15–2 Kings 25).[7] These regnal formulas are structured as follows:

1. Introduction:
   a. Synchronistic formula ("in the year N of B (king of Israel/Judah")
   b. Accession formula ("A began to reign over Israel/Judah")[8]
   c. Age at accession (Judean kings only; "A was N years old when he began to reign")
   d. Length of reign ("he reigned [over Israel] in Samaria N years" or "N years he reigned in Jerusalem")

    e.   Name of queen mother (Judean kings only; "the name of his mother was C")

    f.   Theological verdict

2. Conclusion:

    a.   Source citation

    b.   Death and burial

    c.   Notice of succession[9]

There are minor variations in the order and wording of these formulas throughout 1 and 2 Kings. Richard Nelson draws attention to the following variations.[10] First, in most cases, the accession formula follows the synchronistic formula (e.g., 1 Kings 16:8). However, occasionally, the accession formula precedes the synchronism (e.g., 1 Kings 15:25). Second, the age at accession is missing for Abijam and Asa (1 Kings 15:1, 9). Third, we find variations in the use of active or passive verbs in the burial formulas.[11]

The frame, in its final form, is a Deuteronomistic composition. The theological verdicts, which reflect the overall theme(s) of the Dtr History, and the source citations, are also the literary creations of Dtr. However, the rest of the information—if not the actual wording of the relevant formulas—contained in the frame (especially chronological information) must have been derived from chronistic sources, such as king-lists or chronicles.

Scholars have debated about the origins of the regnal formulas, especially the synchronistic formulas, the accession formulas and the formulas that record the length of a king's reign. For example, A. Jepsen attributes the whole frame to the author of a synchronistic chronicle.[12] According to Shoshana Bin-Nun, most of the regnal formulas in the frame originated in two king-lists, one originating in Judah and the other in Israel.[13] On the other hand, Richard Nelson argues that the Dtr historians composed most, if not all, of the formulas.[14] In the following pages, we will examine three regnal formulas (the synchronistic formula, the accession formula, and the formula that records the length of reign). We will argue that these formulas originated from Israelite chronicles. We will discover parallels to these particular formulas in the Babylonian chronicles. Moreover, in some cases, the wording of the respective regnal formulas is remarkably similar to those formulas found in the Babylonian chronicles.

The Dtr frame opens with a synchronism. The frame synchronizes the accession of a Judean king with the regnal year of an Israelite king and vice versa. A similar concern to synchronize the reigns of two (or more) neighboring kings is present in the Babylonian chronicles. In Chronicle 1, for example, we find many references to the accession of Assyrian and Elamite kings. In each case, the same regnal formula is used: "Year N of A (king of Babylon): B ascended the throne in (Assyria or Elam)." For example, Chronicle 1 i.9–10 reads: "The fifth year of Nabu-nasir: Humbannikash (I) ascended the throne in Elam."[15] Similarly, Chronicle 24 synchronizes the reigns of certain Babylonian kings with their Assyrian counterparts (Reverse lines 2–6).[16] Chronicle 24 is significant because we find two versions of the synchronistic formula. For example, in line 2, we read, "[Adad-nerari (II)] (was) the king of Assyria at the time of [Shamash-mudammi]q." On the other hand, in line 3, we read, "[At the time of Nabu-shu]ma-ukin (I), Tukul[ti-Ninurta (II) (was) the king of] Assyria" (ABC, 181–182). These examples provide evidence that the author of a chronicle varied the wording of a formula. Therefore, we should expect to find similar variations in 1 and 2 Kings.

We do not have to assume that the synchronistic information, found in 1 and 2 Kings, was either derived from a synchronistic source[17] or created by the Dtr composer. The Babylonian chronicles date the accession of a neighboring king to the regnal year of a Babylonian king. Thus, it is certainly possible, if not probable, that an Israelite chronicle would mention the year that a Judean king ascended the throne just as a Judean chronicle would do the same for an Israelite king. The Babylonian chronicles mention the accession of Assyrian and Elamite kings because Babylon bordered upon, and often fought against, these nations. Similarly, we would expect Israelite and Judean chronicles to display a parallel interest in the royal succession of their sister nation. In other words, Dtr probably derived the synchronistic information from two sources. When Dtr wanted to date the beginning of a Judean king's reign, she derived that information from the Israelite chronicle, which would obviously date that accession to the regnal year of an Israelite king. Similarly, when Dtr wanted to date the beginning of an Israelite king's reign, he sought that information in the Judean chronicle.[18]

There are two basic variations of the accession formula in 1 and 2 Kings. For most of the Judean kings, the formula is, "A (son of B) became king of Judah."[19] For the remaining Judean kings and for all the Israelite kings that have one, the accession formula is, "A (son of B) began to reign over Judah/Israel."[20] In both types, the perfect form of the verb מָלַךְ has an ingressive value. The verb refers to the beginning of the king's reign. The second half of the formula designates the territorial limits of the king's reign.[21]

We also find an accession formula in the Babylonian chronicles: "PN ascended the throne in Babylon." This same formula is also used for the accession of Assyrian and Elamite kings.[22] As in the case of the synchronistic formula, we also find variations in the wording of the accession formula. For example, in Chronicle 1 i.16, the words, "in Babylon" are lacking (ABC, p. 72) and in ii.23, we read: "he (Sennacherib) put Bel-ibni on the throne in Babylon" (p. 77). Moreover, unlike the accession formulas of Chronicle 1, Chronicle 2, lines 14–15 provides an exact date for the accession of Nabopolassar (p. 88). An exact date is also given for the accession of Nebuchadnezzar II in Chronicle 5 Obverse line 11 (p. 100).

The Dtr frame and the Babylonian chronicles are also similar in their use of a formula to record the length of a king's reign. In her study of this particular formula in 1 and 2 Kings, Shoshana Bin-Nun discerned two types.[23] The first type is used for Israelite kings and begins with the verb מלך: "and there reigned A (the son of B) over Israel in Tirzah/Samaria N years" or "and he reigned over Israel in Samaria N years" (e.g., 1 Kings 15:25, 33; 16:8, 29). The second type is used for Judean kings and begins with the number of years: "and N years reigned he in Jerusalem" (e.g., 1 Kings 15:1, 9). On the basis of a comparison with similar formulas that are used in the Book of Judges and in the Book of Samuel, Bin-Nun claims that the first type was an Israelite version of the regnal formula and the second type was a Judean version.[24] While I agree with her analysis of these two types of formula, I disagree with her conclusions about the generic origin of the formulas. According to Bin-Nun, these two types of formula originated in two king-lists, an Israelite king-list and a Judean king-list. I contend that, rather than originating in two king-lists, these formulas originated in two chronicles, an Israelite chronicle and a Judean chronicle. These formulas are closer in form to similar formulas in the Babylonian chronicles. Unlike the Mesopotamian king-lists, which merely record the length of a king's reign, the Babylonian chronicles emphasize the location of the king's reign.[25]

At the end of each king's reign, the Neo-Babylonian Chronicle Series (Chronicles 1–7) records the length of reign. For Babylonian kings, the formula reads, "N years PN ruled Babylon." For example, the account of King Nabu-nasir's reign concludes as follows: "For fourteen years Nabu-nasir ruled Babylon." In both the accession formula and the concluding formula, the Babylonian chronicles emphasize the capital city of the royal reign. The king ascended the throne "in Babylon" and he ruled N years as "king of Babylon."[26]

A similar emphasis upon the royal capital can be observed in the Israelite and Judean formulas. The Israelite kings ruled N years "in Tirzah" or "in Samaria."[27] The Judean kings ruled N years "in Jerusalem."[28] Further emphasis upon the royal capital can be seen in the concluding burial formula. Israelite kings were buried "in Samaria" (e.g., 1 Kings 16:28; 2 Kings 13:9, 13; 14:16). Judean kings were buried "in the city of David" (e.g., 1 Kings 15:8, 24; 22:51).

In summary, we find close parallels to some of the regnal formulas in 1 and 2 Kings within the Babylonian chronicles. This suggests that DtrH derived these formulas from ancient Israelite chronicles.

The Chronistic Reports

The final piece of evidence for the existence of Israelite chronicles is the presence of dated reports in 1 and 2 Kings. These reports are similar to passages found in the Babylonian chronicles. All the reports begin with a reference to the regnal year of a Judean or Israelite king. Additionally, all the dated reports in 1 and 2 Kings describe a foreign invasion and the siege of the royal capital. Finally, all these reports display a uniform linguistic style.

The first dated report is found in 1 Kings 14:25–28. This report describes the invasion of Judah by King Shishak of Egypt who "came up against Jerusalem" (עָלָה...עַל־יְרוּשָׁלִַם) in the fifth year of King Rehoboam of Judah. During this invasion, King Shishak seized the treasures of "the temple" (בֵּית יְהוָה) and the treasures of "the palace" (בֵּית הַמֶּלֶךְ). The report uses the third person narrative style to describe the actions of both the Egyptian king and the Judean king. The verbal sequence consists of a temporal clause (...בַּשָּׁנָה יְהִי‎וַ) followed by a perfect verb (עָלָה) followed by a waw consecutive imperfect (וַיִּקַּח).

The second dated report has two versions. A shorter version is found in 2 Kings 17:6 and a longer version is found in 2 Kings 18:9–11. Both versions describe an Assyrian invasion of Israel, the capture of Samaria and the exile of the Israelite population to Assyria. The shorter version dates these events to the ninth year of King Hoshea of Israel, whereas the longer version synchronizes these events with the reign of King

Hezekiah of Judah.[29] According to 18:9, King Shalmaneser of Assyria "came up against Samaria and besieged it" (עַל־שֹׁמְרוֹן וַיָּצַר עָלֶיהָ... עָלָה). In the ninth year of King Hoshea, Shalmaneser "captured" (לכד) Samaria and exiled the Israelite population into Assyria (17:6; 18:11). Like the first example, the report uses the third person narrative style. The verbal sequence consists of a temporal clause (בִּשְׁנַת...; 18:9, ...בַּשָּׁנָה וַיְהִי) plus a perfect verb (17:6, לָכַד; 18:9, עָלָה) followed by a waw consecutive imperfect (17:6, וַיֶּגֶל; 18:9, וַיָּצַר).

The third dated report describes the invasion of Judah by King Sennacherib of Assyria in the fourteenth year of King Hezekiah (2 Kings 18:13–16).[30] According to this report, King Sennacherib "came up against all the fortified cities of Judah and captured them" (וַיִּתְפְּשֵׂם עַל...עָלָה כָּל־עָרֵי יְהוּדָה הַבְּצֻרוֹת). In order to pay the tribute demanded by the Assyrians, Hezekiah used the treasures of "the temple" (בֵּית־יְהוָה) and the treasures of "the palace" (בֵּית הַמֶּלֶךְ). The verbal sequence consists of a temporal clause (וּבְאַרְבַּע...שָׁנָה) plus perfect verb (עָלָה) followed by waw consecutive imperfect (וַיִּתְפְּשֵׂם).

Finally, in 2 Kings 25, we find a series of dated reports that narrate the final days of the kingdom of Judah. The first report (vv. 1–2) describes the siege of Jerusalem by the army of King Nebuchadnezzar of Babylon (עַל־יְרוּשָׁלַםִ...בָּא). The second report (vv. 3–7) narrates the fall of Jerusalem and the capture (תפש) of King Zedekiah. The third report (vv. 8–12) narrates the burning of "the temple" (בֵּית־יְהוָה) and of "the palace" (בֵּית הַמֶּלֶךְ) as well as the exile of the Jerusalem population. In the first report and in the third report, the verbal sequence is similar to that found in the other dated reports; temporal clause (v. 1, בִּשְׁנַת וַיְהִי; v. 8,...וּבַחֹדֶשׁ) plus perfect verb (v. 1, 8: בָּא) followed by waw consecutive imperfect (v. 1, וַיִּחַן; v. 8, וַיִּשְׂרֹף). The verbal sequence of the second report differs from the other reports in that a waw consecutive imperfect follows the temporal clause.

The dated reports of 1 and 2 Kings are very similar to the chronistic reports found in the Babylonian chronicles. These similarities include the structure (beginning the report with a date), content (invasions of the national homeland and the consequences for the temple), and style (third person narrative style, verbal sequence and use of certain key verbs). Let us examine one example from Chronicle 1 i.1–5:

[*The third year of Nabu-nasir,*] king of Babylon: Tiglath-pileser (III) ascended the throne in Assyria. In that same year [the king of Assyria] went down to

Akkad, plundered Rabbilu and Hamranu, and abducted the gods of Shapazzu. (Grayson's italics, ABC, p. 70f)

In this example, the chronicle describes an Assyrian invasion of Babylonia and the subsequent plundering of various cities. Among the items that were plundered were the divine images of Shapazzu. In other words, like the dated reports of 1 and 2 Kings, the chronicle narrates how a military invasion affected the treasures of a temple. Just as the biblical examples from 1 and 2 Kings used the verb עלה "to go up" plus the preposition עַל to describe a military invasion, so this example from the Babylonian chronicles uses the verb *arādu* "to go down" plus the preposition *ana*.[31] Just as King Shishak "took" (לקח) the temple treasures in 1 Kings 14:26, so King Tiglath-pileser "plundered" (*habātu*) the Babylonian towns of Rabbilu and Hamranu and "abducted" (*abāku*) the divine images of Shapazzu.[32] The verbal sequence of this example is also similar to that found in the biblical reports. In this case, we have a temporal clause (MU BI) followed by a preterite plus enclitic -*ma* (*ur-dam-ma*) followed by a sequence of perfect verbs (*ih-ta-bat...i-ta-bak*). According to Richard Caplice, "this sequence, pret. + -*ma* + perf. (the so-called sequence of tenses or "*consecutio temporum*"), expresses past actions performed in sequence."[33] This sequence is the Akkadian equivalent to the perfect + waw consecutive imperfect narrative sequence that we observed in the dated reports of 1 and 2 Kings.

In summary, we have examined the Dtr framework of 1 and 2 Kings. This framework contains evidence for the existence of Israelite and Judean chronistic sources. The Dtr historian(s) named these chronicles, "the book of the annual actions of the kings of Israel" and "the book of the annual actions of the kings of Judah." From these two chronicles, Dtr derived the regnal formulas and chronistic reports.

NOTES

[1] Examples can be found in 1 Kings 14:19, 29; 15:7, 23, 31; 16:5, 14, 20, 27; 2 Kings 1:18; 8:23; 10:34. At the end of the account of King Solomon's reign (1 Kings 11:41), we also find a single reference to "the book of the deeds of Solomon." There

is a possibility that this source was also a chronicle. However, according to J. Liver, the fact that Solomon's wisdom was apparently a major theme of the source suggests that it was not a chronicle. See "The Book of the Acts of Solomon," *Biblica* 48 (1967): 75–101. Van Seters also emphasizes the differences between this source and the Babylonian chronicles (van Seters, *In Search of History*, 302). Since there is some doubt as to whether this source was a chronicle, I will concentrate my investigation on "the book of the annual actions of the kings of Israel" and "the book of the annual actions of the kings of Judah."

2   According to BDB, 399, the plural form of דֹי can refer to an annual period of time (e.g., 1 Sam. 27:7; Lev. 25:29; Judges 17:10). The phrase, "the annual actions" was probably a "fixed form" (GKC, paragraph 129 d, page 420).

3   In contrast, the annalistic inscriptions of the Assyrians and Egyptians narrate the military exploits of individual kings.

4   Other examples can be found in 1 Kings 15:7, 31; 16:14; 2 Kings 1:18; 8:23; 14:15; 15:6, 21, 26, 36; 16:19.

5   Chronicle 22 and 24 display an interest in the building activity of the Babylonian kings. See Chronicle 22 i.8; iii.8 (ABC, p. 174); Chronicle 24 Obverse lines 11, 13 (p. 181).

6   For example, in Chronicle 1 i.14–18, we find an account of two rebellions in Babylon (ABC, 72).

7   We find a concluding passage for Jehu's reign in 2 Kings 10:34–36 but no introductory passage. The account of Athaliah's reign in 2 Kings 11 does not contain any Dtr frame.

8   The accession formula precedes the synchronistic formula in six cases. Five of these cases involve Israelite kings (1 Kings 15:25; 16:29; 22:52; 2 Kings 3:1; 15:13) and the sixth case involves King Jehoshaphat of Judah (1 Kings 22:41). The frames for the remaining Israelite kings have no accession formula.

9   For example, see 1 Kings 15:9–11, 23f; 16:29f and 22:39f; 2 Kings 15:33f and 16:5f.

10   Richard D. Nelson, *The Double Redaction of the Deuteronomistic History*, JSOT Supplement Series 18 (Sheffield: JSOT Press, 1981), 32–36.

11   According to Nelson, "Twelve times the historian uses the Niphal of *qbr*, but seven times we find the active voice" (Ibid., 35). For example, see 1 Kings 15:8 (active) and 15:24 (passive).

12   A. Jepsen, *Die Quellen des Königsbuches* (Halle: Max Niemeyer, 1956), 30–40.

13   Shoshana R. Bin-Nun, "Formulas from Royal Records of Israel and of Judah," *VT* 18 (1968): 414–432. According to van Seters, these two king-lists were used as the framework for the later reconstruction of the Israelite chronicles known as the "book of the annual actions of the kings of Judah/Israel" (van Seters, *In Search of History*, 298).

14   Nelson, *Double Redaction*, 29–42. Nelson claims that the regnal formulas can be used as evidence for a double redaction of the Deuteronomistic History.

15   ABC, 71. C.f., i.1f; i.38–40; ii.32–35; iii.13–16; iii.19–27.

16   This chronicle is significant because we find two variations of the synchronistic formula. For example, in line 2, we read, "[Adad-nerari (II)] (was) the king of Assyria at the time of [Shamash-mudammi]q." On the other hand, in line 3, we read, "[At the time of Nabu-shu]ma-ukin (I), Tukul[ti-Ninurta (II) (was) the king of] Assyria" (Ibid., 181f). These examples provide evidence that the chronicler varied the wording of a formula in the same chronicle.

17   Two examples of ancient Near Eastern synchronistic documents are the Synchronistic History (Chronicle 21 in ABC, 51–56, 157–170) and the so-called "Synchronistic Chronicle" (ANET, 272–274).

18   In a footnote, Bin-Nun acknowledges the possibility of two different origins for the synchronistic formulas: "The fact that the numbers contained in the framework are based upon two opposite systems of reckoning...points to different sources.... This would mean, that the Judean synchronisms were composed in Israel and the Israelite ones in Judah, as far as they were original. Some contradictory numbers may find their natural explanation, if they are understood as originating with the different royal courts." (Bin-Nun, "Formulas," 426).

19   1 Kings 15:9; 2 Kings 8:16; 8:25; 14:1; 15:1; 15:32; 16:1; 18:1. An alternative translation is, "A son of B began to reign as king of Judah."

20   1 Kings 15:1; 15:25; 16:29; 22:41. 1 Kings 22:52 and 2 Kings 3:1 add "in Samaria."

21   מֶלֶךְ + עַל refers to the territory of the kingdom and/or the population over which the king ruled (e.g., 1 Sam. 8:9, 11; 12:14). מֶלֶךְ + בְּ (e.g., "in Samaria") refers to the royal capital. (e.g., Josh. 13:10, 12; Jud. 4:2; 2 Sam. 5:5).

22   See Chronicle 1 i.2, 10, 27f, 40; ii.35; iii.9, 15f, 27, 38; iv.13, 33.

23   Bin-Nun, "Formulas," 419–421.

24   Ibid., 419–422. For rulers from the northern tribes of Israel, the Book of Judges contains the following formula, "and he judged Israel N years" (e.g., Judg. 10:2, 3; 12:7, 11, 14. In these cases, the verb precedes the number of years. For the first few Judean kings, the Book of Samuel contains the following formula, "and N years

reigned he" (e.g., 1 Sam. 13:1; 2 Sam. 2:10; 5:4). In these cases, the formula is connected to another formula that records the age at accession and the verb follows the number of years.

25 Examples of Mesopotamian king-lists, which record the length of a king's reign but do not emphasize the location of a king's reign include: Babylonian king-list A; Babylonian king-list B; the Assyrian king-list; the Uruk king-list from Kandalanu to Seleucus II; and a Seleucid king-list (ANET, 271f, 564–567).

26 Chronicle 1 i.12 (ABC, 72). Interestingly, a slightly different wording occurs when an Assyrian king ruled both Babylon and Assyria. Instead of the city-name Babylon, the country-name Akkad is used: "N years PN ruled Akkad and Assyria" (e.g., Chronicle 1 i.25f, 30, p. 72f).

27 For references to "in Tirzah," see 1 Kings 15:33; 16:8, 15. 1 Kings 16:23f records the change of royal capital from Tirzah to Samaria. For references to "in Samaria," see 1 Kings 16:29; 2 Kings 13:1. 1 Kings 22:52 and 2 Kings 3:1 include the reference to the royal capital in the accession formula.

28 For example, see 1 Kings 15:1, 10; 22:42; 2 Kings 12:1. Dtr places even more emphasis upon the royal capital in 1 Kings 14:21.

29 The existence of two versions may be further evidence that Dtr had access to two chronistic sources, an Israelite chronicle and a Judean chronicle.

30 Verses 17f set the scene for the passage that follows (18:19–19:37) and is, therefore, separate from the dated report. Moreover, 18:13–16 is similar in content to 1 Kings 14:25–28. Therefore, the dated report consists of 2 Kings 18:13–16.

31 See Chronicle 1 ii.1, 26f, 36f (ABC, p. 75–78).

32 See Chronicle 1 ii.26f, 36–39, 46f; ii.48–iii.1.

33 Richard Caplice, *Introduction to Akkadian*. Studia Pohl: Series Maior 9 (Rome: Biblical Institute Press, 1988), 32.

CHAPTER FIVE

Time and Space in Haggai-Zechariah 1–8

A Bakhtinian analysis examines the relation between an individual utterance and its genre. As the typical form of utterances, genres are general and repeatable, whereas an utterance is unique. However, we can only determine the uniqueness of an utterance by comparing the actual utterance with its genre. As Morson and Emerson observe:

> We need genres to understand specific acts, Bakhtin argued, but in understanding genre we have not understood everything that is important about those acts or literary works. Genre provides the 'given,' but the work or act provides the 'created,' something new. As he would eventually elaborate, each act of speech and each literary work uses the resources of the genre in a specific way in response to a specific individual situation.[1]

By examining how an author uses the literary resources of a genre, we can better understand the individual utterance. In the case of the whole utterance of Haggai-Zechariah 1–8, we can better understand this text by examining the composer's use of the chronistic genre.

In this chapter, we will analyze the whole utterance of Haggai-Zechariah 1–8. We will begin by analyzing the chronotope. Specifically, we will compare the chronotope of Haggai-Zechariah 1–8 with the chronistic chronotope. This literary analysis will enable us to reconstruct the socio-historical context of the utterance because, as we have seen, the literary representation of time and space is organically related to the historical time and the social space in which the chronotope was developed. We will conclude by examining the socio-political function of the chronotope.

The Chronotope

A chronotope is the literary representation of time, of space, and of the human actor. Like any other text, the whole utterance of Haggai-Zechariah 1–8 also conceives time and space in a particular way. The use of a chronistic genre suggests that Haggai-Zechariah 1–8 and the Babylonian chronicles share a similar chronotopic perspective. By comparing the chronotope of Haggai-Zechariah 1–8 with the chronotope of the Babylonian chronicles, we will discover that the composer of Haggai-Zechariah 1–8 has transformed the chronotopic worldview of the chronicles.

The word of Yahweh

In contrast to the Babylonian chronicles, which focus on the military actions of the kings, Haggai-Zechariah 1–8 focuses on the word of Yahweh. Like the chronicles, each chronistic report of Haggai-Zechariah 1–8 begins with a date (Hag. 1:1; 1:15b–2:1; 2:10; 2:20; Zech. 1:1; 1:7; 7:1). Unlike the chronicles, however, Haggai-Zechariah 1–8 connects these dates with word event formulas ("the word of Yahweh came"). These formulas introduce prophetic oracles and/or visions. In other words, the chronistic reports of Haggai-Zechariah 1–8 document the revelation and the proclamation of Yahweh's word. Significantly, the chronistic reports of Hag. 1:1–15a and Zech. 1:1–6 also document the audience's response to the prophetic proclamation. Therefore, Haggai-Zechariah 1–8 does not date and record the actions of human kings but rather dates and records the word of Yahweh or, as H. W. Wolff expresses it, "the confronting event of God's word."[2]

Like other prophetic texts, Haggai-Zechariah 1–8 uses royal and mythological language to conceptualize the revelation of Yahweh's word. The word of Yahweh is the judicial decree of King Yahweh, as it is revealed in the divine council. Carol and Eric Meyers summarize this understanding of Yahweh's word as follows:

> Drawing upon mythological or royal language, Israelite literature envisions Yahweh as a king or judge who sits in council and proclaims his orders. In this conception, prophets are members of the council who act as couriers to deliver God's judgment to the people. The prophets utter the appropriate formulas to clarify the source of the message, the fact of its being transmitted, and the authority of its contents. The oracle itself, according to such a paradigm, has

the force of a decree of judgment, emanating as it does from the council of Yahweh.³

Haggai-Zechariah 1–8 conveys this understanding of Yahweh's word by means of the following literary characteristics. First, the language of the word event formula and the message formula is similar to the language of royal decrees. Second, the use of the divine title, Yahweh Sebaoth, in the message formula, and elsewhere in Haggai-Zechariah 1–8, represents Yahweh as the divine king. Third, the visions of Zechariah portray the revelation of Yahweh's word as occurring in the divine council of King Yahweh.

As we observed in Chapter Two, one of the literary characteristics of Haggai-Zechariah 1–8, which distinguishes this text from its canonical context, is the use of the word event formula (*Wortereignisformel*) and the message formula (*Botenformel*). These two formulas represent the two steps by which a message was sent in the ancient Near East: the transmission ("word event formula") and the delivery ("message formula"). Preceding these two steps is the commissioning of the messenger.⁴ The word event formula ("the word of Yahweh came") documents the revelation of God's word as a historical event in the life of the prophet.⁵ The message formula ("thus says Yahweh Sebaoth") establishes the authority of the prophetic proclamation of God's word.⁶ The prophets proclaim the word of Yahweh in the name of Yahweh Sebaoth.

The language of these two formulas resembles the language of royal decrees. For example, we find a parallel to the word event formula in the formulaic introduction to Neo-Assyrian royal decrees. These royal decrees begin, *amāt šarri ana* PN ("word/proclamation/decree of the king to PN").⁷ According to Holladay, the *amāt šarri* was "an especially authoritative, compelling mode of address (equivalent to 'edict of the king')" and, therefore, should be distinguished from the introduction to personal correspondences.⁸ Similarly, as the language of the word event formula suggests, the word of Yahweh, in Haggai-Zechariah 1–8, is the authoritative decree of King Yahweh.

In 2 Kings 18//Isaiah 36, we find two decrees of King Sennacherib. In these two decrees, Sennacherib urges Hezekiah and the inhabitants of Jerusalem to submit to Assyrian rule (2 Kings 18:19–25, 28–35). The second decree of Sennacherib is called "the word of the king" (הַמֶּלֶךְ־

דְּבַר), which is the Hebrew equivalent of the Akkadian phrase *amāt šarri* (v. 28). Additionally, in both decrees, Rabshakeh, the royal herald of Sennacherib, uses a message formula (כֹּה־אָמַר הַמֶּלֶךְ) to introduce the decree (vv. 19, 29).

The "written decree" (מִכְתָּב) of Cyrus, which authorized the rebuilding of the Jerusalem temple (see 2 Chronicles 36:22–23//Ezra 1:1–2), is another example of an ancient Near Eastern royal decree. Like the previous examples from 2 Kings 18, this particular decree begins with a message formula: "Thus says Cyrus, king of Persia" (2 Chronicles 36:23).

The preceding examples demonstrate that the language of the word event formula and the message formula, as they are used in Haggai-Zechariah 1–8, resembles the language of royal decrees. Another biblical text explicitly refers to the word of Yahweh, as proclaimed by Haggai and Zechariah, as the "decree" (טְעֵם) of God. Throughout the book of Ezra, the Persian kings "issue decrees" (שִׂים טְעֵם).[9] These royal decrees are written, archival, documents that have the binding authority of law.[10] According to Ezra 6:14, the Jerusalem temple was rebuilt in accordance with both the "decree" of God, as it was proclaimed by Haggai and Zechariah (see Ezra 5:1–2), and the "decrees" of Cyrus, Darius and Artaxerxes, as they are recorded in Ezra 6:3–12:

> The elders of Judah built and prospered through the prophesying of Haggai, the prophet, and Zechariah son of Iddo. They completed the rebuilding according to the decree (טְעֵם) of the God of Israel and according to the decree (טְעֵם) of Cyrus, Darius and Artaxerxes, king of Persia.[11]

Obviously, the author of Ezra considered the prophetic message of Haggai and Zechariah to be the authoritative decree of King Yahweh. On the basis of the analogy between the prophetic word and the written decrees of the Persian kings, we can also surmise that the author of Ezra was referring to a written text. This text probably included the prophecies of both prophets, that is, the book of Haggai-Zechariah 1–8.

The word of Yahweh, in Haggai-Zechariah 1–8, also resembles the decrees of the gods in mythological texts. Like human kings, the divine kings of the mythological world also issue decrees. In his examination of the divine council in Canaanite and early Israelite literature, E. T. Mullen compares the word event formula and the message formula of Israelite prophetic literature with similar formulas found in Ugaritic mythological texts.[12] In these latter texts, the decrees of El, in his role as the divine king, are introduced as follows:

taḥûmu ṭôri 'ili 'abiki	Message of Bull, El, your father,
huwātu luṭpāni ḥātikiki	Word of Kindly One, your patriarch.[13]

According to Mullen, the stylistic connection between the word event formula and the message formula in Israelite prophetic literature parallels the Ugaritic message formula *thm//hwt*.[14] The prophets, in Haggai-Zechariah 1–8, proclaim the *dĕḇar* of Yahweh just as the messenger-deity, in Ugaritic mythological texts, proclaims the *taḥûmu/huwātu* of El.[15]

Just as El issues decrees in Ugaritic mythology, so Marduk issues authoritative decrees in the Enuma Elish. According to the Enuma Elish of Babylon, Marduk's word is powerful and authoritative. His word is authoritative because he is the king of the gods. Thus, in Tablet 4, we read:

> (The gods) erected for him a princely throne. Facing his fathers, he sat down, presiding. Thou art the most honored of the great gods, thy decree is unrivaled, thy command is Anu.... From this day unchangeable shall be thy pronouncement. To raise or bring low—these shall be (in) thy hand. Thy utterance shall come true, thy command shall not be doubted.[16]

Upon witnessing the creative power of Marduk's word, the divine assembly proclaims him king (line 28).[17] As the divine king, Marduk issues decrees from the divine council.

In summary, the language of the word event formula and the message formula resembles the language of royal decrees. The use of these two formulas in Haggai-Zechariah 1–8 portrays Yahweh as the divine king who issues decrees. The word of Yahweh is the decree of King Yahweh.

The use of the divine title, Yahweh Sebaoth, is another indication that Haggai-Zechariah 1–8 conceptualizes the word of Yahweh as the decree of King Yahweh. As Carol and Eric Meyers observe, the occurrences of this divine title are "disproportionately frequent" in Haggai-Zechariah 1–8.[18] In this prophetic text, the title occurs in the message formula ("thus says Yahweh Sebaoth") as well as in the prophetic utterance formula ("oracle of Yahweh Sebaoth").[19] Alongside these prophetic formulas which establish the authority of the prophetic word, the title is also used in reference to the temple (Hag. 1:14; Zech. 7:3; 8:3, 9, 21f), Zechariah's prophetic commission (Zech. 2:13, 15; 4:9; 6:15; 7:12), and the wrath of Yahweh (Zech. 1:6, 12). While problems remain concerning the interpretation of this title,[20] most scholars agree that Yahweh Sebaoth is a royal title.[21] Therefore, the prominent use of this royal title in Haggai-Zechariah 1–8 provides further evidence that the composer depicts the word of Yahweh as the decree of King Yahweh.

The royal title, Yahweh Sebaoth, is associated with three distinct biblical themes. As we will discover, the chronotope of Haggai-Zechariah 1–8 displays each one of these themes. First, as the title suggests, Yahweh Sebaoth is the king of the heavenly hosts (Ps. 24:10; Isa. 6:1–5; Jer. 46:18; 48:1).[22] As such, Yahweh is the supreme deity in the divine council.[23] From the divine council, Yahweh issues decrees of judgment, which declare the future destiny of a group or individual.[24] The decrees of the divine council are delivered by the "messengers" of the council. The prophets are the means by which Yahweh reveals God's will to humankind (Isa. 6; Jer. 23:18–22). Thus, according to Patrick Miller:

> The prophet was the one who stood in the council of Yahweh. His task was the proclamation of the will and message of Yahweh as declared in the heavenly assembly.[25]

As we will discover, this conception of the prophetic role is also found in Haggai-Zechariah 1–8. We will say more about this conception when we examine the temporal perspective of Haggai-Zechariah 1–8.

Second, Yahweh Sebaoth, the divine king, is "enthroned upon the cherubim" (1 Sam. 4:4; 2 Sam. 6:2; Isa. 37:16). This formulaic phrase is associated with the ark of the covenant and its original resting place in Shiloh and its ultimate resting place in the Solomonic temple.[26] As Ollenburger observes, "The placement of the ark in the temple on Zion thus signified the dwelling of God as king in Jerusalem."[27] In other words, Yahweh Sebaoth, the heavenly king, reigns on earth in the temple of Jerusalem. We will say more about the temple as the dwelling place of Yahweh Sebaoth when we examine the spatial perspective of Haggai-Zechariah 1–8.

Third, as the king of the heavenly hosts, Yahweh Sebaoth is the divine warrior who establishes order in the cosmic realm by defeating the gods of chaos (Ps. 24; 48). Thus, according to Seow:

יהוה צבאות was perceived as the divine warrior who, having fought and won cosmogonic battle, had gained ascendancy in the divine council as the supreme deity, the king over all the heavenly hosts.[28]

Yahweh Sebaoth also establishes order in the earthly realm by defeating the enemies of Israel.[29] We will say more about this particular conception of Yahweh Sebaoth as the divine warrior when we examine the divine image in Haggai-Zechariah 1–8.

In summary, the use of the title, Yahweh Sebaoth, is another literary means by which Haggai-Zechariah 1–8 portrays the word of Yahweh as the royal decree of King Yahweh. As the use of the title in the message formula suggests, the word of Yahweh is the decree of Yahweh Sebaoth, the heavenly king.

According to the visions of Zechariah, the revelation of Yahweh's royal decree occurs in the divine council of Yahweh Sebaoth. Three visions, in particular, portray scenes in the divine council (Zech. 1:7–17; 3:1–10; 6:1–8). In each scene, the divine council is the setting for the revelation of a decree of Yahweh Sebaoth.

According to N. Tidwell, these three visions share the same three structural elements as other biblical texts that portray scenes in the divine council.[30] First, the narrative opens with a description of a session of the divine council (Zech. 1:8; 3:1; 6:1–3).[31] In Zechariah's fourth vision, Zechariah sees a vision of a trial scene in the council chambers of Yahweh (Zech. 3:1).[32] The council scene in Zechariah 3 is very similar to the council scenes described in Job 1–2. In Zech. 3, Joshua, the high priest, is portrayed as the defendant. "The messenger of Yahweh" (יהוה מַלְאַךְ) is the judge. "The satan" (הַשָּׂטָן) is the prosecuting attorney.

Both the first vision (Zech. 1:8) and the last vision (Zech. 6:1–3) describe a scene at, or near, Yahweh's cosmic abode.[33] In the first vision, Zechariah sees a horseman "standing among the myrtle trees near the cosmic deep" (1:8) and, in his last vision, Zechariah sees four chariots "coming out from between two bronze mountains" (6:1). The combined references to "the myrtle trees" (הַהֲדַסִּים),[34] "the cosmic deep" (מְצֻלָה),[35] and "the bronze mountains" (נְחֹשֶׁת הָרֵי)[36] resemble other descriptions of the heavenly king's abode in both biblical and Ugaritic texts.[37] Mullen summarizes his discussion on the cosmic abode of El as follows:

We have thus established the nature of the cosmic abode of El as it is reflected in both Canaanite and Israelite traditions. As we have shown, the mount of El was the *ḫuršānu*, the place of entrance to both the Underworld and Heaven. It was the place of judgment, the seat of the divine council. The tent-dwelling of the aged deity lay there, at the sources of the life-giving rivers. It formed the cosmic center of the earth, the region of Paradise. From there the high god delivered his decree from within the divine council. It was this mountain which became the central focus of the mythology of the high god and his council.[38]

According to the mythological tradition of Ugarit and Israel, the cosmic abode of the heavenly king "was the seat of the divine council."[39] In Zechariah's first vision, Yahweh's representatives, in the guise of horsemen, have just completed their mission of patrolling the earth and have returned to present their report to the divine council (see Zech. 1:10–11). In the last vision, Yahweh's representatives, in the guise of charioteers, present themselves before the divine council in preparation for another patrolling mission on earth (see Zech. 6:5-8).

Second, the council-scene narrative continues with a dialogue. The dialogue climaxes with the intervention of one particular participant (Zech. 1:9–12; 3:2–5; 6:4–7).[40] In the fourth vision, Yahweh rebukes the Satan for accusing Joshua and commands the attendants of the council to remove Joshua's filthy clothes (Zech. 3:2–4). The dialogue comes to a climax with the prophet interrupting the proceedings to command the attendants to place a "clean turban" on Joshua's head (v. 5).[41] In the council-scene of Zechariah's first vision, the horse riders report on the peaceful status of the earth (1:11). On hearing the report, "the messenger of Yahweh" intervenes by lamenting the sorrowful situation of Jerusalem and the other cities of Judah (1:12). In the council-scene of Zechariah's last vision, Yahweh's messenger tells Zechariah that the four chariots are about to patrol the earth (6:5–6). The account climaxes with the messenger issuing the command, "Go, patrol the earth" (v. 7).

Finally, the council-scene concludes with the word of Yahweh. According to Tidwell, the concluding word of Yahweh "determines the future destiny of that person or group whose affairs have been under review" (Zech. 1:13–17; 3:6–7; 6:8).[42] In the fourth vision, the messenger of Yahweh "admonishes" Joshua with a judicial decree of Yahweh Sebaoth (Zech. 3:6–7). As Petersen observes, the idiom עוד ב:

> is particularly at home in the legal context. The phrase can mean "testify against" (Deut. 4:26; 30:19; 31:28), or more generally (as here), "admonish, warn, or enjoin." Such legal language serves to establish a direct linkage between the oracular material and the just completed vision. Both vision and oracle are set in the legal assembly, the divine council.[43]

Like the prophets Haggai and Zechariah, the angelic messenger uses a message formula ("thus says Yahweh Sebaoth") to introduce and to authenticate the decree of Yahweh. The actual decree rewards Joshua with regular access to the divine council as long as Joshua obeys Yahweh's requirements by performing his high priestly duties in the temple (v. 7).[44]

In the first vision, Yahweh responds to the lament of the messenger with "kind and comforting words" (Zech. 1:13). The messenger then turns to Zechariah and commands him to "proclaim" two oracles (vv. 14–16 and v. 17).[45] Each oracle begins with an imperative command to proclaim and a message formula ("thus says Yahweh Sebaoth"). In the first oracle, Yahweh assures Jerusalem and Zion that Yahweh will return to the rebuilt temple (v. 16). The second oracle contains the promise that "Yahweh will again comfort Zion and again choose Jerusalem" (v. 17).

In the eighth vision, the messenger of Yahweh "summons" Zechariah to pay close attention to the closing statement of the vision (v. 8).[46] The messenger of Yahweh, speaking on Yahweh's behalf, declares that the charioteers who went to the north have caused Yahweh's spirit to rest in the land of the north. I understand this ambiguous statement to be a declaration of Yahweh's rule over Babylon and the Persian Empire.[47]

In summary, as Tidwell claims, the first, fourth and eighth visions share a similar basic structure. All three visions portray the revelation of Yahweh's word as occurring in the divine council of Yahweh Sebaoth. They all begin with a description of a council-scene. They all record a dialogue occurring in the council. They all conclude with a decree of Yahweh. In the first vision, Yahweh decrees the future destiny of Jerusalem: Yahweh will again comfort Zion and again choose Jerusalem to be God's dwelling place. In the fourth vision, Yahweh decrees the future destiny of Joshua: Joshua will have regular access to the divine council. Finally, in the eighth vision, Yahweh declares his rule over Babylon and the Persian Empire.

These decrees of Yahweh, which conclude the three council-scenes, summarize the three main themes of Haggai-Zechariah 1–8. First, the word of Yahweh, in Haggai-Zechariah 1–8, decrees the future destiny of Judah. Throughout Haggai-Zechariah 1–8, the new era of blessing is contingent upon the rebuilding of the Jerusalem temple. For example, in Hag. 1:2–11, Yahweh blames the poor harvest on the lack of progress on the rebuilding project. In Hag. 2:15–19, Yahweh declares that he will bless the land now that the foundations of the temple have been laid. Similarly, in Zech. 8:9–13, Yahweh contrasts the poverty and lawlessness of the period before the founding of the temple with the future prosperity of the land.

Second, the word of Yahweh, in Haggai-Zechariah 1–8, also decrees the future destiny of the leaders of Judah, Joshua and Zerubbabel. The future destiny of Joshua and Zerubbabel is also contingent upon their attitude and actions toward the temple of Jerusalem. In Haggai, Yahweh designates Zerubbabel to be his servant and his chosen one (2:23) because of Zerubbabel's role in rebuilding the temple. The vision of Zech. 4 (vv. 1–6a, 10b–14) portrays Joshua and Zerubbabel as two olive trees that stand beside the temple lampstand. The so-called "oracular insertion" of Zech. 4:6b–10a focuses on Zerubbabel's responsibility to rebuild the temple. Finally, according to Zech. 6:12–15, Joshua (the priest) and Zerubbabel (Branch) will rule in cooperative harmony.[48]

Third, the word of Yahweh, in Haggai-Zechariah 1–8, declares the universal rule of Yahweh Sebaoth. Haggai-Zechariah 1–8 declares Yahweh Sebaoth to be "the lord of all the earth" (Zech. 6:5). As we might expect, Yahweh rules from the temple in Jerusalem. For example, in Hag. 2:6–9, Yahweh declares his intention to defeat the nations and to establish his rule in the temple. According to Zech. 4:10b, the seven lamps of the temple lampstand symbolize "the eyes of Yahweh which rove about through all the earth." Similarly, the first vision (Zech. 1:8–17) and the eighth vision (Zech. 6:1–8) symbolize Yahweh's universal rule by means of horse riders or charioteers who patrol the whole earth. Finally, according to Zech. 8:20–23, "many peoples and strong nations" will acknowledge Yahweh's universal rule by coming to Jerusalem "to seek Yahweh Sebaoth."

In summary, Haggai-Zechariah 1–8 documents the word of Yahweh. Using royal and mythological language, Haggai-Zechariah 1–8 conceptualizes the word of Yahweh as the decree of King Yahweh. The revelation of Yahweh's word occurs in the divine council. The word of Yahweh, as it is revealed in Haggai-Zechariah 1–8, not only decrees the future destiny of Judah and its leaders, Joshua and Zerubbabel, but also declares the universal rule of Yahweh Sebaoth.

The temporal perspective

In contrast to the Babylonian chronicles, which conceptualize the passage of time by means of a succession of kings, Haggai-Zechariah

1–8 visualizes time in terms of a succession of prophets. Prophets, not kings, proclaim the word of Yahweh. The combination of two prophetic collections into a single text is the most obvious indication that Haggai-Zechariah 1–8 conceives time in terms of a prophetic succession. Time progresses as Zechariah succeeds Haggai as the one who proclaims the word of Yahweh. Haggai-Zechariah 1–8 also refers to the prophetic succession prior to Haggai and Zechariah. Zech. 1:4–6 and 7:7–14 place Haggai and Zechariah in the same line of succession as the "former prophets" (הַנְּבִיאִים הָרִאשֹׁנִים).[49] Therefore, Haggai-Zechariah 1–8 does not document the actions of a series of kings but rather documents the word of Yahweh as proclaimed by a series of prophets.

All the prophets, in the prophetic succession, proclaim the word of Yahweh in the name of Yahweh Sebaoth. The use of the word event formula, in Haggai-Zechariah 1–8, demonstrates that the word of Yahweh was revealed to both Haggai (Hag. 1:1; 2:1, 10, 20) and Zechariah (Zech. 1:1, 7; 7:1). Although Haggai-Zechariah 1–8 does not use the formula in connection with the "former prophets," it does refer to "the words" of Yahweh that were revealed to and proclaimed by the "former prophets" (see Zech. 1:6a and 7:12). Additionally, all the prophets—Haggai, Zechariah, and the "former prophets"—use the same message formula ("thus says Yahweh Sebaoth") to authenticate their prophetic proclamations of Yahweh's word (Hag. 1:2, 5, 7; Zech. 1:3, 4; 7:9; 8:2). In other words, all the prophets, in the prophetic succession, proclaim Yahweh's royal decree in the name of Yahweh Sebaoth.

Just as the Babylonian chronicles describe each king's reign in terms of the same basic actions (e.g., muster the troops and march to war), so Haggai-Zechariah 1–8 depicts the prophets as proclaiming the same basic message. The word of Yahweh remains the same whether it is proclaimed by Haggai or by Zechariah or by the "former prophets." Thus, Zech. 1:5–6a contrasts the temporal existence of the prophets with the eternal veracity of Yahweh's word. Prophets come and go, but the word of Yahweh endures forever.

As we have already discovered, Haggai and Zechariah proclaim the same basic message. Both prophets claim that the founding of the temple marks the beginning of a new era of blessing for "the remnant" of Judah (see Hag. 2:15–19 and Zech. 8:9–13). Second, both prophets designate Joshua and Zerubbabel as the two divinely ordained leaders of Judah (see Hag. 2:20–23 and Zech. 6:9–15). Finally, both prophets declare that

Yahweh Sebaoth will rule over all the earth from his dwelling place in the Jerusalem temple (see Hag. 2:6–9 and Zech. 1:14–17).

Haggai-Zechariah 1–8 also depicts Zechariah as proclaiming the same basic themes as the "former prophets." According to Zech. 1:3–4, Zechariah proclaimed a similar message of repentance as the "former prophets:"

> Thus says Yahweh Sebaoth: Return (שׁוּבוּ) to me, says Yahweh Sebaoth, so that I may return to you, says Yahweh Sebaoth. Do not be like your ancestors to whom the former prophets proclaimed, saying, Thus says Yahweh Sebaoth: Return (שׁוּבוּ) from your evil ways and from your evil deeds. But they did not listen and they did not pay attention to me, says Yahweh.

Both Zechariah and the "former prophets" use the imperative form of the verb שׁוּב to urge their respective audiences to "return" to Yahweh.[50]

According to Zech. 7:7, 9–10 and 8:16–17, Zechariah also proclaimed a similar ethical message as the "former prophets." Zech. 7:7, 9–10 summarizes the moral teaching of the "former prophets:"

> Were not these the words (הַדְּבָרִים) which Yahweh proclaimed by the hand of the former prophets...? Thus says Yahweh Sebaoth, saying: Render true judgments. Deal kindly and mercifully with one another. Do not oppress the widow, the orphan, the alien or the poor. Do not devise evil in your hearts against one another.

Zech. 8:16–17 summarizes the moral teaching of Zechariah:

> These are the words (הַדְּבָרִים) that you shall do: Speak truthfully to one another. Render true and perfect justice in your gates. Do not devise evil in your hearts against one another. Do not love false oaths because all these are what I hate, says Yahweh.

Like the "former prophets," Zechariah proclaims four "words" (הַדְּבָרִים) or ethical demands. In both cases, these "words" consist of two positive stipulations followed by two negative stipulations. Moreover, both Zechariah and the "former prophets" urge their respective audiences to render true justice and not to devise evil against one another.[51]

According to the chronotopic worldview of Haggai-Zechariah 1–8, the prophets are the messengers of the divine council of Yahweh Sebaoth.[52] Thus, Hag. 1:13 refers to the prophet Haggai as "the messenger of Yahweh" (מַלְאַךְ יהוה). As we observed earlier, all the prophets use the message formula ("thus says Yahweh Sebaoth") to authenticate their prophetic proclamations. Just as Yahweh "sends" other prophetic messengers in the Old Testament, so Yahweh Sebaoth "sends" Haggai, Zechariah, and the "former prophets" (Hag. 1:12; Zech. 2:13, 15; 4:9; 6:15; and 7:12). Finally, the references to "the messenger of Yahweh" (יהוה מַלְאַךְ) or "the messenger who spoke with me" (בִּ֖י הַדֹּבֵ֥ר הַמַּלְאָ֖ךְ) in Zech. 1:7–6:15 emphasize the necessity of having an intermediary who knows the will of the divine council.

In summary, Haggai-Zechariah 1–8 conceptualizes time from the perspective of the prophetic succession. The movement of time is associated with a series of prophets who proclaim the word of Yahweh. This series of prophets consists of the "former prophets," Haggai, and Zechariah. Haggai-Zechariah 1–8 portrays all these prophets as the messengers of Yahweh Sebaoth.

The spatial perspective

Like the chronotope of the chronicles, the chronotope of Haggai-Zechariah 1–8 has, as its basic geographical point of reference, the capital city. In the Babylonian chronicles, the geographic centrality of Babylon is primarily due to the city's unique status as the dwelling place of the king. In Haggai-Zechariah 1–8, however, the geographic centrality of Jerusalem is solely because of the city's unique status as the dwelling place of Yahweh Sebaoth. Therefore, in contrast to the chronicles, which conceptualize space from the perspective of the palace, Haggai-Zechariah 1–8 conceptualizes space from the perspective of the temple.

As we observed in chapter three, the geographic centrality of Babylon, in the Babylonian chronicles, is also due to the city's status as the dwelling place of Marduk. The ideal king returns to Babylon in order to enrich the city and to celebrate the Akitu festival. However, the chronicles primarily emphasize Babylon's status as a royal center rather than as a cultic center. In contrast, Haggai-Zechariah 1–8 emphasizes Jerusalem's status as the dwelling place of Yahweh Sebaoth.

The three main themes of the word of Yahweh, as they are summarized in the prophetic proclamations of Haggai and Zechariah, reflect this spatial perspective. First, both prophets equate the dawning of a new era of blessing for "the remnant" with the founding of the Jerusalem temple (see Hag. 2:18–19 and Zech. 8:9–13). Second, both prophets designate Joshua and Zerubbabel as the two divinely ordained leaders of Judah as long as Zerubbabel completes the reconstruction of the temple and Joshua fulfills his priestly work in the temple (see Hag. 2:20–23; Zech. 3:6–10 and Zech. 6:9–15). Finally, both prophets declare that Yahweh Sebaoth will rule over all the earth from his palace in the Jerusalem temple (see Hag. 2:6–9 and Zech. 1:14–17).

The structural arrangement of the visions, in Zech. 1:7–6:15, reinforces the impression that the chronotope of Haggai-Zechariah 1–8 conceives space from the perspective of the Jerusalem temple. As Paul Hanson observes, the structural arrangement of the visions focuses on the temple as the center of a symbolic universe.[53] Thus, the visions, in their present arrangement, form a chiasmus in which the two visions of Zechariah 3–4 form the center. The eight visions are as follows: vision 1 (Zech. 1:7–17), vision 2 (2:1–4), vision 3 (2:5–9), vision 4 (3:1–10), vision 5 (4:1–14), vision 6 (5:1–4), vision 7 (5:5–11), and vision 8 (6:1–8). Although most scholars agree that the visions are arranged as a chiasmus, they differ in their understanding of the arrangement of the chiasmus. For example, Hanson considers the original series of seven visions to have the following chiasmus: a b b¹ c d d¹ a¹.[54] Baldwin understands the series of eight visions to have a different chiasmic arrangement: a b b¹ c c¹ b² b³ a¹.[55] Carol and Eric Meyers understand the visions to have the following arrangement: a b c d d¹ c¹ b¹ a¹.[56] However, all these scholars agree that the two visions of Zech. 3–4 form the center of the chiasmus.

In the final form of these two visions, the political authority of Joshua (Zech. 3) and Zerubbabel (Zech. 4) is contingent upon their responsibilities in the temple of Yahweh. Thus, Zech. 3:7 defines Joshua's leadership role in terms of his priestly responsibilities in the "house" of Yahweh. Similarly, Zech. 4:6b–10a defines Zerubbabel's leadership role in terms of his work as the rebuilder of the temple.[57]

According to the chronotopic worldview of Haggai-Zechariah 1–8, the temple of Jerusalem is the dwelling place of Yahweh Sebaoth. In the literary context of an oracle of Yahweh Sebaoth, Yahweh refers to the temple as "my house" (בֵּיתִי) in Hag. 1:9, Zech. 1:16, and 3:7. Elsewhere in Haggai-Zechariah 1–8, the composer calls the temple "the house of Yahweh Sebaoth" (בֵּית־יהוה צְבָאוֹת) in Hag. 1:14, Zech. 7:3, and 8:9. Drawing upon the Zion tradition, Haggai-Zechariah 1–8 also refers to the temple mount as "the mountain of Yahweh Sebaoth" (הַר־יהוה צְבָאוֹת)

in Zech. 8:3. Finally, Yahweh Sebaoth declares his intention to dwell in the midst of the people in Hag. 2:5, Zech. 2:14–15, and 8:3.

Within Haggai-Zechariah 1–8, the people's obedience or disobedience of the prophetic word is the basis for Yahweh's triumphant return to the temple of Jerusalem. It is only after the people obeyed Haggai's demand to rebuild the temple that Yahweh assures them, "I am with you" (Haggai 1:12–13). Similarly, in Zech. 1:1–6, the return of Yahweh to dwell among the people, presumably in the rebuilt temple, depends upon the people's obedience. References to the "former prophets" reinforce the urgency of obedience to the prophetic word by reminding the readers of the consequences of disobedience. The people disobeyed the word of Yahweh, as proclaimed by the "former prophets," and the result was the judgment of Yahweh, the destruction of Jerusalem, and the exile (Zech. 1:4–5; 7:7–14). By obeying the word of Yahweh, as proclaimed by Haggai and Zechariah, the people will ensure God's continuing presence in the rebuilt temple of Jerusalem.

In summary, Haggai-Zechariah 1–8 conceptualizes space from the perspective of the temple in Jerusalem. The temple plays an important role not only in the three major themes of Yahweh's word but also in the chiastic arrangement of Zechariah's visions. Haggai-Zechariah 1–8 portrays the temple as the dwelling place of Yahweh Sebaoth. However, Yahweh's presence in the temple is ultimately dependent upon the people's obedience of Yahweh's prophetic word.

The divine image

As we observed in a previous chapter, the Babylonian chronicles create an image of an ideal king. The ideal king is a warrior who protects and enriches Babylon. Rather than create an image of a human king, the composer of Haggai-Zechariah 1–8 creates an image of the divine king. Yahweh Sebaoth is the divine warrior who protects and enriches Jerusalem.

The image of Yahweh as the divine warrior is the primary metaphor that connects the three main themes of Haggai-Zechariah 1–8. As the divine warrior, Yahweh Sebaoth will defeat the kingdoms of the world (see Hag. 2:6–9; Zech. 2:1–4) and designate Zerubbabel as God's chosen messiah (see Hag. 2:20–23). Consequently, Yahweh will establish a new era of blessing for "the remnant" (see Zech. 8) when Yahweh will rule over the entire world (see Zech. 6:1–8).

The structural arrangement of the visions, in Zech. 1:7–6:15, not only focuses on the temple as the center of a symbolic universe but also portrays a "dramatic movement" in which Yahweh Sebaoth, as the divine warrior, reestablishes his rule over all the world.[58] Thus, in Zech. 1:7–17, Yahweh declares his jealousy for Jerusalem and his anger with the nations. In Zech. 2, Yahweh defeats the nations (2:1–4), restores the prosperity of Jerusalem (2:5–9), and declares his intention to dwell in the midst of the people (2:14ff). In Zech. 3–4, Yahweh appoints a diarchic political establishment that will rule from the temple in Jerusalem (see also 6:9–15). In Zech. 5, Yahweh purifies the nation of wickedness and impurity (5:1–11). Finally, in Zech. 6:1–8, Yahweh establishes his rule over the entire world.

Instead of contrasting the actions of successive kings as they impacted the capital city, Haggai-Zechariah 1–8 contrasts the different responses to the prophetic word of Yahweh. The people disobeyed the word of Yahweh, as proclaimed by the "former prophets," and the result was the destruction of Jerusalem and the exile (Zech. 1:5–6a; 7:11–14). In contrast, the people obeyed the word of Yahweh, as proclaimed by Haggai and Zechariah, and the result was the founding of the temple. The new temple symbolized the dawning of a new era of blessing and salvation for "the remnant" (Hag. 1:12–14; 2:6–9, 18–19; Zech. 1:6b, 14–17; 8:9–23). The divine warrior, Yahweh Sebaoth, however, remains the same whether the people obey or disobey Yahweh's word.

In summary, Haggai-Zechariah 1–8 portrays Yahweh Sebaoth as the divine warrior who protects and enriches Jerusalem. If the inhabitants of Jerusalem truly desire the divine king's patronage, then, according to Haggai-Zechariah 1–8, they will respond to the urgency of the prophetic demand to obey the word of Yahweh. Only when the people have submitted to the word of Yahweh and rebuilt the temple can the true, divine king return to Jerusalem, bringing prosperity and blessing to the people. As the human king returns to the capital city in triumph, so shall the divine king return to dwell in the Jerusalem temple, restoring the intended order and blessing to the inhabitants.

In conclusion, like any other text, the whole utterance of Haggai-Zechariah 1–8 conceives time and space in a particular way. In Haggai-Zechariah 1–8, the composer uses a chronistic form to document the prophetic word of Yahweh. By so doing, the composer transforms the worldview of the chronicles. According to the worldview of the chronicles, the king, by his actions, protected and enriched the city and nation. The composer of Haggai-Zechariah 1–8 transforms that worldview by portraying Yahweh as the King. According to Haggai-Zechariah 1–8, the future prosperity of Jerusalem does not depend upon the actions of King Darius (whose regnal years are used simply to date the chronistic reports) but, rather, is dependent upon obedience to the royal decree of Yahweh Sebaoth, as proclaimed by the prophets of Yahweh.

The Socio-Historical Context

The literary chronotope of Haggai-Zechariah 1–8 is organically related to its socio-historical context. As we observed in chapter three, a literary chronotope is developed in the context of a particular socio-historical discourse. Therefore, in this section, we will reconstruct the socio-historical discourse that underlies the literary chronotope of Haggai-Zechariah 1–8. Specifically, we will identify the original participants of the discourse (the addresser and the addressee) as well as its historical situation.

The addresser

In chapter three, we argued that the temple scribes of Esagil composed the Babylonian chronicles. These temple scribes composed the chronicles in order to maintain a record of past kings who did or did not respect the temple. The use of a chronistic form in Haggai-Zechariah 1–8 suggests that a temple scribe also composed this text. Rather than maintain a record of past kings, however, the temple scribe who edited Haggai-Zechariah 1–8 documented the prophetic activity of Haggai and Zechariah.

In his recent book *Prophecy and Apocalypticism*, Stephen Cook raises two methodological problems that are relevant to this inquiry regarding the social identity of the editor of Haggai-Zechariah 1–8. First, we must be careful about using distinctive language and ideas to identify the social setting of a post-exilic text because, in this period, the imitation and borrowing of language was widespread.[59] Second, we must be aware that writers in the post-exilic period increasingly integrated citations and quotations from other written documents into their own works.[60] Both these problems limit the certainty and specificity that we can expect concerning the social identity of the editor of Haggai-Zechariah 1–8.

The first argument to support the hypothesis that a temple scribe edited Haggai-Zechariah 1-8 is the priestly provenance of other prophetic chronicles. Haggai-Zechariah 1–8 is not the only example of a prophetic chronicle. The prophetic books of Jeremiah and Ezekiel also use a chronological framework to shape their respective prophetic content. In addition, the Deuteronomistic History (DtrH) places prophetic material within a chronistic framework. Like Haggai-Zechariah 1–8, these three other biblical texts use a chronistic form to document the revelation of Yahweh's word.

In 1 and 2 Kings, the Deuteronomistic historian frames the accounts of each king's reign with a similar introduction and conclusion. Included in this frame is chronological information. The historian derived this information from two chronistic sources, calling them, "the book of the annual actions of the kings of Judah" and "the book of the annual actions of the kings of Israel." The historian places prophetic material within this chronistic framework. For example, the historian places the account of Jehu's prophecy against Baasha (1 Kings 16:1–4) within the chronistic frame of 1 Kings 15:33–34 and 16:5–7. Consequently, the revelation of Yahweh's word is always associated with, and is usually directed against, the reign of a particular king. For example, just as the word of Yahweh came to Haggai and Zechariah during the reign of Darius, so the word of Yahweh came to Jehu during the reign of Baasha (1 Kings 15:33–16:7).

Jeremiah and Ezekiel provide closer literary parallels to Haggai-Zechariah 1–8. Like Haggai-Zechariah 1–8, the book of Jeremiah dates the revelation of Yahweh's word by using the regnal years of kings. The book of Ezekiel is slightly different in that it dates the revelation of Yahweh's word according to the years of King Jehoiachin's exile in Babylon. Let us compare examples from each book in order to illustrate the formal similarities.

> The word that came to Jeremiah concerning all the people of Judah in the fourth year of Jehoiakiam, son of Josiah, king of Judah (that was the first year of Nebuchadrezzar, king of Babylon). (Jer. 25:1)

The word of Yahweh came to me in the ninth year in the tenth month on the tenth day of the month. (Ezek. 24:1)

In the second year of King Darius, in the sixth month, on the first day of the month, the word of Yahweh came by the hand of Haggai the prophet to Zerubbabel son of Sheatiel, governor of Judah, and to Joshua son of Jehozadak, the high priest. (Hag. 1:1)

Ezekiel and Haggai-Zechariah 1–8 employ this type of chronological information more consistently and frequently than Jeremiah. Walther Zimmerli detects an "increasing precision in the date references" in the prophetic books of the Hebrew Bible. Ezekiel, Haggai and Zechariah 1-8 are the most consistent in their use of dates. Zimmerli suggests that this increasing use of chronological references can be attributed to the priestly habit of "noting all important events in temple annals chronologically."[61]

Two scribal groups are responsible for composing these three other prophetic chronicles (DtrH, Jeremiah, and Ezekiel). The same Deuteronomic group probably transmitted and edited DtrH and Jeremiah.[62] An Ezekiel group transmitted and edited the book of Ezekiel. Both these groups were priestly in provenance. The priestly provenance of the Ezekiel group is most obvious in Ezekiel 40–48. These chapters describe, in visionary form, the restoration of the temple and its priesthood.[63] The priestly provenance of the Deuteronomic group is most obvious in its close association with the Josianic attempt to centralize the cult in the Jerusalem temple.[64] Significantly, the superscriptions of both Jeremiah and Ezekiel claim priestly lineage for the two prophets (Jer. 1:1; Ezek. 1:1–3). Although these three texts now contain post-exilic additions, all received their chronistic shape during the exilic period and, therefore, were composed prior to Haggai-Zechariah 1–8.[65] The priestly provenance of these other prophetic chronicles suggests that a priestly scribe also edited Haggai-Zechariah 1–8.

The second argument to support the hypothesis that a temple scribe edited Haggai-Zechariah 1–8 is its particular interest in the leadership roles of Joshua, the high priest, and Zerubbabel, the governor. Aside from the prophets Haggai and Zechariah, the only characters to be consistently named in Haggai-Zechariah 1–8 are Joshua and Zerubbabel. The prominence of Joshua is based on his role as the cultic leader of the temple. The prominence of Zerubbabel is related to his role as the rebuilder of the temple.

In Haggai-Zechariah 1–8, the power that is conferred upon Joshua makes him a political equal with Zerubbabel. Thus, in Hag. 1:1 and 2:2, the prophet addresses both of them in their official capacities as the overseers of the temple reconstruction project. Zech. 4:1–6a, 10b–14 and 6:9–15 depict Joshua and Zerubbabel as equals in the sight of God. In Zech. 3, Yahweh assures Joshua that he will have direct access to the divine council of Yahweh Sebaoth, thus granting Joshua prophetic authority.

Haggai-Zechariah 1–8 also displays a particular interest in the political role of Zerubbabel. Haggai-Zechariah 1–8 acknowledges Zerubbabel's messianic status as "Branch" (Zech. 6:9–15) and as Yahweh's chosen servant (Hag. 2:20–23). However, as we have seen, Zerubbabel's messianic status is contingent upon the rebuilding of the temple. In other words, the editor of Haggai-Zechariah 1–8 is interested in Zerubbabel because of his role as the rebuilder of the temple. This interest in Zerubbabel and the emphasis on Joshua disclose an agenda that would most likely be attributable to a temple scribe.

The third argument to support the hypothesis that a temple scribe edited Haggai-Zechariah 1–8 is its literary portrayal of Zechariah. As part of its presentation of the prophetic activity of Zechariah, Haggai-Zechariah 1–8 portrays Zechariah as a priestly scribe.

First, according to Haggai-Zechariah 1–8, Zechariah displays a particular interest in the rebuilding of the temple. For example, Zechariah claims to have been present at the founding of the temple on December 18, 520 BCE (Zech. 8:9; 4:6b–10a). In addition, like Haggai, Zechariah attributes the future prosperity of Judah to the rebuilding of the temple (Zech. 8:9–15).

Second, according to the genealogy of Zech. 1:1, the prophet Zechariah came from a priestly lineage. Apparently, he was the grandson of Iddo, one of the priests that returned to Judah from Babylon with Zerubbabel (Neh. 12:4).[66]

Third, according to Haggai-Zechariah 1–8, Zechariah performed priestly and scribal functions. For example, in Zechariah 7–8, Zechariah provides the response to a request for a priestly torah. In Zech. 7:2–3, certain individuals from Bethel come to Jerusalem "to ask the priests of the house of Yahweh Sebaoth and the prophets, Should I mourn and practice abstinence in the fifth month as I have done for so many years?"

Subsequently, Zechariah provides the answer to this inquiry, thus, demonstrating that Zechariah performed a priestly function.

Janet Tollington suggests that the portrayal of Zechariah in Zech. 6:9–15 resembles Priestly passages in Exodus and Number that portray Moses as receiving offerings of silver and gold for the tabernacle (Ex. 25:1–3; 30:11, 16; Num. 7:1–84; 31:54). Just as the offerings of silver and gold received by Moses become a "memorial" (לְזִכָּרוֹן) before Yahweh (Ex. 30:16), so the offerings of silver and gold received by Zechariah become a "memorial" (לְזִכָּרוֹן) in the temple of Yahweh (Zech. 6:14).[67]

The references to the "former prophets" in Zech. 1:1–6 and 7:7–12 suggest that Zechariah also performed a scribal function. These two passages portray Zechariah as one who had access to written collections of prophetic material. On the basis of the similarity between the quotation from the "former prophets" in Zech. 1:4 and texts from Jeremiah and Ezekiel, Petersen concludes:

> One may infer that the author of Zech. 1:4 has viewed such texts as Jer. 11:18; 25:5; 35:15; Ezek. 33:11 as typical of pre-586 prophetic language and has appropriated it as the sort of things such prophets said. This activity on the part of the author of Zech. 1:4 presupposes that he had access to some form of the nascent prophetic collections, one that in the case of Jeremiah included the recently written deuteronomistic prose.[68]

Presumably, these collections would have been kept in the rebuilt temple.[69] In addition, these passages portray Zechariah updating and reinterpreting these earlier prophetic traditions in light of new historical circumstances. In other words, Haggai-Zechariah 1–8 portrays Zechariah as one who preserves and reinterprets written texts. This was the typical activity of temple scribes.[70]

Fourth, the symbolism of Zechariah's visions reflects a cultic background.[71] According to Carol and Eric Meyers, all of Zechariah's visions "legitimize, according to the ancient typology, the rebuilt temple."[72] Moreover, Zechariah borrows much of his imagery from the temple cult. For example, the four horns in Zechariah's second vision (2:1–4) are probably the horns of the altar,[73] and the lampstand in Zechariah's fifth vision (4:1–4) is, undoubtedly, the temple lampstand.[74] Finally, the two visions in Zech. 5 reflect a priestly concern for purity.[75]

In summary, in its presentation of Zechariah's prophetic activity, Haggai-Zechariah 1–8 portrays Zechariah as a priestly scribe. This portrayal of Zechariah as a priestly scribe provides further evidence that a temple scribe edited Haggai-Zechariah 1-8.

The final argument to support the hypothesis that a temple scribe composed Haggai-Zechariah 1-8 is the existence of other scribal efforts to preserve the laws and traditions of local temple cults during the Persian period. As part of the Persian policy of re-establishing local sanctuaries, the Persian imperial administration authorized the use of non-Persian scribes to collect and preserve religious texts associated with the sanctuary.[76] For example, Darius I commissioned the Egyptian priestly scribe Udjahorresnet to re-establish the scribal institution known as the "House of Life." As Raymond Person observes, this mission is

> in all likelihood associated with Darius I's order (preserved in the *Demotic Chronicle*) that a commission be established in order to codify Egyptian laws which were in force at the end of Amasis's reign (526 BCE).[77]

Similarly, later, the Persian imperial administration commissioned the priestly scribe Ezra "to reassert Persian control over the Jerusalem temple cult" by codifying the Mosaic law (Ezra 7).[78] Just as these other priestly scribes sought to preserve the laws and traditions, so the editor of Haggai-Zechariah 1–8 sought to preserve the prophetic words of Haggai and Zechariah. The composer preserved the prophetic words of Haggai and Zechariah because these two prophets supported and encouraged the rebuilding of the temple.

Ezra 3 describes Joshua's and Zerubbabel's efforts to re-establish the temple cult of Jerusalem. Among the tasks performed by these two individuals was the appointment of levitical priests "to supervise the work of the house of Yahweh" (בֵּית־יהוה עַל־מְלֶאכֶת לְנַצֵּחַ; v. 8b). Keeping records must have been among the responsibilities of these levites. In other words, some of these levites were priestly scribes. According to 2 Chron. 34:12–13, some of the levites, appointed by King Josiah to supervise the repair work on the temple, were "scribes" (סוֹפְרִים).

In summary, a temple scribe probably edited Haggai-Zechariah 1–8. Evidence for this conclusion is derivable from the following facts. First, priestly scribes composed other examples of prophetic chronicles, such as DtrH, Jeremiah and Ezekiel. Second, Haggai-Zechariah 1–8 displays a particular interest in the role of Joshua as the cultic leader of the temple and in the role of Zerubbabel as the rebuilder of the temple. Third, Haggai-Zechariah 1–8 portrays Zechariah as a priestly scribe. Finally, the chronistic record of Haggai-Zechariah 1–8 parallels the scribal efforts of other priestly groups who sought to collect and preserve religious texts associated with the temple cult.

The addressee

Having identified the social group that authored the chronotope of Haggai-Zechariah 1–8, let us now identify those whom they were addressing. In chapter three, we argued that the Babylonian chronicles were addressed to the kings of Babylon. The use of the chronistic form in Haggai-Zechariah 1–8 suggests that an analogous audience was the intended recipient of this prophetic chronicle. In this section, we will argue that the intended recipients of Haggai-Zechariah 1–8 were the two leaders of the Persian province of Judah: Joshua, the high priest, and Zerubbabel, the governor.

As we have already observed Haggai-Zechariah 1–8 displays a particular interest in the leadership roles of Joshua and Zerubbabel. The prophetic word of Yahweh explicitly addresses one or both of these individuals in Hag. 1:1–11; 1:15b–2:9; 2:20–23; Zech. 3:6–10; 4:6–10a; and 6:12–15. No other individual or group is addressed as often as Joshua and Zerubbabel. Haggai-Zechariah 1–8 also documents Joshua's and Zerubbabel's response to the prophetic word in Hag. 1:12–15a. Upon hearing the prophetic word, contained in Hag. 1:4–11, Zerubbabel and Joshua "obeyed the voice of Yahweh their God" (v. 12). Joshua and Zerubbabel are also the subjects of the central two visions (Zech. 3:1–5; 4:1–5, 10b–14). All this literary evidence supports the hypothesis that the composer addressed Haggai-Zechariah 1–8 to Joshua and Zerubbabel.

Apart from the literary evidence of the text itself, we can surmise that Joshua and Zerubbabel were the intended audience on the basis of their official roles. According to Hag. 1:1 and 2:2, Zerubbabel was the "governor of Judah" (יְהוּדָה פַּחַת), and Joshua was "the high priest" (הַגָּדוֹל הַכֹּהֵן). Although some uncertainty exists about the historical accuracy and the exact nature of these roles, it is certain that Zerubbabel and Joshua were the official appointees of the Persian crown.[79]

According to Ezra, Cyrus appointed these two individuals to re-establish the temple cult of Jerusalem. Ezra 4:3 specifically states that

Cyrus commanded Zerubbabel and Joshua to rebuild the temple. Ezra 3 documents their compliance with that command. They rebuilt the altar and re-established the daily sacrifices and cultic festivals (vv. 2–5). They hired masons and carpenters to rebuild the temple (v. 7). They appointed priestly supervisors (vv. 8b–9). Finally, they laid the foundation of the temple (vv. 10–13).

In their appointive roles, Zerubbabel and, especially, Joshua would have also functioned as the supervisors of the scribal school charged with preserving the religious texts of the temple. Those in the scribal school would have completed their work, understanding that Joshua and Zerubbabel would have been its primary readers. Among the works written specifically for the benefit of Joshua and Zerubbabel would have been Haggai-Zechariah 1–8.

In summary, Joshua and Zerubbabel, the two official leaders of the Judean community, were the intended recipients of Haggai-Zechariah 1–8. Internal literary citations from Haggai-Zechariah 1–8 demonstrate the preoccupation of the editor with these two figures. In addition, as the official leaders of the community, Joshua and Zerubbabel would have supervised the scribal activity of the temple; therefore, they would have been those for whom the temple scribes primarily intended their work.

The situation

As an utterance, Haggai-Zechariah 1–8 used the chronotopic resources of the chronistic genre "in a specific way in response to a specific individual situation."[80] We have already identified the addresser and the addressee of the utterance. We will now reconstruct the historical situation and, consequently, the socio-historical discourse that underlies the literary chronotope of Haggai-Zechariah 1–8.

Let us begin this reconstruction of the historical situation by determining the approximate date of composition. December 7, 518 BCE is the last recorded date in Haggai-Zechariah 1–8 (see Zech. 7:1). This date serves as the *terminus post quem* for the composition of the whole text. Like Carol and Eric Meyers, we contend that the temple rededication ceremony in 516 or 515 BCE, which is described in Ezra 7:16–18, is the *terminus a quo* of the text.[81]

According to Haggai-Zechariah 1–8, the completion of the temple is an eagerly anticipated future event. In Hag. 2:6–9, the prophet predicts that the completed second temple will be more glorious and more prosperous than the Solomonic temple. The use of the imperfect form of the verb בנה in Zechariah 1:16 and 6:13 suggests that the construction of the temple has not been completed. Notably, the text does not contain any indication that the temple has either been completed or rededicated. Considering the importance of the foundation ceremony in Haggai-Zechariah 1–8 (Hag. 2:18; Zech. 8:9), the absence of any reference to a rededication ceremony is significant. One cannot conceive of the idea that the temple could have been completed and yet have received no mention or documentation in the book of Haggai-Zechariah 1–8.

Second, as we have seen, Haggai-Zechariah 1–8 ascribes special status to Zerubbabel because of his official role as the rebuilder of the temple. According to Zech. 4:9 and 6:12–13, Zerubbabel, as "Branch," will complete the rebuilding of the temple. Hag. 2:23 designates Zerubbabel as Yahweh's servant and Yahweh's chosen one. All this royal language and imagery, associated with Zerubbabel, is surprising because, as Miller and Hayes observe, Zerubbabel "simply disappears from history."[82] The book of Ezra does not mention Zerubbabel in its account of the rededication ceremony (Ezra 6:16–18), the implication being that Zerubbabel played no official part in this pivotal event. The contrast between the high role accorded Zerubbabel in Haggai-Zechariah 1–8 and his complete disappearance from history suggests failed expectations on the part of the biblical tradition. The composition of Haggai-Zechariah 1–8 must have occurred prior to the time of this disappointment. Therefore, this observation gives further credence to the setting of an early date for the composition of Haggai-Zechariah 1–8.

Third, there are indications in Haggai-Zechariah 1–8 that the composer expected the fulfillment of Haggai's and Zechariah's prophetic predictions in the lifetime of the prophets. For example, in Hag. 2:6, we find the use of the unusual phrase, "once again, in a little while" (היא עוֹד אַחַת מְעַט), introducing a prediction of Yahweh's defeat of the nations. As Ackroyd observes, this "somewhat cryptic phrase…presumably must mean that the events are anticipated as taking place in the immediate future."[83] This assertion of the prophecy's immediate fulfillment must have been acceptable to the editor of Haggai-Zechariah 1–8 or it would not have been included in the completed text.

Another indication that the editor of Haggai-Zechariah 1–8 anticipated the fulfillment of Zechariah's predictions is the use of the phrase "then you will know that Yahweh Sebaoth has sent me (to you)" (Zech. 2:13, 15; 4:9; 6:15). The editor expects the fulfillment of

Zechariah's predictions to validate his prophetic authority in the near future. Specifically, as Zech. 4:9 and, to a lesser extent, 6:15 indicate, the editor of Haggai-Zechariah 1–8 considers the completion of the temple to be the most undeniable proof of Zechariah's prophetic authority.

Understanding the composition date of Haggai-Zechariah 1–8 to be early, we can identify the rededication of the temple as the historical situation that underlies the literary utterance of Haggai-Zechariah 1–8. In anticipation of the rededication ceremony, a temple scribe composed the prophetic chronicle of Haggai-Zechariah 1–8.

Since the composition date is early, there is a strong possibility that Zechariah himself was the actual editor. Carol and Eric Meyers come to a similar conclusion:

> Nothing that we have discovered in the two prophets has proved definitive in arguing against the assumption that Haggai and Zechariah were the authors of virtually all that is attributed to them and that Zechariah himself, since his concluding words echo some of Haggai's themes, had a composite work in mind. Zechariah or a close disciple would have united the two small prophetic collections into the form in which they now appear.[84]

We have already seen how the text portrays Zechariah as a priestly scribe. Further indications that Zechariah was the temple scribe who edited Haggai-Zechariah 1–8 is the use of the first person in the references to the prophet Zechariah. The editor consistently refers to Haggai in the third person. However, the editor refers to Zechariah in both the third person and the first person. The editor uses the third person in the word event formulas that introduce each section of Zechariah 1–8 (Zech. 1:1, 7; 7:1). However, the editor uses the first person in the visions of Zechariah (e.g., Zech. 1:8; 2:1; 3:1; 4:1). Significantly, the formulaic phrase, "then you will know that Yahweh Sebaoth has sent me" (Zech. 2:13, 15; 4:9; 6:15) refers to the prophet in the first person. Like other scholars, we contend that Zechariah himself added these phrases to his original prophecies.[85] This use of the first person and the related concern to confirm the prophetic authority of Zechariah on the basis of fulfilled prophecy (see Deut. 18:21–22; Jer. 28:9) provides further evidence that Zechariah edited Haggai-Zechariah 1–8 in anticipation of the rededication of the temple in 516/515 BCE.

Since we have identified the participants of the discourse and the historical situation that underlies this discourse, let us now define the relation between the literary chronotope and its socio-historical setting.

By transforming the chronistic genre to create this prophetic chronicle, the editor of Haggai-Zechariah 1–8 accomplishes three interrelated tasks. First, Zechariah chronicles the role of the prophets in motivating the rebuilding of the temple. Second, Zechariah defends his own prophetic authority. Third, Zechariah proclaims the universal rule of Yahweh Sebaoth.

According to the chronotopic perspective of Haggai-Zechariah 1–8, the people rebuilt the temple in obedience to the prophetic word of Yahweh. In this literary utterance, Zechariah emphasizes the role of the prophets, especially his own role, in facilitating the rebuilding of the temple. By so doing, Zechariah not only de-emphasizes the role of King Darius but also challenges his audience, Joshua and Zerubbabel, to continue obeying the prophetic word. The references to the "former prophets" augment this argument by reminding Joshua and Zerubbabel of the dire consequences of disobedience.

In order to persuade Joshua and Zerubbabel of the necessity of obeying the prophetic word, Zechariah has to defend the legitimacy of his own prophetic ministry. Zechariah expects the completion of the temple and, consequently, the fulfillment of his predictions, to demonstrate his prophetic authenticity. He reinforces this argument by placing himself in the same line of succession as Haggai and the "former prophets."

Finally, Zechariah proclaims the universal rule of Yahweh Sebaoth. According to the chronotopic perspective of Haggai-Zechariah 1–8, the temple is not a symbol of Persian imperial beneficence. The temple is the dwelling place of Yahweh Sebaoth, the lord of all the earth. By obeying the prophetic word of Yahweh, as it is written in Haggai-Zechariah 1–8, Joshua and Zerubbabel can ensure God's presence in the temple as well as God's blessing and support. Moreover, by obeying Yahweh's word, Joshua and Zerubbabel can rule together, in cooperative harmony, as Yahweh's representatives on earth.

In summary, a temple scribe edited Haggai-Zechariah 1–8 in anticipation of the rededication ceremony in 516/515 BCE. This early date for the composition of the text is indicated by: the absence of any reference to the completion of the temple, the important role of Zerubbabel, and the anticipated imminent fulfillment of Haggai's and Zechariah's predictions. The early composition date for the text raises the possibility that Zechariah himself composed Haggai-Zechariah 1–8.

In this text, Zechariah addresses Joshua and Zerubbabel, the two leaders of the Judean community. Zechariah composed this utterance in order to persuade Joshua and Zerubbabel to obey the prophetic word and complete the rebuilding of the temple.

The Socio-Political Function

A Bakhtinian analysis of a literary text concludes with an examination of the socio-political function of the chronotope. As the worldview of a particular social group in a particular historical setting, a chronotope either preserves the socio-political order (ideological function) or subverts it (utopian function). Therefore, we will conclude this chapter by examining the socio-political function of the chronotope of Haggai-Zechariah 1–8. We will argue that the chronotope of Haggai-Zechariah 1–8 performs a utopian function.[86]

We will explore the utopian function of the chronotope by applying Paul Ricoeur's analysis of utopian discourse to this discussion.[87] Like ideology, utopia operates at the same three levels of socio-political discourse. First, at the deepest level of social discourse, utopian discourse "defamiliarizes" the existing social world by opening "a field for alternative ways of living."[88] According to Ricoeur:

> The fantasy of an alternative society and its topographical figuration 'nowhere' works as the most formidable contestation of what is. What some, for example, call cultural revolution proceeds from the possible to the real, from fantasy to reality.[89]

Therefore, in contrast to ideology, which performs an "integrative" function, utopia performs a "subversive" function. At the second level of social discourse, utopias "always imply alternative ways of using power" and, thereby, "call established systems of power into question."[90] On the surface level, utopian discourse tends toward "escapism" if it is not connected with a concrete course of action.[91]

In contrast to the Babylonian chronicles, which performed an ideological function, the chronotope of Haggai-Zechariah 1–8 performed a utopian function. In Haggai-Zechariah 1–8, the composer discloses a utopian vision that subverts the historical reality of Persian imperial rule. In the real world, the Persian imperial machine of King Darius sought to pacify and to control the Judean population by re-establishing the temple cult of Jerusalem. By transforming the chronistic chronotope to present a prophetic perspective on time and space, the editor of Haggai-Zechariah 1–8 subverts this imperial ideology.

First, the use of the chronistic form in Haggai-Zechariah 1–8 would normally mean that Darius, the Persian king, whose regnal years are used in the chronological framework, would be the main actor in the text. However, Haggai-Zechariah 1–8 does not date and record the actions of King Darius but, rather, dates and records the revelation of King Yahweh's word. Therefore, a literary tension exists between the chronistic form, which reflects the historical reality of Persian imperial rule, and the prophetic content, which declares the universal rule of Yahweh Sebaoth.

In the real world, as it is reflected in the chronistic form, King Darius reigns supreme.[92] In the literary world of Haggai-Zechariah 1–8, however, Yahweh Sebaoth is the divine king who decrees the future destiny of Judah and its leaders, Joshua and Zerubbabel. The chronotopic focus on the prophetic word as the decree of King Yahweh subverts the historical reality of Persian rule by revealing a future reality where the kingdoms of the world, including the Persian Empire, are subservient to Yahweh Sebaoth and Yahweh's representatives in Judah.[93]

Second, the use of the chronistic form in Haggai-Zechariah 1–8 would normally means that time would be envisaged from the perspective of the Persian royal succession. However, Haggai-Zechariah 1–8 does not document the actions of a series of kings but rather documents the word of Yahweh as proclaimed by a series of prophets. Therefore, a literary tension exists between the chronistic form, which uses a royal chronology, and the prophetic content, which conceives time in terms of a prophetic succession.

The royal chronology of the chronistic form reflects the historical reality of Persian imperial rule. In order to date the seven sections of Haggai-Zechariah 1–8, the editor had no choice but to use the regnal years of King Darius. However, the editor subverts that reality by presenting a different perspective on time in the prophetic content of Haggai-Zechariah 1–8.

The overlapping dates in the chronological structure of Haggai-Zechariah 1–8 reinforce this act of literary subversion. Rather than date the opening section of Zechariah 1–8 after the last date of Haggai, the editor dates Zech. 1:1–6 in the month prior to the last date in Haggai, thus interrupting the chronological order of the text. This interruption is due to the concern of the editor to place both Haggai and Zechariah at the founding of the temple in the ninth month (Zech. 8:9). By so doing, the editor implies that this paramount cultic event in the life of the city of Jerusalem was in response to the proclamations of both Haggai and Zechariah. The founding of the temple took place because the people obeyed the word of Yahweh, as proclaimed by both Haggai and Zechariah. It did not take place because of any military or cultic action on the part of King Darius.

By conceptualizing time in terms of a prophetic succession, the editor emphasizes the eternal nature of Yahweh's rule. Haggai-Zechariah 1–8 envisions Yahweh Sebaoth as issuing decrees long before the Persian Empire even existed. Thus, there is an inherent theological critique in Haggai-Zechariah 1–8 of earthly rule and rulers as the perspective for dating history and existence. The editor of this work seeks to subjugate the earthly temporal dating of time to an eternal perspective, thus expanding and exploding the narrow view that time can belong to any king or be dated to any rule other than Yahweh's.

Third, the use of a chronistic form would normally mean that the palace of King Darius would be the locus of space in Haggai-Zechariah 1–8. However, Haggai-Zechariah 1–8 focuses not on the royal palace of the Persian king but rather on the temple of Yahweh Sebaoth in Jerusalem. In this juxtaposition, we can observe a literary tension between the chronistic form, which affirms the historical reality of Persian imperial rule, and the prophetic content, which declares the eternal rule of Yahweh Sebaoth. This literary tension is given a geographical correspondence in the competing locations of the palace of Darius and the temple of Yahweh.

By conceptualizing space from the perspective of the temple, Haggai-Zechariah 1–8 not only affirms the importance of the temple in the ongoing life of the Judean community but also subverts the historical reality of Persian imperial rule. According to the chronotopic perspective of Haggai-Zechariah 1–8, the temple of Jerusalem, rather than the Persian royal palace, is the seat of authority and power. This power and authority belong to Yahweh Sebaoth. All the kingdoms of the world, including the Persian Empire, are subservient to Yahweh's universal and eternal rule. This perspective is portrayed graphically in the structural arrangement of Zechariah's visions. Yahweh's universal rule, symbolized by the first and last visions, has its center in the temple of Jerusalem, portrayed symbolically by the lampstand in the fifth vision.

Finally, the use of a chronistic form in Haggai-Zechariah 1–8 would normally mean that King Darius would be portrayed as a mighty warrior. In the real world of history, Darius established his rule over the Persian Empire by defeating all his enemies in the first two years of his reign. However, Haggai-Zechariah 1–8 portrays Yahweh Sebaoth, not Darius, as the warrior who defeats the nations of the world and rules as the universal ruler. Therefore, a literary tension exists between the chronistic form, which reflects the historical reality of Persian imperial rule, and the prophetic content, which declares the universal rule of Yahweh.

Haggai-Zechariah 1–8 subverts the historical reality of Persian imperial rule by providing a different interpretation of history in which Yahweh Sebaoth acts as the divine warrior. First, according to Haggai-Zechariah 1–8, Judah was defeated and exiled because of the wrath of Yahweh on a disobedient nation and not because of the superior might of the enemy nations (see Zech. 1:1–8 and 2:1–4). Second, according to Haggai-Zechariah 1–8, Yahweh Sebaoth, not King Darius, is "the lord of all the earth" (see Zech. 6:1–8). Finally, according to Haggai-Zechariah 1–8, in the future, Yahweh Sebaoth is going "to shake the heavens and the earth, and to overthrow the throne of kingdoms" (Hag. 2:21–22).

The chronotope of Haggai-Zechariah 1–8 presents not only an alternative perspective on time and space but also an alternative way of using power. As such, the chronotope critiques the established system of power. In the real world, Joshua and Zerubbabel rule as the appointed agents of King Darius. In the literary world of Haggai-Zechariah 1–8, Joshua and Zerubbabel rule as the agents of Yahweh Sebaoth. Within the text, the power and prestige enjoyed by these two leaders is dependent not upon the Persian imperial administration but, instead, upon their obedience to the prophetic word of Yahweh.

The chronotope of Haggai-Zechariah 1–8 portrays Yahweh Sebaoth as "the lord of all the earth" whose earthly agents are Joshua and Zerubbabel. This portrayal receives a visionary form in Zech. 4. This vision depicts Joshua and Zerubbabel as two olive trees that stand on either side of a golden lampstand, which represents Yahweh.

According to Haggai-Zechariah 1–8, Joshua and Zerubbabel are Yahweh's acknowledged agents because they obeyed the prophetic command to rebuild the temple (Hag. 1:12–14). Because of their obedience, Yahweh confers upon Zerubbabel the titles of "servant" (Hag. 2:33) and "Branch" (Zech. 3:8 and 6:12), and Yahweh bestows upon Joshua the privilege of direct access to the divine council (Zech. 3:7). Most significantly, the success or failure of Joshua and Zerubbabel is completely dependent not upon their loyalty to the Persian king but, instead, upon their obedience to the prophetic word of the divine king.

Finally, we must determine whether the chronotope of Haggai-Zechariah 1–8, as utopian discourse, is realistic or merely a form of escapism. Haggai-Zechariah 1–8 avoids the charge of escapism by placing its utopian vision in the foreseeable future. The completion of the temple will not only confirm the legitimacy of Zechariah's prophetic authority but also herald the establishment of God's rule on earth.

In summary, the chronotope of Haggai-Zechariah 1–8 performs a utopian socio-political function. It subverts the historical reality of Persian imperial rule by depicting the universal rule of Yahweh. Earthly power stems from King Yahweh and is dependent upon human obedience to the prophetic word. This utopian vision will be confirmed by the correspondence of its predictions to anticipated future events.

In conclusion, a Bakhtinian analysis of Haggai-Zechariah 1–8 reveals new information about this prophetic corpus. An examination of the literary chronotope demonstrates that it is a prophetic transformation of the chronistic genre. The chronotope of Haggai-Zechariah 1–8 uses the chronotopic resources of the chronistic genre to portray Yahweh as king. This literary examination of the chronotope provides new insights about the socio-historical context of Haggai-Zechariah 1–8. As a literary utterance, a temple scribe edited Haggai-Zechariah 1–8. This editor addressed Haggai-Zechariah 1–8 to Joshua and Zerubbabel in anticipation of the rededication ceremony for the Jerusalem temple in 516/515 BCE. Within this socio-historical context, the chronotope of Haggai-Zechariah 1–8 performed a utopian socio-political function. It presented a utopian vision of the future in which Yahweh rules as "the lord of all the earth."

NOTES

[1]   Gary Saul Morson and Caryl Emerson, *Mikhail Bakhtin: Creation of a Prosaics* (Stanford: Stanford University Press, 1990), 89.

2   According to H. W. Wolff, "(T)he final form of the book of Haggai as we have it presents four accounts of the confronting event of God's word." See Wolff, *Haggai*, 17.

3   Meyers and Meyers, *Haggai*, 7. For more detailed discussions on the mythological background to this prophetic "paradigm," see F. M. Cross, *Canaanite Myth and Hebrew Epic* (Cambridge, MA: Harvard University Press, 1973), 177–190 and E. Theodore Mullen, Jr., *The Assembly of the Gods*, Harvard Semitic Monographs (Chico, CA: Scholars Press, 1986), 209–226.

4   Claus Westermann, *Basic Forms of Prophetic Speech* (Louisville: Westminster, 1991), 101.

5   Gerhard von Rad, *Old Testament Theology*, volume 2 (San Francisco: Harper & Row, 1965), 87.

6   According to Klaus Koch, the message formula "legitimises the speaker and compels the hearers to accept the words he utters as coming from the sender of the message." See Klaus Koch, *The Growth of the Biblical Tradition* (New York: Macmillan Publishing Company, 1988), 190.

7   See John S. Holladay, "Assyrian Statecraft and the Prophets of Israel," in *Prophecy in Israel*, ed., David L. Petersen (Philadelphia: Fortress Press, 1987), 130.

8   Ibid., 141, footnote 54. Holladay presents two arguments to support this argument. First, the *amāt šarri* "appears as an introductory formula only in the king's letter." Second, the personal letters of the king use a different introduction: *duppu* PN.

9   For example, see Ezra 4:19, 21; 6:1, 3; 7:13, 21.

10   See Ezra 1:1; 4:23; 5:23; 6:1–2; 7:11; 6:11; 7:26; Dan. 3:10–11.

11   In Ezra 7:21–23, King Artaxerxes "issues a decree" (שִׂים טְעֵם) in which he urges the people of Judah to obey "the decree of the God of heaven" (טְעֵם אֱלָהּ שְׁמַיָּא). In this case, the "decree" of God is the "law" as codified by Ezra (see v. 26).

12   Mullen, *The Assembly of the Gods*, 137–145, 209–226.

13   Ibid., 137.

14   Ibid., 221.

15   Cross, *Canaanite Myth*, 186.

16   Tablet 4, lines 1–9 (ANET, 66).

[17] In lines 21–28, a star (*lumašu*) is destroyed and recreated by the "word" of Marduk.

[18] Meyers and Meyers, *Haggai*, 18.

[19] For example, see Hag. 1:2, 5, 7, 9; Zech. 1:3, 4, 14, 16, 17.

[20] T. N. D. Mettinger lists three problems associated with the title: the meaning of the word *ṣĕbā'ôt*; the grammatical relationship between the two elements in the title; and the origin and background of the title. See T. N. D. Mettinger, *In Search of God: The Meaning and Message of the Everlasting Names* (Philadelphia: Fortress, 1988), 154–157.

[21] Ibid., 123–157; Cross, *Canaanite Myth*, 91–111; and Ben. C. Ollenburger, *Zion the City of the Great King: A Theological Symbol of the Jerusalem Cult*, JSOT Supplement Series 41 (Sheffield: JSOT Press, 1987), 36–52.

[22] One of the problems associated with the title, Yahweh Sebaoth, is the original meaning of צְבָאוֹת. Does it refer to the armies of earthly Israel or the host of heaven? On the basis of a philological analysis of the divine name, Yahweh, and a comparative study of Ugaritic mythological texts, Cross argues that the word צְבָאוֹת refers to "the hosts of heaven" and that יהוה צבאות was originally a divine epithet for El meaning, "he who creates the (heavenly) armies." See Cross, *Canaanite Myth*, 70. However, since ancient Israel conceived the heavenly armies of Yahweh fighting alongside the armies of earthly Israel in their wars, the military aspects of this title has an earthly dimension as well as a heavenly one. See Patrick D. Miller, Jr., *The Divine Warrior in Early Israel* (Cambridge, MA: Harvard University Press, 1973), 151–156.

[23] See Isaiah 6 and 1 Kings 22:19–23 for a portrayal of the divine council with Yahweh as the supreme deity. The hosts of heaven are members of the divine council. As such, they are called "holy ones" in Ps. 89:6–9 and "sons of El" in Ps. 29:1. However, as Mullen observes, the members of the divine council are clearly subservient to Yahweh. See Mullen, *The Assembly of the Gods*, 189–194.

[24] The divine council was both a military assembly and a judicial court. Thus, according to Ps. 82: "God has taken his place in the divine council; in the midst of the gods he holds judgment." See also Job 1–2 and Zech. 3. Mullen comments: "The very *raison d'être* of the council was to pass judgment, in both the heavenly and human spheres." (Ibid., 226).

[25] Miller, *The Divine Warrior*, 68. See also Cross, *Canaanite Myth*, 186–190 and Mullen, *The Assembly of the Gods*, 209–226.

[26] See Mettinger, *In Search of God*, 127–131 and Ollenburger, *Zion the City of the Great King*, 23–52.

27 Ollenburger, *Zion the City of the Great King*, 24. According to Mettinger: "The temple was God's royal site, and the cherubim formed his throne." (Mettinger, *In Search of God*, 133). As Ollenburger observes, because of Yahweh's royal presence in Zion, Zion is thus a symbol of security: "Zion symbolizes security because Yahweh reigns there as the king who conquered the powers of chaos hostile to the cosmis order, and who subdues Israel's potential foes." (Ollenburger, *Zion the City of the Great King*, 71). In other words, Yahweh's royal presence in the temple is intimately related to Yahweh's role as the divine warrior.

28 C. L. Seow, *Myth, Drama, and the Politics of David's Dance* (Atlanta: Scholars Press, 1989), 13.

29 As the literary context of 1 Samuel 4 demonstrates, the Ark of the Covenant not only functioned as the throne of Yahweh in Shiloh/Jerusalem but also functioned as the "holy war palladium." According to Miller: "The holy war palladium, the Ark of the Covenant, was conceived of as the battle station from which Yahweh, the divine warrior, the creator of the divine armies, fought for Israel." (Miller, *The Divine Warrior*, 158).

30 N. L. Tidwell, "*wā'ōmar* (Zech. 3:5) and the Genre of Zechariah's Fourth Vision," *JBL* 94 (1975): 353–355. The other biblical examples of this "council-genre" are: 1 Kings 22:19–22; Isa. 6; Isa. 40; and Job 1–2.

31 See also 1 Kings 22:19; Isa. 6:1–2; Job 1:6; 2:1.

32 The technical language (עֹמֵד לִפְנֵי), the characters, and the action in Zech. 3:1 demonstrate that Zechariah is seeing a vision of the divine council. (Meyers and Meyers, *Haggai*, 182).

33 According to Petersen, the location of the scene in Zech. 1:8 is "a fertile garden near the residence of the deity" rather than the actual dwelling place of Yahweh (Petersen, *Haggai*, 140). Other scholars locate the scenery of 1:8 in "the lowest part of the Kidron valley." See Ralph L. Smith, *Micah-Malachi*, Word Biblical Commentary (Waco: Word Books, 1984), 188 and Baldwin, *Haggai*, 95.

34 LXX reads τῶν ὀρέων = הֶהָרִים ("the mountains"). Since this is obviously an attempt to harmonize the imagery of the first vision with the imagery of the last vision, the MT reading is to be preferred. Within the biblical tradition, the myrtle trees often symbolize peace and fertility (see Isa. 41:19; 55:13). See Chary, *Aggee Zacharie Malachie*, Sources Biblique (Paris: J. Gabalda, 1969), 58 and Petersen, *Haggai*, 140.

35 We can translate the word מְצֻלָה in one of two ways. Like Petersen, I consider this word to be a variant spelling of מְצוּלָה meaning, "depth, deep" and understand it to be a reference to the cosmic deep at the dwelling place of God. See Petersen, *Haggai*, 139 and Chary, *Aggee*, 57. Alternatively, partly on the basis of the LXX

reading τῶν κατασκίων, Carol and Eric Meyers derive the word from the root צלל meaning "to be or grow dark" and translate the word, "the shadows." See Meyers and Meyers, *Haggai*, 110.

36   This reference to the two bronze mountains resembles a Mesopotamian artistic motif that represents Šamaš, the sun-god, rising between two mountains. See Petersen, *Haggai*, 267; Meyers and Meyers, *Haggai*, 319; and Chary, *Aggee*, 105. As Carol and Eric Meyers observe, a mythological meaning is likely because "the cosmic abode of the deities is linked to great mountains." See Meyers and Meyers, *Haggai*, 319.

37   See Chary, *Aggee*, 57–58, 105; Petersen, *Haggai*, 139–140, 267–268.

38   Mullen, *The Assembly of the Gods*, 162.

39   Ibid., 162.

40   See also 1 Kings 22:20–21; Isa. 6:3–8; Isa. 40:1–6; Job 1:7–11; 2:2–5.

41   The Syriac, LXX, Vulgate, and Targum convert the first person verb of MT (וָאֹמַר) in v. 5 to the third person. In other words, the messenger of Yahweh is the speaker of v. 5 rather than the prophet. The third person reading would be more consistent with the preceding dialogue, which makes the reading suspicious. Moreover, as Tidwell observes, the prophet interrupts the proceedings of the divine council in two other council-scenes (Isa. 6:8 and 40:6; Tidwell, "*wā'ōmar*," 349). Therefore, I have retained the MT reading.

42   Tidwell, "*wā'ōmar*," 354. See also 1 Kings 22:22; Isa. 6:9–13; Isa. 40:9–11; Job 1:12; 2:6. After examining the different traditions of the divine council in the ancient Near East (Babylonian, Ugaritic, Israelite), Mullen claims: "In all our traditions of the divine council, its major function is to decree the fate or destiny of a group or an individual. Hebrew tradition reveals this concept most clearly in the pronouncements of the courier of the assembly—the prophet." (Mullen, *The Assembly of the Gods*, 228).

43   Petersen, *Haggai*, 203. The idiom is also used in a prophetic context. See 2 Kings 17:13; Jer. 11:7; Neh. 9:30.

44   Like many other commentators, I consider the apodosis of v. 7 to begin in the last clause of the sentence: "If you will walk in my ways and keep my requirements as well as ruling my house and overseeing my courts, then I will give you access among those who are standing here." As Petersen observes, the particle וְגַם, which introduces the middle two clauses, normally functions as an adverb meaning "in addition, moreover." It does not usually function as the beginning of an apodosis. See Petersen, *Haggai*, 203 and Beuken, *Haggai-Sacharja 1–8*, 190–193.

45   As Petersen observes: "The command to proclaim is, therefore, a command to engage in prophetic activity…. The command introduces a particular message—two oracles that the prophet, as prophet, is supposed to proclaim." See Petersen, *Haggai*, 152.

46   As Carol and Eric Meyers observe, the use of the Hiphil form of the verb זעק followed by an accusative is unusual. They conclude: "The closest biblical analogy for the Hiphil of zᶜq followed by an accusative comes in the vocabulary of mustering, in which a military leader calls forth or summons members of certain tribes or units for military duty (e.g., Judg. 4:10, 13). The implication of such usage for Zechariah is that the prophet is to be fully alert and ready to hear the statement that follows, which appears not only as a climax to this vision but also, since this is the last, as a conclusion to the visionary sequence in its entirety." (Meyers and Meyers, *Haggai*, 328).

47   Commentators disagree about the meaning of this verse. Does it refer to Yahweh's wrath against Babylon (Petersen, *Haggai*, 271) or the salvation of the exiles in Babylon (Chary, *Aggee*, 107) or "God's active presence in world events" (Meyers and Meyers, *Haggai*, 330)? Like Susan Niditch, I consider this verse to be a declaration of Yahweh's universal rule. See Susan Niditch, *The Symbolic Vision in Biblical Tradition* (Chico: Scholars Press, 1983), 159.

48   Since Zech. 4:9 has already stated that Zerubbabel will rebuild the temple, the individual called Branch in Zech. 6:12–13 must be Zerubbabel. As v. 13 implies, the title Branch is a messianic appellation (see Jer. 23:5). In other words, Zech. 6:9–15 ascribes messianic status to Zerubbabel. (see Petersen, *Haggai*, 276). Carol and Eric Meyers argue, however, that Zech. 6:12 is referring to a future Davidic ruler who, unlike Zerubbabel, will not be subservient to the Persians. (Meyers and Meyers, *Haggai*, 356–357).

49   Petersen observes: "the phrase 'the former prophets' occurs only in Zechariah 1–8, and it clearly implies prophetic status for Zechariah. Zechariah stands in a line of prophetic succession." (Petersen, *Haggai*, 132).

50   The use of different prepositions reflects different emphases. On the one hand, according to Zech. 1:3, Zechariah urged his audience to "return to" Yahweh (שׁוּב + אֶל). This could mean either a geographic return, of the exiles, to Jerusalem or a spiritual renewal of the covenant relationship. On the other hand, according to Zech. 1:4, the "former prophets" urged their audience to "return from" (שׁוּב + מִן) or to "repent" of their wickedness. See Petitjean, *Les Oracles*, 30–33.

51   Petersen labels this type of oracle in which we find a series of moral stipulations "an oracle of admonition conditioned by wisdom perspectives." (Petersen, *Haggai*, 289). See also Beuken, *Haggai-Sacharja 1–8*, 123–124.

[52]   Meyers and Meyers, *Haggai*, 7. For a more detailed examination of this prophetic paradigm, see Mullen, *The Assembly of the Gods*, 209–226.

[53]   Paul D. Hanson, "In Defiance of Death: Zechariah's Symbolic Universe," in *Love and Death in the Ancient Near East*, ed., J. H. Marks and R. M. Good (Guilford: Four Quarters Publishing Company, 1987), 176f. See also B. Halpern, "The Ritual Background of Zechariah's Temple Song," *CBQ* 40 (1978): 167–190; and Meyers and Meyers, *Haggai*, liii–lx.

[54]   Hanson, "In Defiance of Death," 176.

[55]   Baldwin, *Haggai*, 85.

[56]   Meyers and Meyers, *Haggai*, lvi.

[57]   The vision of Zech. 4 depicts Yahweh's presence as a temple lampstand and portrays Joshua and Zerubbabel as the two olive trees that stand beside the lampstand. (Petersen, *Haggai*, 217ff; Meyers and Meyers, *Haggai*, 229ff). In other words, the symbolism of the vision, as well as the oracular insertion (vv. 6b–10a), portrays the leadership roles of Joshua and Zerubbabel in terms of their relation to the temple.

[58]   Hanson, "In Defiance of Death," 176f.

[59]   Stephen L. Cook, *Prophecy and Apocalypticism* (Minneapolis: Fortress Press, 1995), 140. Cook provides the following example: "(A)lthough the language of Deuteronomy was characteristic of one specific minority group before the exile, Deuteronomistic idioms and themes were taken up by many groups in the Persian period."

[60]   For example, Cook writes: "Zechariah 1–8 and Zechariah 9–14 draw on written collections of authoritative prophetic material. It is hard to imagine that the language and motifs in these collections would not have influenced the modes of expression of the Zechariah group." (Ibid., 141).

[61]   See Walther Zimmerli, *Ezekiel*, volume 1, Hermeneia (Philadelphia: Fortress Press, 1979), 112f.

[62]   For discussions on the Deuteronomic redaction of Jeremiah, see Joseph Blenkinsopp, *A History of Prophecy in Israel* (Philadelphia: Westminster Press, 1983), 153–169; and Robert P. Carroll, *From Chaos to Covenant* (London: SCM Press, 1981).

[63]   While the book of Ezekiel displays a remarkable structural and thematic unity, most critical scholars would agree with Blenkinsopp's summary statement about the tradition history of the book: "While not a late Second Temple pseudepigraphal work, as suggested by C. C. Torrey and one or two others, in its final form the book is the product of a school which owed allegiance to Ezekiel, which was closely

associated with the cult, and which inherited the ancient traditions of the priesthood as did Ezekiel himself." (Blenkinsopp, *A History of Prophecy in Israel*, 194f).

[64]   Bernhard W. Anderson, *Understanding the Old Testament*, 4th ed. (Englewood Cliffs, NJ: Prentice-Hall, 1986), 373–388. The question of the social identity of the Deuteronomic movement is the subject of much scholarly debate. According to von Rad, northern Israelite rural levitical priests were the carriers of the Deuteronomic tradition. See G. von Rad, *Deuteronomy* (Philadelphia: Westminster Press, 1966). According to Clements, these northern levitical priests composed Deuteronomy in order to reform and to reinterpret the Jerusalem cult tradition. See R. E. Clements, "Deuteronomy and the Jerusalem Cult Tradition," *VT* 15 (1965): 300–12. Nicholson argues that northern Israelite prophetic circles were the carriers of the Deuteronomic tradition. See E. Nicholson, *Deuteronomy and Tradition* (Oxford: Basil Blackwell, 1967). Finally, Weinfeld argues that Jerusalem court scribes were responsible for composing and editing the Deuteronomic literature. See M. Weinfeld, *Deuteronomy and the Deuteronomic School* (Oxford: Clarenden Press, 1972). I am persuaded by Dutcher-Walls' recent argument that the Deuteronomic group probably was a mixed elite grouping of priests, prophets, scribes, court officials, and landed gentry. These different factions joined together in order to increase their own mutual influence and power. See P. Dutcher-Walls, "The Social Location of the Deuteronomists: A Sociological Study of Factional Politics in Late Pre-Exilic Judah," *JSOT* 52 (1991): 77–94.

[65]   Two recent books have argued, persuasively, that the Deuteronomic group and the Ezekiel group continued to edit and revise their respective prophetic texts into the post-exilic period. On the basis of text-critical evidence and thematic evidence, Raymond Person argues for a post-exilic setting for some redactional additions to DtrH and Jeremiah. Similarly, Steven Tuell argues for a post-exilic date for the final form of Ezekiel 40–48. See Raymond F. Person, *Second Zechariah and the Deuteronomic School*, JSOT Supplement Series 167 (Sheffield: JSOT Press, 1993); and Steven Shawn Tuell, *The Law of the Temple in Ezekiel 40-48*, Harvard Semitic Monographs 49 (Atlanta: Scholas Press, 1992).

[66]   Zech. 1:1 offers a slightly different genealogy for Zechariah than Ezra 5:1 and 6:14. According to Zech. 1:1, Zechariah was the son of Berechiah the son of Iddo. According to Ezra, Zechariah was the son of Iddo.

[67]   Tollington, *Tradition and Innovation*, 122–124.

[68]   Petersen, *Haggai*, 132–133).

[69]   According to Stephen Cook, the references to the "former prophets" provide evidence that Zechariah had the official backing of the temple elite. See Cook, *Prophecy and Apocalypticism*, 139. f.n. 60.

70   According to Raymond Person, the primary responsibility of the Deuteronomic scribal school, in the post-exilic period, was to preserve religious texts associated with the temple and to reinterpret earlier traditions in the light of new historical and theological circumstances. (Person, *Second Zechariah*, 162).

71   Baruch Halpern, "The Ritual Background of Zechariah's Temple Song," *CBQ* 40 (1978): 167–190.

72   Meyers and Meyers, *Haggai*, lviii. Carol and Eric Meyers continue: "Throughout the ancient Near East, and in Israel, the construction or restoration of temples was consequent upon a revelation to the king in which the deity gave instructions or approval for the ruler's plan to build or restore a temple, the earthly dwelling for that god. God's revelation to Moses (Exod. 25:8–9) with respect to the tabernacle, and Solomon's dream at Gibeon (1 Kgs 3:5–14) participate in that typology.... Perhaps Zechariah's visions constitute the functional equivalent of the divine revelation to the king." (Ibid.)

73   Halpern, "The Ritual Background," 177–178; Petersen, *Haggai*, 165–166.

74   Meyers and Meyers, *Haggai*, 229–235.

75   Cook, *Prophecy and Apocalypticism*, 142–143.

76   Person, *Second Zechariah*, 158–161.

77   Ibid., 160.

78   Ibid.

79   There are three issues of debate concerning the official titles, "governor of Judah" and "high priest." First, what was the administrative relation between Judah and the larger satrapy of Beyond the River (Eber Nahara)? In other words, was Judah an autonomous province or was it a "sub-province" of Eber Nahara? Second, what were the official responsibilities of the "governor"? Third, when was the title, "high priest," first used as an official designation for the senior priest of the temple? See Petersen, *Haggai*, 23–27; Meyers and Meyers, *Haggai*, 13–17; Tollington, *Tradition and Innovation*, 126–134; Daniel L. Smith, *The Religion of the Landless* (Bloomington, IN: Meyer-Stone Books, 1989), 108–112.

80   Morson and Emerson, *Mikhail Bakhtin*, 89.

81   Meyers and Meyers, *Haggai*, xlv.

82   J. Maxwell Miller & John H. Hayes, *A History of Ancient Israel and Judah* (Philadelphia: Westminister Press, 1986), 459.

83   Ackroyd, *Exile and Restoration* (London: SCM, 1968), 153–154.

84 Meyers and Meyers, *Haggai*, xlvii. See also Tollington, *Tradition and Innovation*, 47.

85 Tollington, *Tradition and Innovation*, 72; Petitjean, *Les Oracles*, 127.

86 Consequently, I disagree with those scholars who maintain that the prophets Haggai and Zechariah, as well as the book(s) that bear their names, provided ideological justification for the existing socio-political order. For example, according to Hanson, Haggai and Zechariah "dedicated themselves to continuity, to preservation of the pre-exilic structures, to maintenance of the status quo." See Paul D. Hanson, *The Dawn of Apocalyptic*, 2d ed. (Philadelphia: Fortress Press, 1989), 247. Similarly, according to Carol and Eric Meyers, the composite work of Haggai-Zechariah 1–8 stood as "the repository of words which expressed the ideological basis for the Second Commonwealth." See Meyers and Meyers, *Haggai*, xliii.

87 Paul Ricoeur, *Lectures on Ideology and Utopia*, ed., George H. Taylor (New York: Columbia University Press, 1986); "Ideology and Utopia," in *From Text to Action: Essays in Hermeneutics, II*, translated by Kathleen Blamey and John B. Thompson (Evanston, Illinois: Northwestern University Press, 1991), 308–324.

88 Ricoeur, "Ideology and Utopia," 320.

89 Ibid.

90 Ibid., 321.

91 As Ricoeur observes, this tendency may explain why utopian discourse is associated with a particular literary genre: "writing becomes a substitute for acting." (Ibid., 322).

92 Petersen comments on the significance of the date in Zech. 1:7, which also uses the Babylonian name for the month, as follows: "Yahweh's activity must be dated to a Persian king and to the Babylonian calendar which the Persians also used. This introductory formula is therefore of great significance. It does more than simply provide a chronological setting in which Yahweh and Israel find themselves. It emphasizes the "foreign" context in which Yahweh and Israel find themselves—one controlled by a foreign ruler and by foreign vocabulary." (Petersen, *Haggai*, 138). Similarly, Carol and Eric Meyers argue that the dating in Haggai-Zechariah 1–8 "reflects an acceptance, in our opinion, of the legitimacy of the Persian rule over Yehud." (Meyers and Meyers, *Haggai*, 5–6).

93 In their discussion on the use of the divine title, Yahweh Sebaoth, in Haggai-Zechariah 1–8, Carol and Eric Meyers claim: Yahweh Sebaoth "reestablishes the preexilic conception of divine presence and expresses the ultimate authority of Yahweh, even over the Persian emperor or any other human king." (Meyers and Meyers, *Haggai*, 19).

CONCLUSION

This study offers a Bakhtinian analysis of Haggai-Zechariah 1–8. The goal of a Bakhtinian literary analysis is to understand the text as a communication event by analyzing its particular use of a genre. In this study, we analyzed the use of the chronistic genre in Haggai-Zechariah 1–8. The use of a chronistic form in the prophetic books of Haggai and Zechariah 1–8 raises three questions that remain the subject of debate. First, what is the relation between Haggai and Zechariah 1–8? Second, what is the relation between the chronistic form and the prophetic content? Third, what is the relation between the chronistic form and the socio-historical context? On the basis of a Bakhtinian analysis, this study proposes answers to these three questions. In this concluding chapter, we will summarize the results of this Bakhtinian analysis and propose some avenues for future research.

In chapter one, we summarized the history of research on the three critical questions listed above and examined the usefulness of Bakhtinian literary theory to answer these questions. Although previous scholars have examined the chronistic form of Haggai and Zechariah 1–8, no other has compared these texts with specific examples of the chronistic genre. In chapter one, we suggest that such a comparison will enable us to resolve the problem of the chronistic form of Haggai and Zechariah 1–8. The "Bakhtin circle" of Mikhail Bakhtin, Pavel Medvedev, and Valentin Voloshinov has provided us with a methodology for making this comparison. A Bakhtinian analysis seeks to understand a literary text by examining its distinctive use of a genre. Such an analysis is obviously applicable in the case of Haggai and Zechariah 1–8.

In chapter two, we argued that Haggai-Zechariah 1–8 is a unified literary utterance. Haggai and Zechariah 1–8 were not separate books, composed by different authors but were instead a single text, composed by the same author. We arrived at this conclusion by examining the structural, thematic and stylistic connections between Haggai and Zechariah 1–8. First, both texts have a chronological structure. A closer examination reveals formal and thematic connections. The overlapping dates reinforce a thematic connection: both prophets were present at the founding of the temple. In addition, the combined use of dates, in Haggai and Zechariah 1–8, creates a symbolically significant total of seven sections. Second, both texts share a common interest in the rebuilding of the temple. In both texts, the rebuilding of the temple marks the beginning of a new era of blessing for the remnant. In addition, both Haggai and Zechariah 1–8 understand the temple to be the center of Yahweh's universal rule as well as the basis for Joshua's and Zerubbabel's political authority. Third, both texts exhibit a similar prophetic style. They consistently use the same two prophetic formulas, the word event formula and the message formula.

In chapter three, we analyzed the genre of the Babylonian chronicles. We began with an analysis of the literary chronotope. All the Babylonian chronicles share a similar perspective on time and space. These chronicles describe the actions of the king from the temporal perspective of the Babylonian royal succession and the spatial perspective of the royal city of Babylon. Moreover, all the chronicles portray an image of the ideal king. The ideal king protects and enriches the city of Babylon.

The literary chronotope of the Babylonian chronicles is organically related to the socio-historical context in which they were composed. The literary chronotope was generated in the context of a socio-historical discourse between the temple of Esagil and the palace of the Babylonian kings. The temple scribes of Esagil composed the chronicles as part of an ongoing socio-political discourse with the Babylonian kings. The scribes wrote the chronicles during a critical period when the political and economic prerogatives of Esagil had recently been eroded by the military actions of certain individual kings. Sennacherib's destruction of Babylon in 689 BCE was the archetypical situation that provoked this discourse between Esagil and the palace.

Reflecting the worldview of the temple scribes in this historical setting, the literary chronotope of the Babylonian chronicles performed an ideological function. The chronistic chronotope is a literary attempt to "preserve" the social order of Esagil in a period of socio-psychological crisis. By composing texts that "chronicle" the reigns of "ideal" and "less-than-ideal" kings, the temple scribes sought to persuade the kings to patronize the cult of Esagil and to maintain the economic health and commerce of the city of Babylon.

In chapter four, we examined the evidence in 1 and 2 Kings to determine whether the chronistic genre also existed in ancient Israel. On the basis of the textual evidence, we determined that the two sources, known as "the book of the annual actions of the kings of Israel" and "the book of the annual actions of the kings of Judah," were the Israelite equivalents of the Babylonian chronicles. These two sources apparently exhibited a similar chronological structure as well as similar themes and language as the Babylonian chronicles.

In chapter five, we examined the use of the chronistic genre in Haggai-Zechariah 1–8. In Haggai-Zechariah 1–8, the editor uses a chronistic form to document the prophetic word of Yahweh. By so doing, the editor transforms the chronotopic worldview of the chronicles. According to the chronicles, the king, by his actions, protected and enriched the temple and city. The editor of Haggai-Zechariah 1–8 transforms that worldview by portraying Yahweh as king. According to this prophetic chronicle, the future prosperity of Jerusalem is not dependent on the military actions of King Darius but is rather dependent upon the reader's obedience to the royal decree of Yahweh Sebaoth, as proclaimed by the prophets of Yahweh.

On the basis of this literary analysis, we reconstructed the socio-historical discourse that underlies the chronotope of Haggai-Zechariah 1–8. We argued that a temple scribe edited Haggai-Zechariah 1–8 in anticipation of the rededication ceremony for the Jerusalem temple in 516/515 BCE. In this literary utterance, the editor addresses Joshua and Zerubbabel, the two leaders of the Judean community. By composing a prophetic chronicle, the editor not only reminds Joshua and Zerubbabel of the prophetic role in facilitating the completion of the temple but also challenges them to obey the prophetic word, as it is contained in the written text of Haggai-Zechariah 1–8.

Finally, we argued that the chronotope of Haggai-Zechariah 1–8, in this particular socio-historical context, performs a utopian socio-political function. It subverts the historical reality of Persian imperial rule by depicting the universal and eternal rule of Yahweh. Earthly power stems from King Yahweh and is dependent upon human obedience to the prophetic word.

Let me now propose two avenues for future research. In this study, we have removed the literary utterance of Haggai-Zechariah 1–8 from its canonical context. Yet, the image of Yahweh as king, which is so prominent in Haggai-Zechariah 1–8, can also be found in Zechariah 9–14. This raises the possibility that the image of God in Zechariah 9–14 is a literary and theological "response" to Haggai-Zechariah 1–8. A Bakhtinian analysis of Zechariah 9–14 may provide insights about not only the literary relation between Haggai-Zechariah 1–8 and Zechariah 9–14 but also the socio-historical discourse that underlies Zechariah 9–14.

Another avenue for future research concerns the other examples of prophetic chronicles. Within the Old Testament, the Deuteronomistic History, Jeremiah, and Ezekiel all use a chronistic form to shape their prophetic content. Just as this Bakhtinian analysis of Haggai-Zechariah 1–8 has enabled us to come to a better understanding of this text as a communication event, so such an analysis might provide similar results for these other prophetic chronicles. From the preceding analysis of Haggai-Zechariah 1–8, we can surmise that the chronistic genre was the most obvious genre for temple scribes to use when dealing with the socio-psychological crisis that resulted from the destruction of the temple. Consequently, further research on the Babylonian chronicles and their similarities and differences with biblical chronicles may provide fresh insights into the socio-historical contexts and socio-political functions of the Deuteronomistic History, Jeremiah, and Ezekiel.

In conclusion, this study not only demonstrates the benefits of a Bakhtinian analysis but also reveals new insights about the generic form, the theological purpose, and the socio-historical setting of Haggai-Zechariah 1–8. In contrast to previous scholars, I have proposed that Haggai-Zechariah 1–8 performed a radical and subversive function in its original socio-historical context. By disclosing a utopian vision of the future, in which Yahweh rules as king, Haggai-Zechariah 1–8 also challenges us to re-examine our loyalties and allegiances.

BIBLIOGRAPHY

Achtemeier, Elizabeth Rice. *Nahum-Malachi.* Interpretation. Atlanta: John Knox Press, 1986.

Ackroyd, Peter R. "Studies in the Book of Haggai." *JJS* 2 (1951): 163–176.

————. "The Book of Haggai and Zechariah I–VIII." *JJS* 3 (1952): 1–13.

————. *Exile and Restoration.* London: SCM Press, 1968.

Amsler, Samuel. "Zacharie et l'Origine de l'Apocalyptique." *VTSup* 22 (1971): 227–231.

Amsler, Samuel, Andre Lacocque, and Rene Vuilleumer. *Aggee, Zacharie, Malachie.* Commentaire de l'Ancien Testament, XIc. Paris: Delachaux and Niestle, 1981.

Bakhtin, M. M. and P. N. Medvedev. *The Formal Method in Literary Scholarship: A Critical Introduction to Sociological Poetics.* Translated by Albert J. Wehrle. Cambridge, Mass.: Harvard University Press, 1985.

Bakhtin, M. M. *The Dialogic Imagination.* Translated by Caryl Emerson and Michael Holquist. Austin: University of Texas Press, 1982.

――――. *Speech Genres and Other Late Essays.* Translated by Vern W. McGee. Austin: University of Texas Press, 1986.

――――. *The Bakhtin Reader: Selected Writings of Bakhtin, Medvedev, Voloshinov.* Edited by Pam Morris. London: Edward Arnold, 1994.

Baldwin, Joyce G. *Haggai, Zechariah, Malachi.* Tyndale Old Testament Commentaries, 24. Downers Grove: InterVarsity Press, 1972.

Barton, John. *Reading the Old Testament:Method in Biblical Study.* Philadelphia: Westminster Press, 1984.

Becker, J. *Messianic Expectation in the Old Testament.* Translated by D. E. Green. Philadelphia: Fortress Press, 1980.

Ben Zvi, Ehud. "Prophets and Prophecy in the Compositional and Redactional Notes in I–II Kings." *ZAW* 105 (1994): 331–351.

Berquist, Jon L. *Judaism in Persia's Shadow: A Social and Historical Approach.* Minneapolis: Fortress Press, 1995.

Beuken, W. A. M. *Haggai-Sacharja 1–8.* Assen: Van Gorcum and Comp., 1967.

Beyse, K-M. *Serubbabel und die Königsertwartungen der Propheten Haggai und Sacharja.* Stuttgart: Calwer Verlag, 1972.

Bin-Nun, Shoshana R. "Formulas from Royal Records of Israel and of Judah." *VT* 18 (1968): 414–432.

Black, J. A. "The New Year Ceremonies in Ancient Babylonia: 'Taking Bel by the Hand' and a Cultic Picnic." *Religion* 11 (1981): 39–59.

Blenkinsopp, Joseph. *Prophecy and Canon: A Contribution to the Study of Jewish Origins.* Notre Dame: University of Notre Dame Press, 1977.

————. *A History of Prophecy in Israel.* Philadelphia: Westminster Press, 1983.

Bright, John. *A History of Israel.* London: SCM Press, 1960.

Brueggemann, Walter. "Trajectories in Old Testament Literature and the Sociology of Ancient Israel." *JBL* 98 (1979): 161–185.

————. *Theology of the Old Testament: Testimony, Dispute, Advocacy.* Minneapolis: Fortress Press, 1997.

Butterworth, Mike. *Structure and the Book of Zechariah.* JSOT Supplement Series, 130. Sheffield: JSOT Press, 1992.

Carroll, Robert P. *When Prophecy Failed.* London: SCM Press, 1979.

————. "Twilight of Prophecy or Dawn of Apocalyptic." *JSOT* 14 (1979): 3–35.

————. *From Chaos to Covenant: Uses of Prophecy in the Book of Jeremiah.* London: SCM Press, 1981.

————. "The Myth of the Empty Land." *Semeia* 59 (1992): 79–93.

————. "So what do we know about the Temple? The Temple in the Prophets." In *Second Temple Studies: 2. Temple Community in the Persian Period*, ed. Tamara C. Eskenazi and Kent H. Richards, 34–51. JSOT Supplement Series, 175. Sheffield: JSOT Press, 1994.

Carter, Charles E. "The Province of Yehud in the Post-Exilic Period: Soundings in Site Distribution and Demography." In *Second Temple Studies: 2. Temple Community in the Persian Period*, ed. Tamara C. Eskenazi and Kent H. Richards, 106–145. JSOT Supplement Series, 175. Sheffield: JSOT Press, 1994.

Chary, Theophane. *Aggee Zacharie Malachie.* Sources Bibliques. Paris: J. Gabalda, 1969.

Childs, Brevard S. *Introduction to the Old Testament as Literature.* Philadelphia: Fortress Press, 1979.

Clark, Katerina and Michael Holquist. *Mikhail Bakhtin.* Cambridge, Mass.: Harvard University Press, 1984.

Clines, David J. A. "Haggai's Temple. Constructed, Deconstructed and Reconstructed." In *Second Temple Studies: 2. Temple Community in the Persian Period,* ed. Tamara C. Eskenazi and Kent H. Richards, 60–87. JSOT Supplement Series, 175. Sheffield: JSOT Press, 1994.

Cogan, Mordechai. "The Chronicler's Use of Chronology as Illuminated by Neo-Assyrian Royal Inscriptions." In *Empirical Models for Biblical Criticism,* ed. Jeffrey H. Tigay, 197–209. Philadelphia: University of Pennsylvania Press, 1985.

Cogan, Morton. *Imperialism and Religion: Assyria, Judah and Israel in the Eighth and Seventh Centuries.* SBL Monograph Series, 19. Missoula: Scholars Press, 1974.

Coggins, R. J. *Haggai, Zechariah, Malachi.* Old Testament Guides. Sheffield: JSOT Press, 1987.

Collins, Terrence. *The Mantle of Elijah: The Redaction Criticism of the Prophetical Books.* The Biblical Seminar, vol. 20. Sheffield: JSOT Press, 1993.

Cook, Stephen L. *Prophecy and Apocalypticism: The Postexilic Setting.* Minneapolis: Fortress Press, 1995.

Cross, Frank M. *Canaanite Myth and Hebrew Epic.* Cambridge, Mass.: Harvard University Press, 1973.

————. "A Reconstruction of the Judean Restoration." *JBL* 94 (1975): 4–18.

Davies, Philip R. "The Society of Biblical Israel." In *Second Temple Studies: 2. Temple Community in the Persian Period*, ed. Tamara C. Eskenazi and Kent H. Richards, 22–33. JSOT Supplement Series, 175. Sheffield: JSOT Press, 1994.

Davies, W. D., and L. Finkelstein. *The Cambridge History of Judaism: vol. 1. Introduction. The Persian Period.* New York: Cambridge University Press, 1984.

Doty, William G. "The Concept of Genre in Literary Analysis." *Proceedings of the SBL* 1972, volume 2, 413–448.

Dumbrell, W. J. "Kingship and Temple in the Post-exilic Period." *Reformed Theological Review* 37 (1978): 33–42.

Eagleton, Terry. *Marxism and Literary Criticism.* Los Angeles: University of California Press, 1976.

———. *Ideology: An Introduction.* New York: Verso, 1991.

———, ed. *Ideology.* London: Longman, 1994.

Eisenstadt, S. N. "Observations and Queries about Sociological Aspects of Imperialism in the Ancient World." In *Power and Propaganda: A Symposium on Ancient Empires*, ed. Mogens Trolle Larsen, 21–33. Copenhagen: Akademisk Forlage, 1979.

Ellis, R. S. *Foundation Deposits in Ancient Mesopotamia.* New Haven: Yale University Press, 1968.

Frankfort, H. *Kingship and the Gods.* Chicago: University of Chicago Press, 1948.

Gardiner, Michael. *The Dialogics of Critique: M. M. Bakhtin and the Theory of Ideology.* London: Routledge, 1992.

Garelli, Paul. "L'Etat et la Legitimie Royale sous L'Empire Assyrien." In *Power and Propaganda: A Symposium on Ancient Empires*, ed.

Mogens Trolle Larsen, 319–329. Copenhagen: Akademisk Forlage, 1979.

Gelston, A. "The Foundations of the Second Temple." *VT* 16 (1966): 232–235.

Good, Robert M. "Zechariah's Second Night Vision (Zech. 2:1–4)." *Biblica* 63 (1982): 56–59.

Gottwald, Norman K. "Social Class and Ideology in Isaiah 40–55: An Eagletonian Reading." *Semeia* 59 (1992): 43–57.

Gray, John. *1 and 2 Kings*. The Old Testament Library. London: SCM Press, 1964.

Grayson, A. Kirk. *Assyrian and Babylonian Chronicles*. Texts from Cuneiform Sources. Locust Valley, N.Y.: J. J. Augustin, 1975.

————. "Histories and Historians of the Ancient Near East: Assyria and Babylonia." *Orientalia* 49 (1980): 140–194.

Green, Barbara. *Mikhail Bakhtin and Biblical Scholarship: An Introduction*. The Society of Biblical Literature Semeia Studies 38. Atlanta: Society of Biblical Literature, 2000.

Halpern, Bruce. "The Ritual Background of Zechariah's Temple Song." *CBQ* 40 (1978): 167–190.

Hals, Ronald M. *Ezekiel*. The Forms of the Old Testament Literature, vol. XIX. Grand Rapids: William B. Eerdmans Publishing Company, 1989.

Hanson, Paul D. *The Dawn of Apocalyptic*. 2d ed. Philadelphia: Fortress Press, 1989.

————. "In Defiance of Death: Zechariah's Symbolic Universe." In *Love and Death in the Ancient Near East*, ed. J. H. Marks, and R. M. Good, 173–179. Guilford: Four Quarters Publishing Company, 1987.

Harrelson, Walter. "The Trial of the High Priest Joshua: Zechariah 3." *Eretz Israel* 16 (1982): 116–124.

Haupt, Paul. "The Visions of Zechariah." *JBL* 32 (1913): 107–122.

Herion, Gary A. "The Role of Historical Narrative in Biblical Thought: The Tendencies Underlying Old Testament Historiography." *JSOT* 21 (1981): 25–57.

Herrmann, Siegfried. *A History of Israel in Old Testament Times.* London: SCM Press, 1975.

Hoffner, Harry A. "Propaganda and Political Justification in Hittite Historiography." In *Unity and Diversity: Essays in the History, Literature, and Religion of the Ancient Near East*, ed. Hans Goedicke and J. J. M. Roberts, 49–62. Baltimore: The Johns Hopkins University Press, 1975.

Holquist, Michael. *Dialogism: Bakhtin and his World.* London: Routledge, 1990.

Horst, Friedrich. "Die Visionsschilderungen der alttestamentlichen Propheten." *Ev.T* 20 (1960): 193–205.

Jacobsen, Thorkild. "Religious Drama in Ancient Mesopotamia." In *Unity and Diversity: Essays on the History, Literature, and Religion of the Ancient Near East*, ed. Hans Goedicke and J. J. M. Roberts, 65–97. Baltimore: The Johns Hopkins University Press, 1975.

————. *The Treasures of Darkness.* New Haven: Yale University Press, 1977.

Jameson, Fredric. *The Political Unconscious: Narrative as a Socially Symbolic Act.* Ithaca, N.Y.: Cornell University Press, 1981.

Jepsen, A. *Die Quellen des Königsbuches.* Halle: Max Niemeyer, 1956.

Jeremias, C. *Die Nachtgesichte des Sacharja.* Göttingen: Vandenhoeck & Ruprecht, 1977.

Jones, G. H. *1 and 2 Kings.* Volume 1. The New Century Bible Commentary. Grand Rapids: William B. Eerdmanns, 1984.

Kline, Meredith G. "The Structure of the Book of Zechariah." *JETS* 34 (1991): 179–193.

Knierim, Rolf. "Criticism of Literary Features, Form, Tradition, and Redaction." In *The Hebrew Bible and its Modern Interpreters*, ed. Douglas A. Knight and Gene M. Tucker, 123–165. Chico: Scholars Press, 1985.

Kuhrt, A. "The Cyrus Cylinder and Achaemenid Imperial Policy." *JSOT* 25 (1983): 83–97.

Laato, Antti. *The Servant of Yahweh and Cyrus: A Reinterpretation of the Exilic Messianic Programme in Isaiah 40–55.* Stockholm: Almqvist and Wiksell International, 1992.

———. *Josiah and David Redivivus: The Historical Josiah and the Messianic Expectations of Exilic and Postexilic Times.* Stockholm: Almqvist and Wiksell International, 1992.

———. "Zachariah 4,6b–10a and the Akkadian Royal Building Inscriptions." *ZAW* 106 (1994): 53–69.

Langdon, Stephen. *Die Neubabylonischen Königsinschriften.* Leipzig: J. C. Hinrich, 1912.

Le Bas, Edwin E. "Zechariah's Enigmatical Contribution to the Corner-stone." *PEQ* (1950): 102–122.

———. "Zechariah's Climax to the Career of the Corner-stone." *PEQ* (1951): 139–155.

Levine, Louis D. "Preliminary Remarks on the Historical Inscriptions of Sennacherib." In *History, Historiography, and Interpretation:*

Studies in Biblical and Cuneiform Literature, ed. H. Tadmor and M. Weinfeld, 58–75. Jerusalem: The Magnes Press, 1984.

Lindblom, J. *Prophecy in Ancient Israel*. Philadelphia: Fortress Press, 1962.

Lipinski, E. "Recherches sur le Livre de Zacharie." *VT* 20 (1970): 25–55.

Liverani, Mario. "The Ideology of the Assyrian Empire." In *Power and Propaganda: A Symposium on Ancient Empires*, ed. Mogens Trolle Larsen, 297–317. Copenhagen: Akademisk Forlage, 1979.

Long, Burke O. "Reports of Visions among the Prophets." *JBL* 95 (1976): 353–365.

————. *1 Kings with an Introduction to Historical Literature*. The Forms of the Old Testament Literature, IX. Grand Rapids: William B. Eerdmans Publishing Company, 1984.

Luckenbill, D. D. *Ancient Records of Assyria and Babylonia*. Volume 2. Chicago: University of Chicago Press, 1927.

Lundquist, John M. "What is a Temple? A Preliminary Typology." In *The Quest for the Kingdom of God*, ed. H. B. Huffmon, F. A. Spina, and A. R. W. Green, 205–219. Winona Lake: Eisenbrauns, 1983.

————. "Temple, Covenant, and Law in the Ancient Near East and in the Old Testament." In *Israel's Apostasy and Restoration*, ed. Avraham Gileadi, 293–305. Grand Rapids: Baker Book House, 1988.

McCready, Wayne O. "The 'Day of Small Things' vs. the Latter Days: Historical Fulfillment or Eschatological Hope?" In *Israel's Apostasy and Restoration*, ed. Avraham Gileadi, 223–236. Grand Rapids: Baker Book House, 1988.

McHardy, W. D. "The Horses in Zechariah."   In *In Memoriam Paul Kahle*, ed. M. Black and G. Fohrer, 174–179. *BZAW* 103. Berlin: Verlag Alfred Topelmann, 1968.

Maisler, B. "Ancient Israelite Historiography." *IEJ* 2 (1952): 82–88.

Marinkovic, Peter. "What does Zechariah 1–8 tell us about the Second Temple?"   In *Second Temple Studies: 2. Temple Community in the Persian Period*, ed. Tamara C. Eskenazi and Kent H. Richards, 88–103. JSOT Supplement Series, 175. Sheffield: JSOT Press, 1994.

Marsh, W. Eugene.   "Redaction Criticism and the Formation of Prophetic Books." *SBL Seminar Papers* 12 (1977): 87–101.

Marti, K. *Das Dodekapropheton erklärt.* Tübingen: Mohr, 1904.

Mason, Rex A. "The Purpose of the 'Editorial Framework' of the Book of Haggai." *VT* 27 (1977): 413–421.

———.   *The Books of Haggai, Zechariah, and Malachi.*   The Cambridge Bible Commentary.   New York: Cambridge University Press, 1977.

———.   "The Prophets of the Restoration."   In *Israel's Prophetic Tradition*, ed. R. Coggins, A Phillips, and M. Knibb, 137–154. New York: Cambridge University Press, 1982.

———.   *Preaching the Tradition: Homily and Hermeneutics after the Exile.* New York: Cambridge University Press, 1990.

Mastin, B. A. "A Note on Zechariah 6:13." *VT* 26 (1976): 113–116.

May, Herbert Gordon.   "A Key to the Interpretation of Zechariah's Visions." *JBL* 57 (1938): 173–184.

Mettinger, T. N. D. *The Dethronement of Sabaoth.* Translated by F. H. Cryer. ConBOT 18. Lund: Gleerup, 1982.

Meyers, Carol L. and Eric M. Meyers. *Haggai, Zechariah 1–8.* The Anchor Bible. New York: Doubleday and Company, 1987.

Miller, J. Maxwell and John H. Hayes. *A History of Ancient Israel and Judah.* Philadelphia: The Westminster Press, 1986.

Miller, Patrick D. and J. J. M. Roberts. *The Hand of the Lord.* Baltimore: The Johns Hopkins University Press, 1977.

Miller, Patrick D. "Faith and Ideology in the Old Testament." In *Magnalia Dei: The Mighty Acts of God,* ed., F. M. Cross, W. E. Lemke, and P. D. Miller, 464–479. Garden City, N.Y.: Doubleday, 1976.

Mitchell, H. G., J. M. P. Smith, and J. A. Brewer. *Haggai, Zechariah, Malachi and Jonah.* ICC. Edinburgh: T. & T. Clark, 1912.

Montgomery, J. A. "Archival Data in the Book of Kings." *JBL* 53 (1934): 46–52.

Morson, Gary Saul and Caryl Emerson. *Mikhail Bakhtin: Creation of a Prosaics.* Stanford, Calif.: Stanford University Press, 1990.

Mullen, E. T. *The Assembly of the Gods: The Divine Council in Canaanite and Early Hebrew Literature.* Harvard Semitic Monographs. Chico, Calif.: Scholars Press, 1980.

Nelson, Richard D. *The Double Redaction of the Deuteronomistic History.* JSOT Supplement Series, 18. Sheffield: JSOT Press, 1981.

Niditch, Susan. *The Symbolic Vision in Biblical Tradition.* Chico: Scholars Press, 1983.

North, Robert. "Zechariah's Seven-Spout Lampstand." *Biblica* 51 (1970): 183–206.

———. "Prophecy to Apocalyptic via Zechariah." *VTSup* 22 (1972): 47–71.

Noth, Martin. *The History of Israel.* 2d Ed. London: A. & C. Black, 1958.

——. *The Deuteronomistic History.* JSOT Supplement Series 15. Sheffield: JSOT Press, 1981.

Nylander, Carl. "Achaemenid Imperial Art."   In *Power and Propaganda: A Symposium on Ancient Empires,* ed. Mogens Trolle Larsen, 345–359. Copenhagen: Akademisk Forlage, 1979.

Ollenburger, B. C. *Zion the City of the Great King.* JSOT Supplement Series, 41. Sheffield: JSOT Press, 1987.

Olmstead, A. T.   *History of the Persian Empire.*   Chicago: The University of Chicago Press, 1948.

Oppenheim, A. Leo. *The Interpretation of Dreams in the Ancient Near East.*   Volume 46, part 3.   Philadelphia: Transactions of the American Philosophical Society, 1956.

——.   *Ancient Mesopotamia: Portrait of a Dead Civilization.* Revised edition. Completed by Erica Reiner. Chicago: University of Chicago Press, 1977.

——. "The Eyes of the Lord." *Orientalia* 88 (1968): 183–206.

Pallis, S. A.   *The Babylonian Akitu Festival.*   Copenhagen: Bianco Lunos Bostrykkes, 1926.

Paul, Shalom M.   "Deutero-Isaiah and Cuneiform Royal Inscriptions." In *Essays in Memory of E. A. Speiser,* ed. William W. Hallo, 180–186.   American Oriental Series, 53.   New Haven: American Oriental Society, 1968.

Person, Raymond F. *Second Zechariah and the Deuteronomic School.* JSOT Supplement Series, 167. Sheffield: JSOT Press, 1993.

Petersen, David L. "Zerubbabel and Jerusalem Temple Reconstruction." *CBQ* 36 (1974): 366–372.

————. "Isaiah 28: A Redaction Critical Study." *SBL Seminar Papers* 17 (1979), volume 2: 101–122.

————. "Zechariah's Visions: A Theological Perspective." *VT* 34 (1984): 195–206.

————. *Haggai and Zechariah 1–8*. The Old Testament Library. Philadelphia: Westminster Press, 1984.

Petitjean, Albert. "La mission de Zorobabel et la reconstruction du temple—Zach. III.8–10." *ETL* 42 (1966): 40–71.

————. *Les Oracles du Proto-Zacharie*. Paris: J. Gabalda, 1969.

Pierce, Ronald W. "A Thematic Development of the Haggai/Zechariah/Malachi Corpus." *JETS* 27 (1984): 401–411.

Pritchard, James B. *Ancient Near Eastern Texts relating to the Old Testament*. 2nd ed. Princeton: Princeton University Press, 1955.

Prokurat, Michael. "Haggai and Zechariah 1–8: A Form Critical Analysis." Ph.D. diss., Graduate Theological Union, 1988.

Redditt, Paul L. "Zerubbabel, Joshua and the Night Visions of Zechariah." *CBQ* 54 (1992): 249–259.

————. *Haggai, Zechariah, Malachi*. The New Century Bible Commentary. Grand Rapids: William B. Eerdman, 1995.

Ricoeur, Paul. *Lectures on Ideology and Utopia*. Edited by George H. Taylor. New York: Columbia University Press, 1986.

————. "Ideology and Utopia." In *From Text to Action: Essays in Hermeneutics*. Translated by Kathleen Blamey and John B. Thompson. Evanston, IL: Northwestern University Press, 1991.

Rudolph, W. *Haggai; Sacharja 1–8; Sacharja 9–14; Maleachi*. KAT 13.1. Gütersloh: Gütersloher Verlagshaus Gerd Mohn, 1976.

Sinclair, Lawrence A. "Redaction of Zechariah 1–8." *Biblical Research* 16 (1971): 36–47.

Smith, Daniel L. *The Religion of the Landless: The Social Context of the Babylonian Exile.* Bloomington: Meyer-Stone Books, 1989.

Smith, Morton. *Palestinian Parties and Politics that Shaped the Old Testament.* London: SCM Press, 1971.

Smith, Ralph L. *Micah-Malachi.* Word Biblical Commentary. Waco: Word Books, 1984.

Soden, Wolfram von. *The Ancient Orient: An Introduction to the Study of the Ancient Near East.* Grand Rapids: William B. Eerdmanns, 1994.

Tadmor, Hayim. "Autobiographical Apology in the Royal Assyrian Literature." In *History, Historiography, and Interpretation: Studies in Biblical and Cuneiform Literature,* ed. H. Tadmor and M. Weinfeld, 36–57. Jerusalem: The Magnes Press, 1984.

Tidwell, N. L. A. "*wā'ōmar* (Zech. 3:5) and the Genre of Zechariah's Fourth Vision." *JBL* 94 (1975): 343–355.

Tollington, Janet E. *Tradition and Innovation in Haggai and Zechariah 1–8.* JSOT Supplement Series, 150. Sheffield: JSOT Press, 1993.

Vanderkam, J. C. "Joshua the High Priest and the Interpretation of Zechariah 3." *CBQ* 53 (1991): 553–570.

Van der Woude, Adam S. "Zion as Primeval Stone in Zechariah 3 and 4." In *Text and Context,* ed. W. Claasen, 237–248. JSOT Supplement Series, 48. Sheffield: JSOT Press, 1988.

Van Hoonacker, A. *Les Douze Petits Prophètes.* Ebib. 6. Paris: Gabalda, 1908.

Van Rooy, Harry V. "Prophet and Society in the Persian Period According to Chronicles." In *Second Temple Studies: 2. Temple*

Community in the Persian Period, ed. Tamara C. Eskenazi and Kent H. Richards, 163–179. JSOT Supplement Series, 175. Sheffield: JSOT Press, 1994.

Van Seters, John. *In Search of History.* New Haven: Yale University Press, 1983.

Wallis, Gerhard. "Erwagungen zu Sacharja VI.9–15." *VTSup* 22 (1971): 232–237.

Weinberg, Joel. *The Citizen-Temple Community.* JSOT Supplement Series, 151. Sheffield: JSOT Press, 1992.

Weinfeld, Moshe. "Zion and Jerusalem as Religious and Political Capital: Ideology and Utopia." In *The Poet and the Historian: Essays in Literary and Historical Biblical Criticism*, ed. Richard E. Friedman, 75–115. Chico: Scholars Press, 1983.

Widengren, Geo. "The Persian Period." In *Israelite and Judaean History*, ed. John H. Hayes and J. Maxwell Miller, 489–538. Philadelphia: Trinity Press International, 1990.

Wiseman, D. J. *Chronicles of the Chaldean Kings (625–556 BC) in the British Museum.* London: British Museum, 1956.

Wolff, Hans Walter. *Haggai: A Commentary.* Minneapolis: Augsburg Publishing House, 1988.

Yamauchi, Edwin M. *Persia and the Bible.* Grand Rapids: Baker Book House, 1990.

Zevit, Ziony. "Deuteronomistic Historiography in 1 Kings 12–2 Kings 17 and the Reinvestiture of the Israelian Cult." *JSOT* 32 (1985): 57–73.

INDEX

Studies in Biblical Literature

This series invites manuscripts from scholars in any area of biblical literature. Both established and innovative methodologies, covering general and particular areas in biblical study, are welcome. The series seeks to make available studies that will make a significant contribution to the ongoing biblical discourse. Scholars who have interests in gender and sociocultural hermeneutics are particularly encouraged to consider this series.

For further information about the series and for the submission of manuscripts, contact:

Hemchand Gossai
Department of Religion
Muhlenberg College
2400 Chew Street
Allentown, PA 18104-5586

To order other books in this series, please contact our Customer Service Department:

(800) 770-LANG (within the U.S.)
(212) 647-7706 (outside the U.S.)
(212) 647-7707 FAX

or browse online by series at:

WWW.PETERLANGUSA.COM